The Role of Context in Language Teachers' Self Development and Motivation

PSYCHOLOGY OF LANGUAGE LEARNING AND TEACHING

Series Editors: **Sarah Mercer**, *Universität Graz, Austria* and **Stephen Ryan**, *Waseda University, Japan*

This international, interdisciplinary book series explores the exciting, emerging field of Psychology of Language Learning and Teaching. It is a series that aims to bring together works which address a diverse range of psychological constructs from a multitude of empirical and theoretical perspectives, but always with a clear focus on their applications within the domain of language learning and teaching. The field is one that integrates various areas of research that have been traditionally discussed as distinct entities, such as motivation, identity, beliefs, strategies and self-regulation, and it also explores other less familiar concepts for a language education audience, such as emotions, the self and positive psychology approaches. In theoretical terms, the new field represents a dynamic interface between psychology and foreign language education and books in the series draw on work from diverse branches of psychology, while remaining determinedly focused on their pedagogic value. In methodological terms, sociocultural and complexity perspectives have drawn attention to the relationships between individuals and their social worlds, leading to a field now marked by methodological pluralism. In view of this, books encompassing quantitative, qualitative and mixed methods studies are all welcomed.

All books in this series are externally peer-reviewed.

Full details of all the books in this series and of all our other publications can be found on http://www.multilingual-matters.com, or by writing to Multilingual Matters, St Nicholas House, 31-34 High Street, Bristol BS1 2AW, UK.

PSYCHOLOGY OF LANGUAGE LEARNING AND TEACHING: 13

The Role of Context in Language Teachers' Self Development and Motivation

Perspectives from Multilingual Settings

Amy S. Thompson

MULTILINGUAL MATTERS
Bristol • Blue Ridge Summit

DOI https://doi.org/10.21832/THOMPS1180
Library of Congress Cataloging in Publication Data
A catalog record for this book is available from the Library of Congress.
Names: Thompson, Amy S., 1979- author.
Title: The Role of Context in Language Teachers' Self Development and
    Motivation: Perspectives from Multilingual Settings/Amy S. Thompson.
Description: Bristol; Blue Ridge Summit: Multilingual Matters, [2021] | Series:
    Psychology of Language Learning and Teaching: 13 | Includes bibliographical
    references. | Summary: "This book unpacks data from conversations with bi-/
    multilingual EFL teachers to provide insights into the formation of ideal teacher
    selves. The author discusses the complexities surrounding the development of the
    teachers' selves and motivation, as well as their intertwinement with the socio-
    political realities of their individual contexts"—Provided by publisher.
Identifiers: LCCN 2020043616 | ISBN 9781800411180 (hardback) |
    ISBN 9781800411173 (paperback) | ISBN 9781800411197 (pdf) |
    ISBN 9781800411203 (epub) | ISBN 9781800411210 (kindle edition)
Subjects: LCSH: English language—Study and teaching—Foreign speakers. | English
    teachers—Foreign countries—Attitudes. | Multilingual education. Classification:
    LCC PE1128.A2 T459 2020 | DDC 428.0071—dc23
LC record available at https://lccn.loc.gov/2020043616

British Library Cataloguing in Publication Data
A catalogue entry for this book is available from the British Library.

ISBN-13: 978-1-80041-118-0 (hbk)
ISBN-13: 978-1-80041-117-3 (pbk)

Multilingual Matters
UK: St Nicholas House, 31-34 High Street, Bristol BS1 2AW, UK.
USA: NBN, Blue Ridge Summit, PA, USA.

Website: www.multilingual-matters.com
Twitter: Multi_Ling_Mat
Facebook: https://www.facebook.com/multilingualmatters
Blog: www.channelviewpublications.wordpress.com

The policy of Multilingual Matters/Channel View Publications is to use papers
that are natural, renewable and recyclable products, made from wood grown in
sustainable forests. In the manufacturing process of our books, and to further
support our policy, preference is given to printers that have FSC and PEFC Chain
of Custody certification. The FSC and/or PEFC logos will appear on those books
where full certification has been granted to the printer concerned.

Typeset by Deanta Global Publishing Services, Chennai, India

Contents

Foreword

Live as if you were to die tomorrow. Learn as if you were to live forever.

Mahatma Gandhi

Amy and I have three things in common (among a myriad of others). First, like her, I am in a privileged position of having taught and educated teachers in my home language, and I have done this in both second language (United States) and foreign language (Chile and the United Arab Emirates) settings, so this means I have had the honor of interacting intimately with amazing educational professionals who teach English as their LX. Second, Amy and I cannot resist a good story – and it is this very trait that makes this book such an incredible read. For me, being privy to others' experiences is the best way to appreciate life's most meaningful insights, and Amy narrates people's stories like no one else can! Third, we both tend to enjoy pushing the parameters of people's comfort zones – 'rattling cages' is what I like calling it.

What I admire most about this book is that Amy advocates for bi-/multilingual language teachers and brilliantly defends her activism with solid argumentation and real-life stories. In my career, I have prepared many English teachers whose home language was not English, and they have inspired me much more than the other way around. I am grateful to them for the guidance they have provided me. With that in mind, I would like to tell a story of my own, and this one comes from Chile where I spent 17 years teaching English and preparing a small segment of their next generation of English teachers.

After spending the first part of my academic career in Chile, I was fortunate to return as a Fulbright Scholar where part of my role was to teach a graduate course in language assessment while simultaneously gathering data concerning the notion of the motivation of 'teachers-as-learners'. Particularly in foreign language settings, the LXs being taught are often not the teachers' first languages, which creates a hybrid where teachers are simultaneously learners of the languages they teach. I am a firm believer that teacher motivation begets learner motivation and vice versa – learners influence their teachers. Lamentably, the opposite is also true: demotivated teachers negatively impact learners, and again this relationship is reciprocal. In fact, Amy brings out this synergy in the narratives of several of her teachers. For example, the Estonian teachers whom she interviewed, Mia and Darja, believe that if their students speak well, it means the teachers speak better. This same interaction between motivation and context is represented in the narratives of the Vietnamese teacher who swells with pride that students crowd into his grammar class; the students are motivating Khiet, the teacher, and he is motivating them. You will also encounter in Amy's narratives a Senegalese teacher, Ablaye, who enjoys surprising people with his English abilities, especially given that schooling is conducted in French; his joy in speaking English inevitably translates to his students.

This leads to questions about the synergy of teacher and learner motivation when embodied in the same person, as is the case with bi-/multilingual teachers. I was so pleased to see that Amy dealt with these questions with great finesse. Her narratives weave a variety of complex phenomena into a cohesive fabric, including teacher selves and their respective contexts from diverse and often remote parts of the world. Such synergy is displayed in every journey of the language educators whom Amy showcases.

Like Amy, I am very curious about such synergy, so I decided to 'eavesdrop' on the inner dialogues of teachers-as-learners when in Chile. To do this, participants' 'teacher-selves' responded to journal entries they themselves wrote as their 'learner-selves'. In practical terms, teacher-learners carried out six tasks two times. The first time they performed the activities, they envisioned themselves as learners and responded afterwards in their journals. The second time, they did the same task, read the entries of themselves as learners, and then wrote comments back to themselves in their role as teachers. What I discovered as I pried into these very private conversations would profoundly change my perspective as a teacher educator and the incredibly beneficial role that bi-/multilingual language teachers play in our global society. Had these teachers not also been learners of the language they taught, they would not have been in the position to provide such sage advice in their journals.

About External 'Ought-to' Expectations

Amy makes it very clear that 'expectations in specific contexts are always relevant in terms of teachers developing an ideal teacher self' (p. 27), and in fact she showcases this notion in her Vietnamese teacher, Khiet, whose parents understood the significant role of English as an international language and the opportunities it would provide their son (see p. 54). Like this English teacher from Vietnam, one of my Chilean teachers echoed the same sentiments:

I had affective factors to learn a second language, since my mother was always a source of motivation to learn English and discover the good things of speaking a second language. Thus, as learners we have to find out how much important and stunning is the fact of speaking a second language, not only to be hired in a good company or make a lot of money, but to incorporate a new way of thinking to understand and be witness of other cultures and far away societies.

About Learning Being a Lifelong Journey

Besides the recognition by bi-/multilingual English teachers of the powerful shaping force of external contextual influences, they also see language learning as a forever endeavor. Amy suggests, 'Particularly relevant for those who teach a language other than their L1, such as the teachers in this project, language learning is a lifelong journey' (p. 135). In fact, Amy quotes María from Argentina who voiced the view that 'learning the language will never end'. One of my Chilean informants agreed:

> my conception of a teacher is that of a person who never stops learning. In this sense, I see the teacher as someone who has a dual role, someone who must never stop seeing himself as a learner too. I am very critical of my own performance and what I do in the classroom. I always end up my lessons by thinking of what were the things I did right and the improvements I should apply. When I work on all these improvements my role as a learner puts itself into practice, that is the point when I see myself as a leaner who is trying to investigate about many things, correcting, editing, improving, getting new information.

In terms of the process being likened to a journey, several of my teacher-learners expressed the analogy poetically:

> Difficulties are a great motivation for me coz I have always thought that the most interesting part of any journey is the road, not the end.

> It is very important to enjoy the journey of learning but you always have to have in mind where you want to go and what you want to achieve.

> I have to become an active agent so that students can fall in love with language and realize that English is not just a class to pass, but an instrument to share emotions and learn from other people and other cultures.

About Understanding Learners Better

In Amy's first chapter, she underscores the value of language teachers learning languages because 'doing so can alter one's perception of the student process' (p. 29) and that learning an additional language expands teachers' awareness of their students' experience. One of my Chilean teacher-learner concurs with the following:

> From my point of view, my learner motivation always interacts with my teacher motivation since my experiences and goals as a learner influence the decisions I make in order to teach. This does not mean I teach the way I would like to learn, but that I always try to provide different tools to my students so they can meet their own goals, depending on their personal styles and interests. This is because as a learner, I can easily understand the fact that a learner may have different areas he or she would like to develop, so as a teacher, I am responsible for providing a variety of teaching and assessing techniques that may help them see if they are reaching those goals or not.

However, according to Amy, the advantage held by bi-/multilingual English teachers is not only having a deeper understanding of learners' processes but they also have the benefit of being intimately familiar with the culture of their students, since in many instances, that culture is shared. Hasani, an Egyptian English as a foreign language (EFL) teacher who is highlighted in this book, put it this way:

> Because I understand my own culture very well, and now I understand some, or a great deal of your culture, so I'm able to make that sort of link. But if anyone from another society, okay, is going to teach a different society, or a different kind of students from a different culture, I think it's, okay, he can teach some sort of language, but he can't create this sort of harmony between the two cultures. (p. 76)

My hope as you read this book is that you take to heart its advocacy for bi-/multilingual English language teachers around the world, listen to their stories with an open heart and let your cage get rattled. My Chilean teachers above along with Amy's informants are just a small sample of why I trust my hope will be fulfilled. The multilingual profiles of Amy's featured teachers provide imitation-worthy role models for future language educators. Enjoy a fascinating read!

Tammy Gregersen

Preface

Do you know what a foreign accent is? It's a sign of bravery.

Amy Chua

This book is the culmination of a 10-year project of collecting and analyzing the narrative data of English teachers in several different contexts worldwide. As such, this project creates an intersection of the work that I have done on individual differences, specifically the development of self (Dörnyei, 2009), and issues related to the use of multiple languages, as well as the advocacy work of language teaching professionals who teach languages other than their first languages (L1s). As Kubanyiova (2019: 394) indicates, research on teacher motivation and self-development necessitates transcending disciplinary boundaries, with the need to 'expand its traditionally psychological boundaries and borrow insights from across the sociolinguistic and critical perspectives on language learning, language teaching and language teachers' lives'. The field of individual differences research has recently begun to emphasize the importance of interactions of self and context, an approach that might have traditionally been conceptualized as a more sociolinguistic framework. Several researchers in the field have paved the way for a more contextualized perspective on individual difference research, making a project such as this book possible. The teachers highlighted in this project have a symbiotic relationship between self and context (Mercer & Williams, 2014a; Ushioda, 2015), a relationship that has helped to form their ideal teacher selves (Hiver, 2013; Hiver & Dörnyei, 2017), thus promoting the interdisciplinary nature of research in teacher motivation.

As will be seen in the narrative data, the themes 'I know how my people think' and 'I'm better than these guys' are present in all of the teacher perceptions. Such comments are highlighted not to discredit those who teach their L1, but instead to emphasize the abilities and positive aspects of traditionally marginalized teachers – the non-native[1] speaker teachers. Native English speaker teachers do not need bolstering; this group has been traditionally privileged, as will be discussed in the review of the literature and in some of the chapters. Just as the 'Black Lives Matter' movement was intended to focus on a group that needed increased equity and support, 'All Lives Matter' disrupted that much needed focus (Victor, 2016). In this project, there is a purposeful emphasis on non-native speaker teachers, not in a traditional comparative sense, but with a focus on these teachers' own 'truth' (Talmy, 2010) and celebrating their diverse backgrounds and expertise (Canagarajah, 2007).

Some of the teacher comments presented in this book might make some readers uncomfortable, whether directly stating that some people hate English because of the American president, or by saying that native-speaking teachers are often not as effective as teachers who share the linguistic and cultural background of their students. These comments were not censored; in fact, they were highlighted and unpacked. Indeed, part of academic work is intended to make people a bit uncomfortable, for this is the way to foster a growth mindset (Dweck & Yeager, 2019). As DiAngelo (2018: xiv) suggests, we should not 'retreat in the face of that discomfort', but instead increase our stamina in confronting issues that might cause discomfort, as being too comfortable leads to complacency. As I am finalizing this project, we are in the middle of what could be conceptualized as two pandemics: COVID-19 and the systemic racism prevalent worldwide, but that is historically and currently especially salient in American society. Both of these pandemics have greatly affected our education system; it is only by facing critical issues of race and discrimination head-on that we can hope to emerge from the 2020–2021 academic year as more inclusive and evolved members of society.

Chapter 1 sets the stage for the subsequent context-specific chapters. Starting with a theoretical overview of the relationship of context and self, issues surrounding non-native speaker status are also discussed and problematized in this chapter, specifically in relation to context and the formation of the ideal teacher self. Providing a framework for the context-specific chapters that follow, this term is explicitly discussed in terms of how being an L1 speaker of a language other than English is part of the formation of the ideal teacher self, an identity that is context-specific. The following chapters (2–8) are a series of case studies, using narrative data from English as a foreign language (EFL) teachers in largely under-studied contexts: Senegal, Vietnam, Egypt, Argentina, Turkey, Ukraine, and Estonia. The contexts, particularly information about the politics involved in language learning and teaching, serve to inform the development of the ideal selves of these EFL teachers. Chapter 9 is a concluding chapter that serves as a discussion of the context-specific chapters and the proceeding theoretical work, as well as to delineate broader concerns in the field.

This book project has survived a move across the country for the start of a new leadership position, as well as the double pandemic in which we find ourselves. Certainly, I could not have completed the project without the support of several people. As such, I would like to thank a number of individuals for helping with this project, such as the editors from Multilingual Matters (particularly Dr Sarah Mercer, series editor, and Ms Laura Longworth, commissioning editor), countless others who have helped with feedback and conversations (particularly Dr Tammy Gregersen, who gave me feedback on my original idea and who wrote the Foreword), and the anonymous reviewers, who helped push this text where it needed to go. I also sought out several friends and colleagues for feedback on the context-specific chapters, particularly when I could not get in touch with the featured teachers: Dr Matilde Olivero (Argentina), Dr Sara Hillman and Dr Emma Trentman (Egypt), Ms Oksana Bomba and Dr Victor Peppard (Ukraine), and additional reviewers Dr Erhan Aslan and Dr Mehmet Öztan for the chapter on Turkey. I am also grateful to Dr Jonathan Hall, who has helped me to think more critically about issues of race and discrimination, particularly in the realm of education. Our conversations have assisted me in being better able to articulate issues of bias found in the field of Applied Linguistics. The efforts of Black faculty to educate others require much emotional labor, labor that often goes unacknowledged; I sincerely thank Dr Hall for taking the time to talk to me, and others, about these critical issues. Most of all, I'm appreciative of my nuclear family (Barbara and Lowery Thompson and Laura, Caroline, and Isabelle Mickail), who always believe in me, and Mehmet Öztan, my life partner, who has kept me sane during this and my other professional endeavors. Finally, I am grateful to the teachers for their willingness to share their stories with me. I hope you enjoy reading about the extraordinary journeys of these teachers as much as I've enjoyed writing about them.

Note

(1) The *non-native* and *nonnative* are interchangeable in the literature. For consistency, I have used *non-native*, unless a direct quote uses *nonnative*.

1 Introduction

Who am I when I speak English?

Claire Kramsch

The relationship between self and context is not straightforward. Although this connection has been studied for decades, questions, such as those that Norton (2020: 159) poses, are still being asked: 'How do we theorize the complex relationship between the language learner and the social world?'. The epigraph to this chapter, 'Who am I when I speak English?' is from Kramsch's afterword from Norton's (2013) revision of her seminal 2000 publication: *Identity and Language Learning*. The question is embedded in a discussion of the historic shift in frameworks in second language acquisition (SLA), which brought about a concern for identity (and, thus, self-concept): interactionist and sociocultural SLA leading to a social turn (Block, 2003), large-scale migrations, and the spread of global English. As Kramsch (2013: 194) states, 'The transformation of English from a national language to a global language gave issues of identity a crucial importance: who am I when I speak English? Or, as Bonny Norton put it, how do I understand my relationship to the world and my possibilities for the future?'. Each individual's relationship with English (or any other language) and the context in which it is used, relates to Mercer's (e.g. 2016) argument: context is not monolithic. It cannot be assumed that one culture equals a singular context, nor can it be assumed that the interaction of context and self will be the same for every person in a similar language use situation. Nonetheless, it is impossible to examine the language learning, use, and motivation of individuals without some understanding of specific sociopolitical realities. With her person-in-context view of motivation, Ushioda (2009) illustrates this point:

> Let me summarise then what I mean by a person-in-context relational view of motivation. I mean a focus on real persons, rather than on learners as theoretical abstractions; a focus on the agency of the individual person as a thinking, feeling human being, with an identity, a personality, a unique history and background, a person with goals, motives

and intentions; a focus on the interaction between this self-reflective intentional agent, and the fluid and complex system of social relations, activities, experiences and multiple micro- and macro-contexts in which the person is embedded, moves, and is inherently part of. (Ushioda, 2009: 220)

The review of the literature in Chapter 1 serves to tease apart (and then bring back together) the complexities revolving around context, development of self, and motivation, culminating in an overview of ideal teacher selves. Chapter 1 prepares the reader for the subsequent chapters in this text: data analysis and discussion of the narratives of non-native speaker (NNS) English language teachers in a variety of understudied contexts intertwined with the sociopolitical realities of the contexts involved. The last part of this chapter includes a methods section for the narrative data collected from the English language educators. For the context-specific chapters in the different sociopolitical contexts, the narrative data is a representation of the English as a foreign language (EFL) instructors' perspectives in relation to their context, including the social interactions therein. Both the sociopolitical realities and the specific social interactions that occur in these realities influence the language learning and teaching processes (Benson, 2019).

Early Forays into the Role of Context in Language Learning

In the field of motivation research, the connection between language learners and the social milieu was detailed in Gardner's (1985) seminal work on the socio-educational (SE) model of motivation. Within this model, Gardner proposed the concept of integrativeness, or the motivation to learn a language because of a desire to become closer to the community that speaks that language. Norton (2020: 156) cites an address that Gardner gave in 2009 at the Canadian Association of Applied Linguistics, detailing that integrativeness is the openness of an individual to integrate aspects of a different culture into their own identity. Gardner (2010) writes that language is not merely the linguistic system but it is also the societal norms that accompany the language in question. Norton (2020: 160) has a similar notion: 'the construct of "language" is not only a linguistic system of words and sentences, but also a social practice in which identities and desires are negotiated in the context of complex and often unequal social relationships'. Indeed, Norton (2020: 153) compared her concept of investment (see also Norton, 2000) and Gardner's of motivation; she argues that both scholars place an importance on the relationship of the learner and society, 'particularly with respect to questions of identity'.

Around the same time as Gardner's (1985) publication, Clément (1980, 1986) proposed a socio-contextual model that examined how language learning was impacted by the macro-societal context. A central part of this model is the concept of ethnolinguistic vitality (ELV) or 'the social and structural characteristics of a language community, which promote its survival' (Rubenfeld & Clément, 2020: 111). An example of ELV is described in Clément and Noels (1992), who found that Francophones identified more strongly with Anglophones in terms of media and symbolic aspects of ethnicity when they were situated in a minority Francophone (i.e. majority Anglophone) context in Canada, such as the province of Ontario. In other words, context plays a role in identity, integration, and thus, language learning motivation and self-concept.

Operationalization of *Context*

Over the years, context has been operationalized in a variety of ways, as Ushioda (2011: 187) indicates: 'the scope of what we mean by learning context can vary greatly, depending on how we choose to circumscribe our analytical lens in terms of environment – e.g., within or beyond the physical, social and cultural boundaries of the classroom setting'. In a subsequent publication, Ushioda (2015: 49) poses the questions, 'how do we identify and delimit the multiple contextual elements that are empirically relevant to motivational development? How narrowly or widely should we focus our contextual lens? ...Should we consider cultural context in the sense of national culture, or local institutional culture, or the "small culture" (Holliday, 1999) of a particular classroom?'. In an earlier publication, Gardner and Clément (1990) indicate three levels of context: that of the language, of a specific encounter, and the larger context of society. Sampasivam and Clément (2014) add to Harwood's (2010) contact space framework, which is a visualization of the types of interactions in a particular context. As described, there are three main types of contact: face-to-face, mass media, and imagined contact. Face-to-face contact is when learners communicate with speakers in that language. Mass media contact is 'in terms of exposure to the L2 and its cultural artifacts' (Sampasivam & Clément, 2014: 32). Imagined contact is related to the vividness part of the ideal self in the second language (L2) Motivational Self System (L2MSS; Dörnyei, 2005, 2009). In a different multipronged view of context, Larsen-Freeman and Cameron (2008: 205) indicate that context is composed of the learner variables (what the learner brings to the situation), the cultural context, the social context, and the pedagogical context.

In terms of the theoretical underpinnings of Dörnyei's (2005, 2009) L2MSS, the two psychological aspects of self (ideal and ought-to) have taken priority in the literature, with very little attention to the learning experience aspect of the L2MSS. As Dörnyei (2019: 22) states 'It was felt right from the beginning that the label L2 Learning Experience was hardly more than a broad, place-holding umbrella term that would need to be fine-tuned at one point, but it appears that the interest in the potentials of the new self-approach has overshadowed this research need, thereby leaving the L2 Learning Experience the Cinderella of the L2 Motivational Self System'. In this recent publication, Dörnyei proposes that learner engagement be equivocated to the learning experience prong of the L2MSS, as engagement is in line with current communicative trends of language pedagogy. It is suggested that the different facets of the learning environment can be 'broken down into more specific meaningful facets' (Dörnyei, 2019: 25), such as the school context, syllabus and teaching materials, learning tasks, one's peers, and the teacher. Arguably, what is missing from this proposal is in which sociopolitical context the learning environment is situated, as this would inevitably have an influence on the school curriculum, as well as on the language teaching methodology. This sociopolitical context is also connected to the concept of the network of relationships (Mercer, 2016) that are formed between actors in a specified context. Another point of view on the integration of the 'learning experience' aspect of the L2MSS comes from Thompson (2017b), who argued that the L2MSS is essentially composed of two parts: the psychological aspects of self (ideal and ought-to, plus the proposed anti-ought-to) and the learning experience, which is language use in context. Specifically talking about the learning experience, Thompson (2017b) states the following:

> The learning experience is the aspect of the L2MSS that looks at the context of the language learning process and the effect of the context on the psychological aspects of self. Target language exchanges are comprised of interactions both in and out of the classroom and include both successful and unsuccessful experiences. As such, there are effects of instructional context and peers, and it is important to note that the language learners themselves can also have an effect on their context (i.e., the influence of context is bidirectional). In the current study, the learning experience aspect of the model specifically relates to the linguistic landscape of the United States and the target language choice. (Thompson, 2017b: 484)

As noted, the learning experience aspect of the L2MSS can be operationalized in a variety of ways (see Dörnyei [2019] for a summary). In this project, the learning experience is most broadly defined as the larger sociopolitical context of the EFL teachers in question.

The EFL-teacher-focused chapters are organized by geographical setting (i.e. country), but it is also relevant to note Mercer's (2016: 13) argument: context is not monolithic but refers to 'multiple levels of contexts stretching from micro-level interactional contexts to macro-level cultures' (see also Serafini, 2020). In other words, it cannot be assumed that every individual's contextual situation has the same external variables, nor can it be assumed that each individual interacts with the context in the same way. Mercer (2016: 12) states that 'acknowledging the role of contexts is only a first step' and posits that further exploration needs to be done to examine the complexities between learner and context. Although the role of context in language learning, self-development, and motivation cannot be ignored, 'At times, cultures and contexts appear to be presented as static, monolithic, external entities which affect individual characteristics in a simple unidirectional manner. Such simplistic views of cultures or contexts risk distorting the nature of an individual's relationship with them and potentially leading to unintended stereotyping and over-generalisations' (Mercer, 2016: 12). As is the case with much of the research on attitudes and beliefs, van Dijk (2009) argues that contexts are subjective, interpretations of which depend on the individual(s) involved. From this argument, Mercer (2016: 16) indicates that 'generalisable simplistic understandings of contexts cannot be assumed to be the same for everyone'. Relating this concept back to Sampasivam and Clément's (2014) updated contact space framework, learners will potentially have a different reaction to the same interlocutor or teacher, will like or dislike different types of music and other cultural artifacts, and will have unique ways of imagining an ideal self. The EFL teachers in this book illustrate their own interaction with languages and contexts; however, it should not be assumed that their experiences speak for all EFL teachers in a similar context. Summarizing the role of context in SLA research, Ushioda (2011: 189) states, 'In short, there is no doubt that context matters in SLA, yet what matters just as much is the individual agency of L2 learners, inherently part of and actively shaping the developing contexts of learning, input and interaction in which they are situated'.

Operationalization of *Self*

The term *self* and how development of the self relates to language learning motivation has been operationalized in a variety of different ways and through the lens of several different frameworks, which Mercer (2016) describes as a cognitive versus contextualized divide. The cognitive selves focus on 'mental representations of self in a more abstract, isolated manner' as opposed to 'more strongly situated definitions of the self in which its contextualised, socially constructed and dynamic character is foregrounded' (Mercer, 2016: 11, see also Turner et al., 2006). Claro (2020) describes the self in terms of two different motivational frameworks: integrativeness is described as having an external referent and the ideal self is described as having an internal referent. As others have indicated, however (e.g. Ushioda, 2014), external referents can be internalized; likewise, individuals can also have an influence on the external referents (i.e. the context). Kostoulas and Mercer (2016) describe what they perceive to be the three milestones in self-related research: Norton's (2000) self-construct of identity; Dörnyei's (2005, 2009) proposal of the

L2MSS; and the most recent concept of self, largely led by Mercer, which looks at individual difference research, including the concept of self, through more holistic theoretical perspectives. Describing this recent trend, Kostoulas and Mercer (2016: 129) write, 'Increasingly, the self is being described through theoretical frames, such as complexity-informed perspectives, that foreground the interconnections and the situated and dynamic nature of individual characteristics'.

One framework that is being used to illustrate the dynamic relationships of the self is that of social networks. Carolan (2013: 3) describes the uniqueness of social network analysis: 'What makes it distinct is that, in addition to focusing on the individual, the relationships that connect that individual to another are of central importance... Relationships defined by connections among individual units—students, teachers, or school districts—are a fundamental aspect of social network analysis'. Mercer (2014a) has used this framework to 'work with contexts and cultures in a truly integrated manner from a complexity perspective' (Mercer, 2016: 20), as '[o]ne suggestion of how to make any complex dynamic system more amenable for research is to conceptualise it as a network' (Mercer, 2015a: 73). Mercer (2014a) explains that her concept of social network theory as it relates to the self was influenced by integrative models and that it documents all relationships of the individual so that the 'context becomes embedded in the network'. Even though the contexts are embedded in the network, the learner can still have 'an explicit relationship with a particular context, such as with a specific class, school, educational institution or culture' (Mercer, 2014a: 65). By researching the self in this fashion, the idea that cultures or contexts are not monolithic is emphasized, as the sense of self emerges through the specific relationships that a learner forms as a result of a multitude of interactions and multiple points in time (Mercer, 2016). Even if two learners in the same context had the same interactions, the perceptions of these interactions would be distinct, thereby forming a different sense of self, as 'there is a mutually constitutive and co-adaptive relationship between internal and social-environmental processes. Identity both moulds and is moulded by shifting relations and social networks' (Ushioda, 2015: 51).

The Dynamic Relationship between Self and Context

In the previous sections, potential operationalizations of both context and self have been proposed; in this section, the relationship between self and context will be explored further. Studies have shown that differing motivational profiles of individuals are 'shaped by components of his/her immediate social context' (Thompson & Vásquez, 2015: 163). In the person-in-context view of motivation, there is a symbiotic relationship between self and context: 'learners shape and are shaped by context' (Ushioda, 2015: 48; see also Serafini, 2020). Mercer (2016: 15) reflects on the multiple time dimensions of the relationship of self and context, indicating that one's current concept of self is formed by past and current experiences, as well as future goals. Conceptualizing different timescales can also aid in examining the distinct relationships and self-formation of individuals in the same context, even down to the same classroom. MacIntyre and Legatto (2011) developed idiodynamic software to measure how learners were feeling during a specific task in very small timescales (second and minutes). Learners were recorded during the same task and were later asked to indicate an increase or decrease of a specific self-related emotion, such as self-confidence or anxiety, while watching the recording. Referencing her 2014b study, Mercer (2016: 17) notes, 'Indeed, potentially the same contextual factor can have quite different significance and implications for different individuals. Thus, in research on situated views of the self, it becomes apparent that it is not the context *per se* that we need to be examining and describing but crucially the learners' own subjective interpretation of the relevance and meaning of respective contextual factors. Researchers must thus take care not to make assumptions about the influence of contextual factors on a learner's sense of self, but rather we need to understand what the individual from their first-person perspective interprets as significant, how and why'. As Polat (2014) describes from his perspective of Turks of Kurdish descent going to school in eastern Turkey, others' perceptions of the learners' selves also relate to the energy put forth in creating an L2 self. 'They continuously contribute to the shaping of their immediate and broader environments (ecologies) while simultaneously being shaped by them... More specifically, L2 learners constantly transform their identity repertoires while participating in communities of practice because they ultimately attempt to re-situate their identities according to the actions of those deemed as experienced and important' (Polat, 2014: 273). Ushioda (2015: 47) has a similar opinion, indicating that 'there is a dynamically evolving relationship between learner and context' as they interact with each other.

Ushioda (2015: 50) also raises the important point regarding operationalizing the contexts that potentially exist within the learner, arguing that memories and experiences create a different kind of context, or 'multiple internal ecosystems'. This point is especially relevant to the subsequent chapters in this book, as the narrative data extrapolates the lived experiences and memories of the EFL teachers featured therein. In reviewing the data for this book, the 'symbiotic and mutually constitutive relationship between contexts and language learners, as captured in the metaphor of a learner-context ecosystem' (Ushioda, 2015: 50) was untangled and analyzed. As Mercer and Williams (2014a: 179) state, 'the self cannot be conceptualised as being abstracted and separated from contexts'.

As is unpacked above, both self and context are complex entities. Understanding and utilizing multiple perspectives to operationalize the concept of self is advised, as Mercer and Williams (2014a: 183) state, 'there cannot be only one best way to research the self'. As Gardner (2010) discusses, and Norton (2020) also references, there are multiple perspectives on different issues in SLA, and it is advantageous to determine, 'what is valuable in each' (Gardner, 2010: 154).

Empirical Studies on Self and Context

For this book project, empirical studies related to self and context were examined. In terms of empirical studies, current issues (2009 to summer of 2020) of 17 journals were carefully reviewed for articles on the relationship between self and context. Instead of carrying out a keyword search within a specific database, each issue was examined individually, looking for the words/phrases related to 'motivation', 'self', and 'attitude' in the titles, abstracts, keywords (if included), and the articles themselves, and approximately 450 relevant articles were found. All of the journals surveyed participate in a double- or triple-blind peer-review process, and almost all of them are indexed on the Social Science Citation Index (SSCI), which is noted below. Although empirical studies were the focus of the search, theoretical articles were also included, as were articles with a shorter format, as in short reports and summaries, teaching issues, brief research reports, and forum articles. When available, the 'online first' or 'early view' versions of the articles were also included. In alphabetical order, the following journals were included: *Applied Linguistics* (SSCI), *Canadian Modern Language Review* (SSCI), *ELT Journal* (SSCI), *Foreign Language Annals* (SSCI), *Journal of Multilingual and Multicultural Development*, *Innovation in Language Learning and Teaching*, *International Journal of Bilingual Education and Bilingualism* (SSCI), *International Journal of Multilingualism*, *Journal for the Psychology of Language Learning* (first issue in 2019), *Language Learning* (SSCI), *Language Learning Journal*, *Language Teaching Research* (SSCI), *Modern Language Journal* (SSCI), *Studies in Second Language Acquisition* (SSCI), *System* (SSCI), *TESOL Journal*, and *TESOL Quarterly* (SSCI).

After identifying relevant articles, each was scrutinized for pertinent information about self and context. Not surprisingly, most of the empirical studies on self focused on the L2MSS self paradigm; as such, the following synthesis primarily emphasizes the relationship among the types of selves in the L2MSS and context. Also included are a few studies about language attitudes that relate to the contexts in the subsequent chapters. Many of the empirical studies take place in contexts such as China, Japan, and Western Europe; however, the focus of the studies presented below are those related to the contexts that are presented in this book. Accordingly, as the following chapters focus on Senegal, Vietnam, Egypt, Argentina, Turkey, Ukraine, and Estonia, details will be given about representative empirical studies from Africa, Southeast Asia, Latin

America, the Middle East/Turkey, and Eastern Europe. As the data from the following chapters is from relatively understudied contexts, not all of these contexts have explicit empirical studies about that context; thus, studies in contexts with geographic, linguistic, and/or cultural similarities are included. For a quantitative synthesis of L2MSS research, see Boo *et al.* (2015); for a qualitative synthesis, see Mendoza and Phung (2019). A section focusing specifically on research related to teacher motivation follows the context-specific overview sections; as such, the context-specific sections provide a broad overview of the motivation research in the specific settings.

Africa

Coetzee-Van Rooy (2014, 2019) is the author of the only examined publications in terms of self in the African context; specifically, she analyzes the L2MSS framework in the Vaal Triangle region of South Africa. In this region of multilingualism as the norm, the author argues that participants can have a multilingual self, a concept similar to what Henry (2017) later proposes. This concept differs from other quantitative work that indicates a distinct ideal self for each language studied (i.e. Dörnyei & Chan, 2013; Thompson, 2017b); however, because of the ostensibly more naturalistic language learning that takes place in the region with languages other than English and Afrikaans, it is possible that the idea of an ideal self for each individual language would need to be reconceptualized in this context. Coetzee-Van Rooy (2014: 124) also describes the multilingual ought-to self for this multilingual region as directing 'people to believe that if they are not multilingual in this society, they do not "fit in", because well-integrated citizens in this society are multilingual'. Indeed, the data shows that most people in this region speak between three and five languages. The 2019 publication emphasizes the naturalistic multilingualism of people in this region, which differs from the classroom-based multilingualism that is the focus of most motivation studies.

Two studies in the African context focused on attitudes toward English: Parmegiani (2010) in South Africa and Dyers and Abongdia (2010) in Cameroon. Parmegiani (2010) was primarily interested in examining attitudes toward ownership of English, particularly of those who had not traditionally been associated with English via the birthright paradigm (i.e. those other than white Europeans). Thus, she collected data from 120 Black South Africans. Most participants in this sample described ownership of English as having to do with both race and native speaker (NS) status; however, 33% of the participants said that anyone who has learned English well or anyone who wished to claim English as 'their' language could claim ownership. In terms of language choice, a majority of the participants felt most comfortable using English for writing an essay or a letter and reading. The only time a majority of the participants perceived using a mother tongue to be more effective was in arguing or discussing feelings (see also Dewaele, 2010). Most participants wanted to learn English to perform well in their studies or to find a better job, but many (77%) of the participants wanted to learn English to effectively communicate with those who have a different first language (L1). The participants did not feel that the NSs were the best speakers of English: 'This study has also shown that equating expertise with "nativeness" is also problematic. In particular, the assumption that a mother tongue gives a speaker the highest level of expertise in any given commutative situation does not reflect the socio-linguistic reality of the students in the sample, who sometimes find it easier to use English to communicate most effectively' (Parmegiani, 2010: 374).

Dyers and Abongdia (2010) discuss the difference between language attitudes and ideologies. The main differences are that attitudes can change depending on a variety of socioeconomic factors, such as age, gender, social class, and education, but ideologies 'are constructed in the interest of a specific social or cultural group, i.e., they are rooted in the socio-economic power and vested interests of dominant groups' (2010: 123). The results, using data from high school students in the Cameroon context, emphasize attitudes toward English. Most of the participants had a more positive attitude toward French than they did toward English, citing 'It is my culture' (2010: 127) or 'French is the language of the people' (2010: 128). Some participants recognized the importance of knowing English as 'a language of the world' (2010: 128), and one even indicated that although they had positive attitudes toward English, they would be punished when speaking English at home as a result of parental attitudes.

Southeast Asia

Lamb (2012, 2013) uses the L2MSS framework to examine the motivation of Indonesian junior high pupils. Lamb (2012) is a quantitative study using 10 variables with a primary focus of looking at student motivation in three different contexts: metropolitan city, provincial town, and rural area. In all three contexts, the ideal self, instrumentality, and international posture have the highest mean scores, indicating that all students in Indonesia, even those in rural areas, are 'well aware of the potential importance of English for themselves and of the possible benefits that could accrue to them by gaining proficiency' (Lamb, 2012: 1009). Looking closer at the three groups, overall, those in areas with larger populations, the metropolitan and provincial areas, patterned more similarly than those in rural areas, likely because of resource and opportunity disparities. For example, those students in rural areas 'found it more difficult to imagine a future English-speaking self' (Lamb, 2012: 1009), leading Lamb (2012: 1014) to indicate 'only [a] partial endorsement here of the importance of the Ideal L2 self in motivating language learners'. In this study, the urban context versus the rural context strongly affected the capability of creating an ideal English self. It is also of note that the ought-to self construct was excluded from the analyses because of the low internal reliability of the items. Via interviews, Lamb (2013) further investigates the ideal self with these participants, specifically those in rural areas who had high ideal selves but lower English proficiency than their provincial and metropolitan counterparts. Two learners from an urban school and another from a rural school with a different profile (low ideal self) were also interviewed for comparison purposes. The future selves of the high ideal self rural learners indicated upward mobility (i.e. teacher, model), but were different in terms of the answers from students in more heavily populated areas (i.e. doctor). The majority of the participants indicated they would like to make their parents proud and have a profession to help others, and all but the participant with a low ideal self indicated a link between future success and English. It is also important to note that for the rural students, while their parents supported their efforts to learn English, they were likely not the role models that helped create the students' ideal selves. Lamb suggests that other, younger, family members might serve as role models for these students. Also important in terms of accessibility is the growing access to technology and social networking making it possible 'to reach across national borders' (Lamb, 2012: 25). In a subsequent study, Lamb (2018) re-examines interview data and subsequent motivational trajectories; the most salient finding was the lasting effect of the researcher on student motivation. Also using the L2MSS framework in the context of Thailand, Siridetkoon and Dewaele (2018: 324) examined the ideal and ought-to selves of Thai students who were studying English plus an additional language. In terms of the ideal self, one finding was the perception that a language other than English (LOTE) gave them a competitive edge; as everyone is expected to know English, only an additional language will help people stand out in the job market: 'students of an L3 had a powerful vision of ideal self to sustain their learning effort despite the presence of global English'. Their motivation fluctuated throughout the learning process, and positive attitudes toward English were not sufficient motivators if the students did not see how English would help them achieve future goals. In terms of LOTEs, 'dislike for other FLs could be overcome by the students' perceived improvement of their performance, necessity, or the idea of future rewards' (Siridetkoon & Dewaele, 2018: 325).

In a different context with a distinct perspective, Trang Thi Thuy Nguyen and Hamid (2016) examine the motivation of Vietnamese ethnic minority students using qualitative data. These eight participants had home languages of Rengao (2), Bahnan (2), Jarai (2), Halang (1), and Jeh (1), and the interview data focuses on their conceptualizations of self in their L1s, Vietnamese, and English. Trang Thi Thuy Nguyen and Hamid (2016: 94) state that 'Connecting their home language to their ethnicity, the students were probably thinking about their possible selves – the image of the person speaking, preserving L1 and identifying with the L1 community they would like to become', indicating the importance of preserving the L1. In terms of Vietnamese and English, the authors state that they are 'manifestations of instrumentality-promotion that belongs to their ideal language self', but in terms of Vietnamese, they also feel obliged to learn it well (ought-to self) to avoid social isolation and the stagnation of opportunities in Vietnamese society. The authors talk about different selves developing in different languages; the participants envision English as providing opportunities for education, international communication, and relationship building. Several of the participants connect the idea of 'knowledge', broadly construed with the idea of an 'ideal Vietnamese self' in terms of access and opportunity. Also in Vietnam, White and Cuong Pham (2017) discuss English language learning in a rural context. Although the framework used is the Bakhtinian construct of chronotope, not the L2MSS, the concepts of visualizing future goals are one of the main discussion points of this study. For example, one of the participants, Phong, uses visualization to contrast two future selves: one who speaks English with more opportunities and one who does not speak English with fewer opportunities. He continues with his English study to 'maximise his life chances and answer not only to the expectations of significant others (such as his parents and grandmother), but also to his own expectation of how he will meet the challenges that may confront him in the top class' (White & Cuong Pham, 2017: 215). It can be seen that imagining an ideal English-speaking self and what that entails in this context is an important part of Phong's English learning motivation.

Latin America

Of the contexts in question, research in Latin America and Africa had the least number of publications of the articles examined. In the Latin American context, there were only two self-related articles found. Kormos and Kiddle (2013) examined how socioeconomic factors (i.e. context) in Chile could affect language learning motivation. In describing this context, like Gao (2010: 400) who indicated the vast socioeconomic disparity in China, Kormos and Kiddle state that Chile, while often classified as the 'most stable country in South America' also experiences 'a high degree of social stratification' with one of the 'most segregated educational systems in the world'. Thirteen latent variables were examined along with the socioeconomic status of the 740 participants in this study. Five socioeconomic class divisions were determined based on household income and parents' education levels: low, lower middle, middle, upper middle, and high. As regards the results involving the L2MSS (i.e. the ideal self – the ought-to self was not included in the data collection), students from upper-middle and high class households had significantly stronger ideal selves than did those students from low, lower-middle, and middle class households. Although relatively little data has been collected on motivation and socioeconomic status, the authors liken their findings to Lamb (2012), who also found lower ideal selves in Indonesian students from rural areas, who were predominantly from lower social classes. Also in the Chilean context, Kormos et al. (2011) analyzed questionnaire data from 518 secondary, university, and language institute students using structural equation modeling. The ideal and ought-to selves, as well as motivated learning behavior, were three of the nine latent variables examined. In all three participant groups, there was a relationship between the ideal self and motivated learning behavior with a stronger relationship for the secondary and university students. The ought-to self did not have a relationship to motivated learning behavior for any of the participant groups. These results are similar to the results in Papi (2010) regarding the relationship of intended learning effort and the ideal self (and not the ought-to self), but are different from the results found in the Chinese (i.e. Li, 2014; You et al., 2016) and Japanese (i.e. Ueki & Takeuchi, 2013) contexts. There was also a relationship between language learning attitudes and the ideal self for all three groups, with the strongest relationship being with the university students. International posture also strongly influenced the students' ideal selves, which is different from the finding in Islam et al. (2013); parental encouragement was found to influence the ought-to self more than any other latent variable. Using frameworks other than the L2MSS, Banegas et al. (2020) examined the reason for the demotivation of English language student-teachers in a teacher education program in Argentina to complete written assignments. The initial lack of authenticity was the reason for the initial demotivation; motivation increased with the goal of learning to write for publication. In the Brazilian context, Castro (2018) examined the motivation fluctuations of a student enrolled in a teaching English as a foreign language (TEFL) program. A self-identified low-level learner at the outset of the 16-month observation period, the student's motivation was strengthened due to a variety of factors, the most prominent being his language advisor who coached him in the learning process.

The Middle East and Turkey

Of the contexts involved in this project, most publications on context and self were from the Middle East and Turkey; as such, a few relevant studies are highlighted here. Much of the L2MSS research in this region involves large-scale, quantitative studies from Iran. For example, using the ideal and ought-to selves from the L2MSS, as well as the added dimensions of English anxiety and intended effort, Papi (2010) analyzed data from 1011 Iranian high school students. Based on the results of structural equation modeling, the ideal self and the learning experience (operationalized in this study as the English classes themselves) had the strongest relationship to the intended learning effort. As can be expected, the ought-to self had the strongest relationship to English anxiety, with the ideal self and the learning experience having inverse relationships. It is important to note that some of the relationships were quite weak (i.e. the learning experience to English anxiety at −0.16), although all of the relationships were significant, perhaps owing to the large sample size. Papi and Teimouri (2014) collected data from a similar population (i.e. 1278 secondary students learning English in Iran) and found results that supported those of Papi (2010) in terms of anxiety. As was found in Papi (2010), a strong ideal self seems to be the most important for high levels of motivated learning behavior, with the difference in ought-to self strengths less relevant. However, the group with the lowest ought-to self had relatively higher proficiency and lower anxiety, indicating that, like other studies, strong ought-to selves can have a negative relationship to proficiency (i.e. Liu & Thompson, 2018).

Taking a closer look at the ought-to self facet of the L2MSS, Teimouri (2017) followed in the footsteps of Thompson and Vásquez (2015) by applying the own/other dichotomy of the L2MSS to the ought-to self guide. Via principle component analysis (PCA), Teimouri confirmed that the ought-to self could be conceptualized into an 'own' component and an 'other' component, whereas this was not the case for the ideal self (although see Thompson [2017b] for an example of an exploratory factor analysis [EFA] that found a division in the ideal self of the second foreign language learned). Using regression models, Teimouri found that the ideal self most strongly predicted intended learning effort, followed by the ought-to self/own. The ought-to self/others was also a significant predictor, but at a lower level. The inverse was true for anxiety: the ought-to self/others was the strongest predictor, followed by the ought-to self/own. The ideal self did not significantly predict anxiety. The results of the regression models for intended effort and anxiety support the results from Papi (2010) and Papi and Teimouri (2014) for these constructs. Regression models were also carried out for willingness to communicate (WTC) (ideal self only), joy (ideal self and ought-to self/own), and shame (all three selves).

Using similar quantitative methods in a different context, Islam et al. (2013) examined the motivation of 1000 undergraduate students in Pakistan. The authors used 12 scales that had been used in previous studies: cultural interest, attitudes toward the L2 community, integrativeness, instrumentality (promotion), instrumentality (prevention), English anxiety, milieu, intended learning effort, ideal L2 self, ought-to L2 self, attitudes to learning English, and international posture. A new construct, national interest, was developed to focus specifically on the importance of English in the context of Pakistan. The regression model found that attitude toward learning English most strongly predicted intended learning efforts, followed closely by ideal self and milieu. Other predictors were international posture, cultural interest, and the ought-to self. Regression analyses were also carried out with the three components of the L2MSS used as criterion measures. As expected, instrumentality (prevention) was the strongest predictor of the ought-to self and instrumentality (promotion) was the strongest predictor of the ideal self; neither of these predictors contributed to the other self in the models. The new construct, national interest, contributed to the ideal self and the learning experience, but not to the ought-to self. National interest was a stronger predictor than international posture in this study, indicating that the participants valued learning English for use in their own context, rather than internationally. Using both quantitative and qualitative methods in a multilingual Pakistani context, Rasool and Winke (2019) found that the learners of English in this study did not necessarily use native speakers as models for language learning goals. Also, although this context was more multilingual than other Pakistani contexts researched, Rasool and Winke (2019: 60) found the L2MSS framework equally valid to use with English learners in this setting, and they encourage researchers to keep the language learning context in mind, particularly the 'colonial legacy attached to English'.

Two recent articles investigated the L2MSS framework in rural contexts. In the context of rural Yemen, Al-Murtadha (2019) found that weekly visualization sessions enhanced the students WTC; techniques other than visualization were also found to help develop the ideal self. This study provides practical information on how teachers in a variety of contexts can help students create strong ideal selves. In Iraq, Hajar (2018) discussed the motivational path of a student from a rural setting, Noura, who needed a higher test of English as a foreign language (TOEFL) score to attend a postgraduate program in the UK. Her context originally constrained her language learning: 'This situation was clearly influenced by political and societal factors in Iraq along with the rigid practices of most of her English teachers in under-resourced rural schools' (Hajar, 2018: 425). Noura's vision of 'being the first woman in her village to complete her higher studies abroad, and her aspirations to demonstrate an accurate and positive picture of Islam and participate in the economic development of Iraq (i.e. individual and national interest)' (Hajar, 2018: 425) were the factors that motivated her to develop in English, a development that was also supported by a Canadian coworker.

In the Turkish context, Thompson and Erdil-Moody (2016) examined the ideal and ought-to selves of university students through the lens of two different operationalizations of multilingualism. The first operationalization defined bilinguals as those who had only studied English and multilinguals as those with experience with more than one foreign language. The second operationalization was perceived positive language interaction (PPLI) – an emic perspective of multilingualism that indicates that learners can be defined as multilingual only if they can perceive positive interactions between the foreign languages studied (i.e. perceiving how learning Spanish could help with learning Japanese). The number of participants in each group for both operationalizations of multilingualism was similar. Although the effect size was larger for the PPLI/NPPLI distinction, a significant difference was found between groups for both operationalizations of multilingualism. No significant difference was found with the ought-to self. A secondary point of inquiry was that of potential gender differences with the selves: no significant difference was found between male and female learners for either the ideal or ought-to self.

Polat and Schallert (2013), one of the only studies in this region that focuses on motivation to learn a LOTE, collected data from 121 Kurdish adolescents regarding their Turkish learning with a focus on accent and pronunciation (see also Polat, 2014). In a regression model with 'native-like' accent in Turkish as the criterion measure, Turkish identification positively predicted a native-like accent, whereas Kurdish identification negatively predicted it. The ideal self was not a significant predictor of Kurdish adolescents' native-like accents in Turkish. Context was especially relevant in this study, considering the historic sociopolitical conflicts with Turkish and Kurdish speakers. The authors suggest that, 'learners can attain near-native L2 accent without demonstrating low levels of identification with their native language as long as they also maintain high level of identification with the L2 community' (Polat & Schallert, 2013: 758).

Europe

As the L2MSS was first conceptualized by Dörnyei (originally from Hungary with a scholastic life in the UK), it is perhaps not surprising that the L2MSS framework is frequently used in the European context. In the context of Eastern Europe, Csizér and Lukács (2010) document English negatively affecting Hungarian students' motivation to learn German, particularly if these students are not able to learn the languages in the desired order. Earlier studies by Csizér and colleagues that are not included in this review also examine the role of multiple languages with the development of selves. Additionally, these authors examine the L2MSS in tandem with other aspects of motivation in Hungary. For example, Csizér and Tankó (2017) analyze the relationship of self-regulatory control strategies, writing, and motivation. Related to the L2MSS, those with higher reported use of control strategies also seem to have a more developed ideal self, 'which shows that the control of present activities is linked to future visions' (Csizér & Tankó, 2017: 398). In Csizér *et al.* (2010), the motivation of dyslexic students is examined. As does the motivation of non-dyslexic students, the motivation of these participants greatly fluctuated throughout the language learning process. Another main, perhaps expected, finding was the negative language learning self concepts that these participants had; in some cases 'the discrepancy between their actual and ideal selves was often so great that they gave up language learning or did not invest sufficient energy in it' (Csizér *et al.*, 2010: 484). Comparing several contexts (Bulgaria, Germany, the Netherlands, and Spain), Busse (2017) examined attitudes toward English versus LOTEs in these contexts. Bulgarian student answers stood out in several ways. For example, the Bulgarian students placed more importance on the teacher effect of influencing attitudes than on the status of English. Additionally, comments on ability were mentioned least by Bulgarian students. Some of the students in this study showed a positive attitude toward languages in general. As a Bulgarian student said, 'Languages are an important part of the kind of people we want to become' (Busse, 2017: 576).

In terms of attitudes toward Russian, one of the languages discussed in both the Estonian and Ukrainian narratives, in a study that focused on the task motivation of L1 German students studying Russian in Germany, Mozgalina (2015) found three reasons that her participants were studying Russian, other than the language requirement: wanting to learn a language outside of the Germanic or Romance classification (also see the anti-ought-to self, Thompson, 2017a), having friends or partners from Russia (ideal self), and usefulness for future employment (ought-to self). This motivation is quite different from the relationship with Russian for those in the former Soviet Union, such as Estonia and Ukraine. In contexts such as Germany, attitudes toward Russian lack the emotional charge that some individuals living in the former Soviet Union have toward the language.

Teacher Motivation and the Development of Ideal Teacher Selves

As indicated in the preface, research on teacher motivation inevitably necessitates an interdisciplinary approach. Merging the fields of individual differences in SLA and sociolinguistic approaches, this project focuses on issues of teacher self-development and context. Kubanyiova (2019) summarized the synthesis of approaches:

> Drawing from insights from across these multiple domains might lend an instructive transdisciplinary perspective on the future shape, scope, and directions for teacher motivation research; that is, a perspective that engages more systematically with the broader sociocultural and ideological as well as psychological layers of language teachers' work on the one hand and which seeks to integrate the knowledge base of

other disciplinary domains, such as sociolinguistics and second language acquisition (SLA) on the other. (Kubanyiova, 2019: 392)

In the same 2019 publication, Kubanyiova provides three metaphors to examine teacher motivation: *complexity*, *figured worlds*, and *acts of imagination*. In terms of complexity, she specifically highlights studies that connect student engagement and teacher motivation with a focus on the uniqueness of relationships formed in all contexts. The metaphor of *figured worlds* is a direct connection of teachers and their contexts, which is the focus of this current project: 'the metaphor of figured worlds lends a distinctly sociocultural and, crucially, ideological and socio-political perspective on understanding the worlds in which teachers are invested as they learn to support their students' (Kubanyiova, 2019: 398). Directly related to the concept of possible selves, and thus to the formation of the ideal teacher self, *acts of imagination* refers to the vision of who language teachers would like to become, particularly as it relates to the larger context: 'what kinds of images are at the heart of teachers' acts of imagination, what are the sociocultural, historical, political, or linguistic circumstances that may have given rise to those images… and, most importantly, what difference do they make to their students' language learning experience in the classroom and beyond?' (Kubanyiova, 2019: 400). It is clear that the issues surrounding teacher motivation cannot be explored from a singular perspective.

Teacher motivation has been examined from a variety of different perspectives, such as vision (Kalaja, 2016), visual identity (Brandão, 2018), identity positioning (Kim, 2017), language teacher cognition (Kubanyiova & Feryok, 2015), as well as connected areas such as teacher commitment (Moodie & Feryok, 2015), teacher emotions (Golombek & Doran, 2014; Martínez Agudo, 2018) and socio-emotional competencies (Gkonou & Mercer, 2018), teacher autonomy development (Dikilitaş & Mumford, 2020), teacher attitudes toward students (Dewaele & Mercer, 2018), teacher motivational strategy use (Erdil-Moody & Thompson, 2020; Karimi & Zade, 2019; Waddington, 2018) and WTC (Sato, 2019), sustained flow/directed motivational currents (Ibrahim & Al-Hoorie, 2019), and teacher resilience (Hiver, 2018). Job satisfaction is also related to teacher motivation (Bernaus, 2020), as are issues related to resources (Gao & Xu, 2014; Zhai, 2019). Hiver *et al.* (2018) explore general issues of teacher motivation, including motivation for entering the teaching profession. Reasons such as job stability and retirement benefits are cited, as well as others. A motivation for entering into the teaching profession that is especially relevant for this current project is that of the status of English: 'in the era of globalisation, English proficiency can be perceived as a measure of affluence and social savviness. Thus, the implicit social values and interest in foreign cultures that accompanies English language use can create EFL teachers' global orientation and function as a source influencing teachers to enter the profession' (Hiver *et al.*, 2018: 25, see also Baleghizadeh & Gordani, 2012; Kim *et al.*, 2014). An overview of these and other topics can be found in Mercer and Kostoulas' (2018) edited collection of issues surrounding language teacher psychology; the following sections focus specifically on ideal teacher selves.

Overview of the development of ideal teacher selves

Of the numerous studies on the development of language learning selves, relatively few focus on the development of teacher selves. Indeed, relatively few studies focus on the teacher side of learning, even though 'understanding language teacher psychology is centrally related to an understanding of the psychology of their learners, too' (Mercer & Kostoulas, 2018: 3). Of the studies focusing on teachers, most involve teachers of English, with a few exceptions. In the context of the United States, Thompson and Vásquez (2015) examine the language learning narratives of teachers of German, Italian, and Chinese, and Thompson (2017a) focuses on teachers of Arabic and Chinese, although teacher education is not the main focus of either of these studies. In the Chinese context, Tao *et al.* (2019) discuss the ideal and ought-to selves of LOTE university faculty in China, especially when it comes to the expectation of publishing in English, a language that is neither their L1 nor the language that they teach. Valmori and de Costa (2016) primarily used data from English teachers in Italy, although their participants included one teacher of Spanish and one of French. Although a variety of aspects are discussed in these teacher motivation articles, the focus of this section is on issues surrounding the formation of their ideal selves, as the relationship of self and context is the overarching theme of this project.

Of the studies on teacher motivation discussed here, and indeed in much of the literature on teacher motivation, the teachers in question are oftentimes not L1 users of the language they teach. Perhaps unsurprisingly, a common theme arises throughout: the perception of less-than-adequate proficiency of the target language. It should be noted, however, that this was not a common theme found with the teachers in this project. As specified in Valmori and de Costa (2016: 102), 'Most of the interviewees set high proficiency standards for themselves and stated that their goal as learners was to become like a native speaker', which was a strong part of their development of their ideal teacher selves. These participants indicated that upon graduation, they had good proficiency but that they needed further development of their language skills to be, in their opinion, effective teachers. However, depending on the level of English that they were required to teach, in some cases the impetus for improving was not present. A colleague's attitude of not wanting to 'waste time' on professional development was reported by one of the participants in the study: 'He said that the level [of his students] was so low that he didn't even need a degree for the English he was teaching [...] The context is so demotivating' (Valmori & de Costa, 2016: 104). That being said, all of the participants in the Valmori and de Costa study seemed to have created an ideal self that was a 'native speaker' of the language taught, a goal that many have argued is not realistic. Having unrealistic goals for an ideal self may cause demotivation in the long term; as Dörnyei (2009) emphasizes, images and goals used in the creation of the ideal self will only be effective if they are realistic and attainable.

In some cases, the ideal teacher self that has been developed by certain teachers is not congruent with some classroom activities, such as allowing students to interact and to engage in communicative activities during class. Such was the case for Tamara, Kubanyiova's (2015) case study participant. Through interviews, the themes of 'control, authority, dominance, and leadership' emerged, and 'Tamara's desire to lead was integral to her deeply internalised language teacher' (Kubanyiova, 2015: 577) and her ideal teacher self image 'as a well-organised and highly competent language educator who is in full charge of the teaching process and a primary knower in her interaction with the students clearly clashed with some of the pedagogical objectives of classroom context mode' (Kubanyiova, 2015: 579). It is not clear what contextual factors have led Tamara to create this ideal teacher self image, but the author suggests that awareness-raising would be insufficient to make her rethink her practices. Instead a 'transformation of her vision' (Kubanyiova, 2015: 579) would be necessary to relinquish a bit of the classroom control that she so craves.

The theme of a multitude of obligations for teachers also emerged from the previous research. For example, in the Korean context, Guilloteaux (2013) presents evidence that teachers tend to underuse motivational strategies in the classroom, indicating that motivating students is not a priority for these teachers, which is likely due to the context. Specifically, Guilloteaux (2013: 11) explains that 'teachers are often exhausted by institutional demands and sociocultural constraints' related to the emphasis on class time spent toward test prep, large class sizes, and a heavy administrative workload. Guilloteaux (2013: 12) also states that 'Korean teachers may need more practice at giving specific positive feedback'. Based on the data presented, it can be extrapolated that these teachers' ideal selves do not include a teacher-as-motivator aspect.

Also in the Korean context, Hiver (2013) investigated why his participants (seven in-service Korean English teachers) wanted to participate in a government-sponsored six-month training course. Repairing inadequacies of the self (prevention) and enhancing the self (promotion) were the two main reasons he found, and the third finding, adhering to normative obligations, was less significant for these teachers (Hiver, 2013: 215). Like the participants in the Valmori and de Costa study, Hiver found that these teachers were not secure in terms of their English language abilities (operationalized as self-efficacy), which motivated them to seek out professional development workshops such as the one described in this study. As Hiver (2013: 216) describes, 'The overwhelming majority of these positive future self images, however, relate to the participants' ideals as expert language users. Curiously, these teachers tended to respond to questions about "self as a teacher" with answers restricted to language proficiency issues, rather than strictly about teacher identity'. One of the participants stated that 'I always want to be as good as a native speaking teacher in a native speaking country… One day I'm going to study abroad and I'm going to prove that I'm as good as the rest of them' (Hiver, 2013: 216), which is a sentiment reflected by the Turkish teachers in the current book project. This comment is especially interesting as it expresses the desire for native-like proficiency while simultaneously indicating an inclination to attempt this challenge. The desire to 'prove' oneself in light of a difficult situation is akin to Thompson's (2017a) idea of an *anti-ought-to self*, the self that is conceptualized by the desire to succeed in the face of challenges or to do something that others believe to be difficult or impossible. Like those participants in Guilloteaux's study, enhancing student motivation was not a priority for these teachers; instead, the focus was on their own English language proficiency.

Looking at teacher selves from a different angle, in a teacher self scale validation study, Karimi and Norouzi (2019) looked at latent variables in three possible language teacher self-questionnaires: the ideal, feared, and ought-to language teacher selves. Particularly relevant to the current study are the sub-scales of the ideal language teacher self-questionnaire. The first latent variable, *self as an expert in pedagogy*, 'reveals that teachers' pedagogy-relevant visions of themselves as teachers are central to their ideal selves… this finding further indicates that teachers' images of their ideal selves are linked to their students' (Karimi & Norouzi, 2019: 54). The second latent variable in this questionnaire, *self as an expert language user*, 'reflects teachers' aspirations for developing native-like language proficiency and lends support to the previous finding that language teachers' images of themselves are primarily those of native-like linguistic experts' (Karimi & Norouzi, 2019: 54), findings which resonate with other studies on language teacher motivation (Hiver, 2013; Valmori & de Costa, 2016). The last two latent variables in the ideal teacher self-questionnaire are *self as a socially/professionally recognized teacher* and *self as a teacher interested in professional development*. Aspects of these sub-areas of an ideal language teacher self can be found in the context-specific chapters in this book.

Gao and Xu (2014) also present data regarding English teachers' ideal self development in rural areas in China. Like the participants in Guilloteaux's study, these participants indicated that teaching comes with a heavy workload (2014: 158) and an overreliance on test scores (2014: 162); unlike those in the other studies, these Chinese participants also cited low pay as a demotivator (2014: 158). The ideal selves of these teachers began to be shaped once they started interacting with students and saw the progress that these students made with their help; external validation, such as winning a teaching award or publishing an article also helped with the ideal self formation. They also indicated that role models, such as a previous English teacher or a family member, influenced their love for English (Gao & Xu, 2014: 160). As in many contexts, these teachers found a discrepancy in what they wanted to achieve as teachers and what was expected of them in terms of school administration and society; thus, they experienced a clash between their ideal and ought-to teacher selves. Like participants in other studies, these Chinese teachers had a focus on improving their own English language proficiency as an integral part of forming an ideal teacher self (Gao & Xu, 2014: 159), and several indicated that teaching in the context of a rural school did not afford them opportunities to improve their English, as one participant notes: 'In rural schools, English teachers had no environment for learning [...] In the villages, there was no money for us to have any professional development [...] We just could not keep teaching with the world shut to us' (Gao & Xu, 2014: 163). Another participant states that she does not wish to teach in secondary school because it will not provide her with opportunities to improve her English: she 'wanted to maintain the knowledge acquired from her master's studies, particularly English competence, which has been consistently at the core of her visions of "ideal self"' (Gao & Xu, 2014: 164). Although not specific to language teaching, Zhai (2019: 88) discussed teacher motivation development in rural contexts in China, finding that 'rural teacher motivation is a complex construct. It includes two layers: "to be a teacher" and "to be a teacher in the rural area"'. In the context of the United States, Thompson (in press) examines and compares trends of university LOTE study in a rural and an urban setting, particularly examining the trends of external resistance found in these contexts and student resistance to persevere nonetheless (anti-ought-to self). The study also provides illustrative examples from experienced K-12 teachers in a rural context and how they helped their students in these contexts develop ideal Spanish selves.

The connection of non-native speaker status and the ideal teacher self

Several studies that illustrate a potential link between non-native speaker identity of English teachers and the formation of the ideal teacher self are subsequently highlighted; however, a problematization of the term 'non-native speaker' first needs to be unpacked. For years, the terms 'native speaker' and 'non-native speaker' have been used to describe learners and teachers in what can be interpreted as a deficit model of categorization. Recently, scholars such as Dewaele, Ortega,

Cook, and others have argued for a shift in terminology away from 'non-native speaker'. Scholars such as Ortega (i.e. 2013) and Cook (i.e. 1999) have argued for 'L2 user', while Dewaele (2018) has argued for 'LX user', so as to not indicate the superiority of one language over another and to also highlight that learners can be multicompetent in more than one language. In terms of language instruction, many scholars, such as Kramsch (2014: 305), have argued that native speaker instruction isn't the goal: 'The real living monolingual NS in all his/her phonological, stylistic, ethnic, and social diversity was never the goal of instruction... The purpose is not to abandon all standard pedagogic norms of language use as the goal of instruction. It is, rather, to strive to make our students into multilingual individuals, sensitive to linguistic, cultural, and above all, semiotic diversity, and willing to engage with difference, that is, to grapple with differences in social, cultural, political, and religious world-views'. This statement resonates with Ortega's (2013) argument to reduce the monolingual bias in the field of SLA, and as Aneja (2016) postulates, there may not be a need to conceptualize native speaker and non-native speaker categories at all (see also Aslan & Thompson, 2017). One aspect is clear, as Rothman and Treffers-Daller (2014: 97–98) indicate: 'We can no longer afford to be tolerant of the hegemony of monolingualism as the standard and the sole proprietor of the native label, as such would be to deny the linguistic reality of a world where multilingualism is the majority state of linguistic knowledge'. Additionally, Kuteeva (2014) warns of the common misconception that academic competence in English equals native-like proficiency, and Selvi (2014) discusses the misconceptions about the teaching English to speakers of other languages (TESOL) non-native speaker teacher (NNST) movement.

In terms of the labels used in this project, several considerations were given. When possible, the term 'L2 user' is preferred; however, as much of the previous literature on this topic uses the term 'non-native' speaker, this term is also used when discussing these specific studies. In terms of the discussions with the participants of this project, the terms 'native speaker' and 'non-native speaker' were used because of familiarity and clarity; this was also how these participants self-identified. The last consideration is the self-identification of those L2 users/non-native speakers themselves in the field. Several advocacy and special interest groups have co-opted this term for their own use, with a strong sense of identity intertwined. For example, the group 'TEFL Equity Advocates & Academy' has on the homepage of their website: 'Download this FREE checklist to learn easy, actionable tips that you can immediately use to start promoting equal professional opportunities for both "native" and "non-native speaker" teachers' (https://teflequityadvocates.com/). Also, TESOL International has a special interest section called '"Nonnative" English Speaker Teachers Interest Section (NNEST-IS)'. The term 'non-native' was recently put into quotation marks, the rationale for which is described as follows: 'The quotation marks surrounding the word "Non-native" was purposefully added to denote the idea that teachers may position themselves (and others), and be positioned, as "non-native"' (https://nnest.moussu.net/history.html). With the added quotations around the term 'Nonnative' came revised objectives of the special interest group:

- promote, develop, and advance academic and professional awareness of the experiences of 'NNEST' professionals in the field;
- stimulate scholarship, research, and professional development within the IS, by sponsoring special projects, sessions at the TESOL convention, webinars and publications;
- provide members with opportunities to learn about the continuum of perspectives that study and address privilege-marginalization;
- contribute to the cultivation of a non-discriminatory professional environment for all TESOL members, through a focus on teachers positioning themselves and/or are positioned as 'NNESTs';
- connect with other critically oriented professional communities within and beyond TESOL International, in unity and in recognition that privilege-marginalization manifests in ways unaddressed by the scope of the IS.

Thus, in terms of terminology, care must be taken to allow teachers to position themselves as they see fit, while at the same time, acknowledging and fighting against the marginalization that still exists surrounding the topics of teaching a language other than the L1.

Indeed, despite the boom of writing and theorizing on this topic in recent years (see Kamhi-Stein [2016] for an overview), there still seems to be a native/non-native speaker divide, particularly when it comes to language teaching in some contexts. Kumaravadivelu (2016) questions why inadequacies still exist, such as pay discrepancies for native versus non-native speaker teachers (also see Ruecker & Ives, 2015). Ruecker and Ives (2015: 751) also document the intersection of race and perceived nativeness in many Southeast Asian advertisements for English language teachers: 'they delimit who qualifies as a native speaker through the use of repeated images of White teachers and text demanding that teachers produce passports from a list of predominantly White, inner-circle countries' (see also Holliday & Aboshiha, 2009; Todd & Pojanapunya, 2009). Jenkins (2017: 375) and Charles (2019: 5) also address issues of race and perceived nativeness, specifically in terms of Blackness: Jenkins describes jobs 'mysteriously' becoming 'filled' after his race was revealed and Charles (2019: 1) describes Black teachers of English in South Korea who 'assumed the identity of cultural ambassadors' not only of the English language, but also for their 'racial and ethnic backgrounds as Black Americans'. Fan and Jong (2019: 13) present case study data of a Chinese student in an English as a second language (ESL) teacher preparation course in the United States and calls for more work on 'unpacking the understandings of Asian ethnic English language teachers about their raciolinguistic identities'. Swearingen (2019) provides a synthesis from research on the identity development of non-native English-speaking teacher candidates in North American TESOL programs.

In terms of hiring practices, Trent (2012) discusses a native speaker teacher government initiative in Hong Kong and illustrates the antagonism it creates between the administrators and the different groups of teachers. Jenkins (2017) outlines discriminatory hiring practices worldwide and encourages professionals to raise awareness on this issue in part by collecting data on publishing about these discriminatory hiring practices. Recent literature has offered suggestions on how to empower those who teach in a language other than their L1 (Burri, 2018), and there is some evidence that, at least from the students' perspectives in some cases, native and non-native speaker teachers are equal in terms of pedagogy. For example, Aslan and Thompson (2017) created a series of carefully constructed semantic differential scale items involving teacher characteristics, collecting 76 responses from ESL students taking classes at an intensive English language program that, at that time, employed 23 native speaker English teachers and 19 non-native speaker English teachers (i.e. an almost balanced number). Of the 27 adjective pairs, there was only one significant difference in student perception: the students found the non-native speaker English teachers to be significantly more creative than the native speaker English teachers. These results indicate that when the politically and culturally charged terms 'native' and 'non-native' are not mentioned, students are likely not to perceive a difference in the quality of their English language instruction between these two groups of instructors, providing evidence that perceived differences by other stakeholders (administrators, parents, etc.) are perhaps culturally or socially constructed, as opposed to being based on the linguistic and teaching capabilities of the teachers in question.

Regarding the role of different types of non-native speaker teacher identity in forming a pedagogical style, Zheng (2017) examined the identity of two international teaching assistants (ITAs) teaching English composition: Ming from China and Sara from Egypt. There were examples of Ming struggling with the preconceived ideas that her students had about her: 'Often her knowledge about English language and literature was not considered legitimate because she was viewed as someone from a non-English-speaking country' (Zheng, 2017: 35). In Sara's case, with her dual Egyptian-British nationalities, she was very much aware of the native speaker bias in Egypt, as she was often seen as having a higher rank than the 'local' Egyptian teachers: 'She was seen as a native speaker of English by her Egyptian colleagues who would ask her questions about the English language. She felt slightly guilty about having this privilege, especially after reading articles that examined the native speaker construct in the MATESOL Program. However, Sara never hid her British identity and used it to her advantage' (Zheng, 2017: 38). These two ITAs used their identity as international students/instructors and their language abilities in different ways. Sara was successful at developing a translingual pedagogy, whereas Ming was less so; this relates to several factors including the validation of their identities as English speakers: 'Ming, who learned English as a foreign language in China, sensed others' prejudice with regard to her legitimacy as an English teacher. By contrast, Sara, who grew up speaking British English and was educated through an English-medium education, found her linguistic identity as a bilingual English–Arabic speaker validated in the United States' (Zheng, 2017: 41). Although Zheng does not explicitly bring up this point in the discussion, it would seem that it was Sara's bilingual/bicultural identity in relation to her context that gave her the confidence and freedom to use her linguistic skills to her advantage in the classroom, and it seems that using multiple languages in her pedagogy is part of her ideal teacher self. This is perhaps similar to an L1 English speaker using Spanish to their advantage in an English language classroom in the context of the United States, a situation that exerts privilege in terms of language status and would perhaps be viewed differently than an L1 Spanish speaker similarly using Spanish in an English language classroom in the same context. Even though both teachers might want to develop translingual pedagogy, the L1 Spanish speaker, like Ming in Zheng's study, would not enjoy the same privileges in doing so. Even non-native speaker teachers with considerable teaching experience, such as Puja in Wolff and de Costa (2017), struggle with feelings of insufficiency and even illegitimacy and need to develop strategies for adapting to the expectations of a new context. TESOL programs need to help lead the process to engage and legitimate English teachers from all backgrounds (e.g. Ilieva, 2010). With proper support from mentors, who are often instructors in TESOL programs, a strong ideal teacher self can be developed in harmony with the teachers' language backgrounds. This can be seen in Xia's development in her TESOL program (illustrated in Park, 2012: 141), when, as a result of a mentor, she becomes more confident in her English ability and status: 'I want to improve my English but not for the purpose of being identified as an NES [native English speaker]'. Similarly, Nuske (2018) discusses a TESOL graduate student's (Linlin) shift in attitude over a three-year period toward China English. Upon starting the TESOL program, Linlin's ideal teacher self was that of a native English speaker; however, by the end of her program, she was more open to different varieties of English. Schreiber (2019) also analyzes a shift in attitude vis-à-vis standard inner-circle English. The facilitated virtual exchanges between English teachers in Sri Lanka and MA TESL students in New York helped both groups visualize the importance of multilingualism in language teaching and to challenge the superiority of the language abilities of inner-circle speakers. For an overview of non-native English teacher identity, see Yuan (2019).

Expectations in specific contexts are always relevant in terms of teachers developing an ideal teacher self. Similar to the participants in Guilloteaux (2013), Hayes (2009) found that the context of teaching in rural Thailand affected how teachers developed their ideal selves. The participants started their careers wanting to use student-centered activities and only English in their classes, but because of the context (i.e. perceived lack of need for English, focus on language testing at a national level, etc.), the participants often had to adjust their teaching styles. Lack of resources, similar to Gao and Xu (2014), was also cited as an obstacle in Hayes (2009). In summary, Hayes (2009: 9) encourages 'ELT classroom practice as a response to the locally-situated needs of the participants' as opposed to 'a monolithic view of ELT based on western conceptions of idealised practice', ending with the following sentiment: 'Teachers' nativeness in this respect needs to be given its due prominence in understandings of teaching and learning English as a foreign language in context, rather than disproportionate attention paid to "nonnativeness" in terms of English language competence'.

In the literature, non-native speaker teachers often indicate a need for self-improvement in the area of pronunciation (i.e. Thompson & Fioramonte, 2012; Wolff & de Costa, 2017). As Solano-Campos (2014: 423) states about her own journey in developing an ideal teacher self, 'I saw native-like proficiency as the ultimate trait of a good language learner, and I saw my English learning journey as a journey towards nativeness... Once I started teaching, I became more preoccupied with the thought that my accent and pronunciation would affect my credibility as an English teaching professional'. In the Hong Kong context, Cheung and Sung (2016: 59) found that 13 out of 18 participants strove for 'native-like' pronunciation: 'In particular, these participants' desire for a native-like accent in pursuing a positive self-image could be explained by their perceived association of native-speaker pronunciation with status and prestige, and these positive attributes associated with native-speaker pronunciation appear to be closely related to the participants' perception of native-speaker as the "best" English'. However, a few participants chose to speak with a 'local' accent because of issues relating to identity: 'By choosing to use a local accent of English, they could avoid any native speaker associations, since a native-like accent could potentially index a native-speaker identity, typically associated with Anglophone countries and/or cultures, which may be perceived to be at odds with their desired lingua-cultural identity' (Cheung & Sung, 2016: 61). The question of how teacher accent can affect student development has also been posed. Studies, such as that of Levis *et al.* (2016), have found that the native speaker versus non-native speaker status of teachers did not significantly affect students' comprehensibility and accentedness improvement. Huensch and Thompson (2017) also reported a lack of non-native speaker teachers bias in their LOTE participants. Murphy (2014) suggests the non-native speaker models of pronunciation should be incorporated into English language classrooms to help coun-teract the deficit model that many have about non-native speaker speech.

Additionally, Ma (2012), as have several others (e.g. Chun, 2014), indicates that teachers who share the students' L1 in an EFL context (i.e. L2 users) have certain advantages in the classroom due to empathy for the language learning process and shared cultural knowledge (see Moussu and Llurda [2008] for an overview of non-native speaker teacher advantages). For example, Chun (2014: 574) found that students believed that Korean English teachers 'were judged to be more effective in helping students with the psychological aspects of language learning and in hav-ing sensitivity to students' needs, because of the shared L1 and experience as language learners'. The author explicitly pointed out that although the native speaker and non-native speaker teachers had differing strengths, 'this does not mean that one of the groups is better'. In the Chinese con-text, Rao (2010: 63) pointed out that some of the students were dissatisfied with the insensitivity of native speaker teachers to the students' process of learning English as they: 'have not gone through the complex process of learning the English language as a foreign language' and thus lack insight into the 'typical problems of Chinese students and are unable to anticipate the language difficulties for us'; the lack of knowledge of the students' L1 also contributed to the perceived insensitivity of the learning pro-cess. Todd and Pojanapunya (2009: 30) found that 'In the current study, although students explicitly prefer NESTs, unconsciously they exhibit no real preference and they actually feel warmer towards non-NESTs'. Cop-land et al. (2020) encourage a deeper understanding of the lived classroom experiences of native English speaker teachers (NESTs) and local English teachers (LETs), as there has been a research–reality disconnect.

When it comes to teaching level, however, some research has shown that informal school policies in some contexts tend to place non-native speaker teachers in lower levels: 'I observed that some teachers in the school held preconceived deficit notions of NNESTs. Mainly, I sensed an unspoken agreement that NNESTs were not equipped to teach students in the higher grades' (Solano-Campos, 2014: 427). The non-native speaker teachers of Spanish in Thompson and Fioramonte (2012: 574) indicated similar feelings, whether it be an 'unspoken rule' by program administra-tion, as Susan indicates: 'they hire the native speakers and they give them the more advanced classes' or if it is a matter of self-confidence in teaching higher levels, as indicated by Tipa: 'For me, at the level that I'm teaching – Spanish I, II, III, IV – I would say there is not much difference [for NS ver-sus NNS]. But, in the higher levels, I would say that there is a difference. That I, for example, won't be able to teach literature. I know for sure'.

Yoo (2014) addresses the idea of a conceptualized 'ideal English teacher' outside of the L2MSS framework. Swinging the pendulum to the other side of the superiority of the native speaker teacher argument, he argues that only non-native speaker teachers can be ideal teachers because 'Although native teachers can try to experience this unfamiliarity by learning another language, they will never be able to experience the unfamiliarity of English and its foreignness that their students are experiencing'; therefore, 'The "ideal teacher" thus seems a category reserved only for non-native teachers as only non-native teachers can experience, or have already experienced, the reality of English for people learning it: "a function of its unfamiliarity"' (Yoo, 2014: 85). Approaching the topic from a different angle, Ellis (2013) uses the categories of plurilingual and monolingual teachers instead of the native/non-native speaker teacher dichotomy. She found that plurilinguals have different attitudes toward language learning than do their monolingual counterparts: 'Plurilingual teachers described their language proficiency in confident, neutral terms which suggested that language learning is normal and natural, and challenging but possible' (Ellis, 2013: 457) and 'The monolinguals' talk instead characterised language learning as fraught with difficulty and charged with the potential for embarrassment and failure. Their comments tended towards self-berating and suggested that the monolinguals see language learning as desirable but something they have failed to achieve' (Ellis, 2013: 459). The results and discussion in this study highlight the value of learning languages for a language practitioner, as doing so can alter one's perception of the student process. It is also similar to Henry's (2017) concept of an ideal multilingual self (a self that perceives learning multiple languages to be an ideal) and Coetzee-Van Rooy's (2014) concept of an ought-to multilingual self (a self that needs multiple languages to thrive in a specific context). Unlike Yoo's (2014) argument, the process of learning an additional language (any language) helps teachers understand the language learning process that their students undergo (see also Selvi [2011] for commentary on alternative naming practices for non-native speaker teachers). As Ellis (2016) illustrates, the linguistic identities of language teachers are complex, whether they are teaching their first language or a language learned later in life.

Bringing It All Together: Context and the Learner–Teacher Duality

As was discussed in the first part of this chapter, the concept of *self* and *context* are complex and dynamic. Furthering the complexity relates to discussions about creation of self, either as a teacher, or as a language learner. For example, Papi and Abdollahzadeh (2012) examined the relationship between teachers' use of motivational strategies and student motivational behaviors and found a significant relationship between the two. However, there is often an embodiment of teacher and student in the same individual, as many of the language teachers worldwide, including all of those highlighted in this project, are non-native speakers of the language they teach. As Gregersen and MacIntyre (2015: 216) note, 'Surprisingly little research has been done on the interplay of teacher motivation and learner motivation, and we know even less about the synergy of teacher and learner motivation when embodied in the same person'. And as Mercer (2015b: 151) aptly states about a participant, 'the "teacher self" domain appears to be an integral part and subdomain of her overall EFL self'.

As many language teachers do, the teachers in this project 'balance the identities of being lifelong learners of English as a foreign language who also teach that language' (Gregersen & MacIntyre, 2015: 264) and sometimes struggle to balance the duality of these roles. Participants in Gregersen and MacIntyre's (2015: 266) study were very much aware of the interaction of their language student and language teacher roles, as participant 11 indicates: 'I would dare to state that the relationship between my learner and teacher motivation is cyclic and they are in constant interaction'. The participants also made comments regarding constantly being a learner, even after becoming a teacher, and the influences that their experiences as a learner had on their teacher selves.

This book project brings together a variety of complex phenomena, specifically the embodiment of self and context in several EFL teachers. Through the relationship between context and self, as well as the student–teacher duality of these teachers, each context-specific chapter takes the reader on a journey through the lived reality of the featured teachers. Through the themes that emerged via the narrative data, an exploration of development of self, with the complexities that this process entails, unfolds for each of the teachers.

Rationale for the Research Approach Taken

The research approach to the current project is a narrative-based qualitative approach. As Savin-Baden and Howell-Major (2013: 238) state, using a narrative approach is a way 'to discover information that the participants themselves may not realize'. Focusing on 'the lived experience, motivations and realities of language learners as uniquely individual "people" is among the greatest strengths and contributions of qualitative approaches to researching motivation' (Ushioda, 2020: 202), and helps to clarify the integration of selves to context. Benson (2019: 66) indicates that qualitative methods such as case studies are used in order to put the focus on 'the individual in social context, rather than the social context itself', and Linde (1993: 219), in her text on life stories which have similar characteristics to narratives, discusses how life stories allow for an expression of self: 'Life stories express our sense of self – who we are, how we are related to others, and how we became that person. They are also one very important means by which we communicate our sense of self to others and negotiate it with others', and as Serafini (2020: 150) indicates, 'both large-scale replication and small-scale exploratory studies in order to address the broader question of the extent to which the self is situated' are needed to take the conceptualization of self past a generic global construct. As such, the relationship between the context and self of EFL teachers is qualitatively explored in this study.

Norton (2013: 58–60) discusses six ideas that guide her investigations of identity and language learning. Although she discusses them in the context of primarily ethnographic research, for this book, three of the concepts are particularly relevant and were used as guiding principles of inquiry. As such, the data analysis and the presentation of excerpts in the chapters are guided by these principles:

(1) 'The researchers are interested in the way individuals make sense of their own experience'.
(2) 'The researchers are interested in locating their research within a historical context'.
(3) 'The researchers reject the view that any research can claim to be objective or unbiased'.

In the following sections, the manner in which these principles guided the analysis and presentation of data in this book project is delineated.

(1) *The researchers are interested in the way individuals make sense of their own experience*

The discussions with the featured teachers in the subsequent chapters were not interviews in the traditional sense; rather, it was akin to what Ushioda (2020) describes as the 'wine and conversation' way of collecting qualitative data. As Ushioda (2020: 198) indicates, the '"wine and conversation" metaphor suggests that facilitating the free flow of ideas and perspectives can generate richly interesting and meaningful insights, which is the essence of qualitative inquiry'.

All of the discussions started with the teachers introducing themselves and describing what their teaching setting was like. The exact prompts varied for each participant or pair of participants, depending on previous interactions and the manner in which the pre-discussion took place. Overall, however, the purpose of asking the teachers to describe their classrooms served to gather background data and was also a warm-up topic to help the teachers ease into the discussion, as a description of the classroom setting itself (number of students, textbooks/materials used, curricular issues, language or instruction) is a fairly objective, non-emotional task. As an example, the start of the discussion with Ablaye, the teacher from Senegal, is as follows: 'So, to start with, I want to ask some questions about your language classroom. What does the typical English lesson look like? What are the materials that you use, the number of students, anything that you can think of?'

The remainder of the discussions were primarily guided by the teachers' comments. Although there were general topics that I wanted to address, how they were specifically discussed varied greatly from participant to participant. The general topics covered in all of the discussions were the classroom context and the role of the instructor; the role of English and LOTEs in the context where they were situated; their own attitudes toward and experiences with English and LOTEs; and opinions about being a teacher of a non-native language (English). In this project, these EFL teachers are positioned as the experts with their diverse language backgrounds and teaching experiences celebrated (i.e. Canagarajah, 2007), and although the terms 'native speaker' and 'non-native speaker' create an unnecessary division, which is arguably irrelevant (i.e. Aslan & Thompson, 2017), these terms are used in the discussions because of their familiarity to the participants involved. The preferred L2 user (i.e. Ortega, 2012) might not have been clear to these EFL teachers, and thus, the more traditional terms were used.

In terms of the topics at hand, in many cases, the teachers brought up these topics on their own; these were the instances that provided the richest data. For example, in the discussion with the Estonian teachers, Darja and Mia, the topic of Russian was brought up when talking about the school setting, as well as later in the discussion. As such, asking about attitudes toward Russian fit naturally into the flow of the conversation. In the case of the discussion with Turkish teachers, Barış and Musa, no mention of any other language was brought up until toward the end of the discussion when I asked: 'What about other languages?... Do you have other languages that you speak or have studied in the past?' as I was curious as to why no other languages other than Turkish and English had been mentioned. As it turns out, although the teachers had had experience with French and German, neither language formed an important part of their language learning or teaching self, as neither had much experience with or attachment to LOTEs; thus, a discussion of this topic was not included in the data analysis for the Turkish teachers. As Ushioda (2020: 206) intuits, 'After all, the "wine and conversation" approach, as with all conversations, is necessarily an interactive process involving exchange of perspectives and co-construction of ideas. In this respect, the qualitative research interview is not a data "elicitation" tool in the strict sense of the term, since the data emerging from the interview is dynamically co-constructed by research and participant (Mann, 2016)'.

Because the conversations were narrative in nature in order to allow the freedom of the teachers to make sense of their own experiences, as opposed to a traditional interview of questions asked and responses recorded, not all of the same themes emerged in the same way through the discussion. As such, the context-specific chapters are formed with the most salient topics from each conversation in terms of self and context, with no set structure for all chapters. Attempting to structure all chapters with the same organization, or indeed the same prompts for all participants, would seem forced, as the data collection method did not lend itself to such rigidity.

(2) *The researchers are interested in locating their research within a historical context*

This aspect of Norton's discussion is central to the organization of this book. Each chapter provides a brief historical background of the political influences on language use in each country (i.e. King, 2016). The current role of English in the society of each context is discussed, both pulling from empirical research on this topic and using the descriptions provided by the EFL teachers. I asked these English teachers to tell me their stories in relation to the linguistic and political contexts of the various settings and countries. The person-in-context chapters do not pretend to be a comprehensive overview of the linguistic and political history of each country, but rather the contextualized lived experiences of one or two remarkable individuals in each context who have agreed to share their stories with me. As Ushioda (2020: 203) indicates, qualitative inquiry, as has been used for this project, 'has contributed also to a different way of conceptualizing language learning that takes account of their context-bound histories, social relationships and lived experiences as well as individuality' and that in the person-in-context approach (Ushioda, 2009), individuals are conceptualized as those who are 'inherently part of, act upon and contribute to shaping the social, cultural and physical environments with which they interact' (Ushioda, 2015: 48). Ushioda (2015: 48) also reminds us that we also need to take into account 'psychological and historical elements of the evolving context that are internal to the learner, such as memories and experiences'.

While looking at data from a person-in-context perspective in which an individual is situated in a specific sociopolitical environment, researchers also need to remember Mercer's (2016) discussion of culture as not being monolithic, but as ever-changing entities. Individuals in the same context can have dramatically different interactions with this context; thus, one must assume variation in the person–context dichotomy: 'We need to appreciate that these [contexts] are in themselves complex dynamic systems and, more crucially in respect to learner characteristics, these are not objective monolithic external variables' (Mercer, 2016: 24). At the same time, while thinking about conceptualizing the context as an internal variable of the self, as opposed to something external and separate, Mercer (2016: 25) warns that we should not allow contexts to become invisible and that 'contexts need to be implicitly integrated into understandings of all learner characteristics, but at the same time, we will need to discuss them explicitly to ensure their continuing visibility, such as exploring and showing explicitly how contexts are embedded in relationships'.

As such, in each context-specific chapter of this book, information about the social and political history as it relates to languages used in that context is provided. An overview of the context starts each chapter, and additional information is interwoven with excerpts from the EFL teacher discussions. An example of a similar approach for providing the linguistic history to situate the data was used in Dyers and Abongdia's (2010) study of attitudes and ideologies of Francophone students learning English in Cameroon. As such, the relationship between context and the selves of the EFL teachers is salient for the readers and it can be seen how they are 'shaped by their personal histories and social-contextual interactions' (Ushioda, 2020: 208).

(3) *The researchers reject the view that any research can claim to be objective or unbiased*

The narratives utilized are the perspectives of these specific English teachers; as such, we must remember that the participants represent their specific truth about the EFL context they are discussing, and that this truth should not be generalized to be representative of the whole country, or of other teachers in the same context (Pavlenko, 2007; Talmy, 2010). Mercer (2016: 17) indicates that different individuals will inevitably have distinct reactions to the same context; thus, what needs to be described is not only the context, but more importantly, 'the learners' own subjective interpretation of the relevance and meaning of respective contextual factors... we need to understand what the individual from their first-person perspective interprets as significant, how and why'. Similarly, Linde (1993: 102) illustrates that it is not the concern of the researcher to determine the truth of the stories elicited. She also indicates that the narrative elicited in and of itself is a form of context, as a narrative 'is not a soliloquy; it is told to someone, and it must elicit some response from its addressee'. Considering the co-constructed nature of a narrative, the narrative itself would differ depending on the researcher involved. The potential non-neutrality of qualitative research should not be concerning but should be carefully monitored during data collection and interpretation (Ushioda, 2020).

Related to the co-construction of the narratives in this project, it is also imperative to indicate my own positionality and subjectivities. As an L1 speaker of English, I have enjoyed a privileged position in the field of English language teaching. I am aware of biases that often, and unfortunately, exist toward non-native speaker teachers of English, and although I have fought against that bias in both formal (Aslan & Thompson, 2017) and informal (Thompson, 2017c) contexts, I have never been a non-native speaker teacher of English and have never faced discrimination because of my L1 when teaching English. However, I have also had the experiences of teaching LOTEs, and in these cases, I was indeed a non-native speaker teacher. As described in Thompson and Fioramonte (2012), there are also widespread biases for non-native speaker teachers of all languages, although as English is the most widely taught in the international context, and thus, the most monetized, the biases toward non-native speaker teachers of English are more overt and salient. Also, although I developed a strong rapport with all participants before the data collection, it should be acknowledged that at the time of the conversations, I had a PhD, a position in a research university, was involved in teacher development at this university and, in the case of the exchange teachers, volunteered as a mentor. As is described in a subsequent section, every effort was made to mitigate the potential power imbalance between the participants and me during our conversations.

At times, individuals who read this book might disagree with the content in some of the narrative excerpts. Linde (1993: 219) also states that narratives 'express our sense of self – who we are, how we are related to others, and how we became that person'. Thus, narratives are not portrayals of 'truth' in the broad sense of the word but are rather the constructed 'truth' from the perspective of the participants (Talmy, 2010). The excerpts in this book are the teachers' construction of their perception of reality, which by default is subjective. The goal of this book is not to determine what is true or not true in a specific context but to interpret the selves of the teachers in relation to their sociopolitical contexts and the relationships therein.

Participants: The English Language Teachers in Focus

The focus of this book is the lived realities of a selection of EFL teachers whose L1s are LOTEs. The analyses that you will find in these chapters are comprised of data both from personal acquaintances/colleagues and from a group of teachers who were on an exchange program at the University of South Florida in the spring of 2010. Volunteering to serve as a mentor to this teacher group, I spent that semester interacting with these teachers in a variety of ways: dining, attending events, and even providing canoeing instruction in the alligator-laden Hillsborough River. As I got to know this group of teachers and started learning about their backgrounds and teaching experiences, I had a strong urge to record longer discussions about their experiences; thus, the project was born. Teachers from five different countries volunteered to have a conversation recorded, and I had the discussions with either one or two teachers from each context represented: Senegal (one teacher: Ablaye), Egypt (one teacher: Hasani), Argentina (two teachers: María and Carolina), Ukraine (two teachers: Oleksandra and Lavra), and Estonia (two teachers: Mia and Darja). Through additional personal networks, I also collected experiences from one teacher from Vietnam (Khiet) and two teachers from Turkey (Musa and Barış). The names used in this book are language-specific pseudonyms, which were chosen either by the teachers or by me and either approved by the participant (if I could get in contact with them) or verified for appropriateness by an external party familiar with the context.

The order of the context-specific chapters is as follows: Senegal, Vietnam, Egypt, Argentina, Turkey, Ukraine, and Estonia. The order is intended to flow via similarities of sociopolitical linguistic influences: the French influence on Senegal, Vietnam, and Egypt; the Anglophone influence on Egypt and Argentina; the Russian influence on Ukraine and Estonia; and so on. Part of the rationale for this project was to provide information on understudied contexts, and examples of teachers-actors in these contexts, so that readers could gain information about settings that do not typically play a large role in the literature about self and context.

Point of Inquiry

The overarching point of inquiry for this project was to understand the symbiotic relationship between these EFL teachers' selves and the context in which they were situated. To achieve this goal, the discussions were centered around the classroom context and the role of the instructor; the role of English and LOTEs in the context where they were situated; their students' and their own attitudes toward and experiences with English and LOTEs; and opinions about being a teacher of a non-native language (English).

Procedure

Each context-specific chapter contains excerpts of narrative data gathered from bi-/multilingual English teachers from understudied contexts (Senegal, Vietnam, Egypt, Argentina, Turkey, Ukraine, and Estonia). The discussions, either one-on-one with me (Senegal, Vietnam, and Egypt) or with two teachers from the same country and me (Argentina, Turkey, Ukraine, and Estonia), were conducted with those participants on a teacher exchange program or with personal acquaintances/colleagues (sample of convenience). The decision to meet with participants individually or in groups of two was due to scheduling constraints; although the dynamic inevitably changes when there are either one or two participants per session, I was careful to engage both participants equally in the two-participant conversations so that each participant had a chance to discuss the topic at hand. In recruiting teachers who were on the exchange program for the project, I arranged a conversation with the teachers who volunteered. Only one conversation from this group of exchange teachers (a teacher from the Dominican Republic) did not result in a chapter because of the brevity of the conversation. After the data collection with the exchange teachers, I reached out to colleagues from Vietnam and Turkey to have a broader representation of contexts. The goal of the contexts to be included was to have representation from countries other than from North America, Western Europe, and East Asia (China, Japan, and Korea). The resulting chapters include understudied contexts from around the world: North Africa (Egypt), West Africa (Senegal),

Southeast Asia (Vietnam), South America (Argentina), Eastern Europe (Estonia and Ukraine), and a country split between Eastern Europe and Asia (Turkey). The meetings took place in informal environments – in a participant's apartment, in a campus office, or at a restaurant. Because of my relationship with the participants, either as a mentor in the exchange program or through personal relationships, the interactions took the form of a casual discussion among acquaintances, rather than a formal data elicitation collection procedure (Ushioda, 2020).

The conversations, varying in length from 45 minutes to 1 hour and 20 minutes, were audio-recorded and transcribed. As stated in a previous section, all of the discussions started with a question regarding the teachers' own classroom context. Some variation of the following prompt was provided: 'Can you describe what a typical English lesson looks like in your classroom? You can discuss activities, materials, number of students, typical layout of classroom, technologies used, use of L1 in the classroom, or anything else'. Although there were topics that I was keen to address, I let the teachers primarily guide the conversations, raising questions when appropriate. As such, there was no specific order or specific wording for the prompts given or questions asked; below are the additional topics covered in the discussions and a sample wording of the guiding question or prompt for each topic:

- Role of English and LOTEs in the specific context:
  - Could you give a brief description of the role that English has in your country/environment? For example, is it used for politics, business, schooling, etc.? What about LOTEs?
  - What types of opportunities do your students have to speak English outside of the classroom?
- Experience with attitudes toward English and LOTEs:
  - Have you had an experience with a LOTE? What was the context?
  - Do you have a certain kind of emotional attachment or some type of personal relationship with English? What about with a LOTE?
  - Do you have any role models for your language learning?
- Opinions about being a teacher of a non-native language (English) and other teacher issues:
  - What are the language skills that you feel most comfortable/most uncomfortable with in your language teaching (e.g. listening, speaking, reading, writing, grammar, classroom management)?
  - What are your thoughts and feelings about both the advantages and the challenges of being an non-native speaker teacher of English?
  - Have you ever had someone question or compliment your ability in English?

No direct questions were asked about participants' definitions of ideal teachers; the ideal teacher selves presented in each context-specific chapter were constructed based on the conversations about teaching and learning in general with language attitudes and examples provided being the basis for this compilation.

The transcripts were read multiple times to engage in data coding. Concept coding (or analytic coding) was first employed to find excerpts related to elements of self and the relationship of self to context. For the second round of coding, pattern coding was used to identify similarly coded data (Saldaña, 2016). The themes presented in each context-specific chapter are the salient themes that emerged for each teacher or teacher dyad. All of the excerpts presented give insight into the teachers' concept of self and how that relates to their particular context. As Mercer (2016: 11) indicated for her study, I also 'reflect[ed] on and explore[d] understandings about the dynamic interplay between a learner's L2 self and contexts' in the data analysis for the subsequent chapters. After the initial recording, I spent several years transcribing and analysing these discussions, as well as searching for and reading background information about the countries from where these EFL teachers hailed.

In discussing narrative analysis, Thompson and Vásquez (2015: 161) highlight that narratives 'provide the opportunity for language learners to reflect back upon their lifelong language learning processes', and in the case of these teachers, their teaching processes and other experiences as well. Because of the relationships formed between the teachers and me, discussions took place both before and after the data collection process; however, in analyzing these retrospective thoughts, the representations of the ideas in this project are primarily those that were articulated by the teachers at the time of data collection with additional information added during the member-checking process in some instances. I am not an expert on any of the contexts represented in the context-specific chapters and was the sole data coder. Thus, in line with ethical research for case studies and in terms of member-checking (Hornberger, 2006) and increasing the reliability of my interpretations, I attempted to contact each of the participants whose narratives wer used. I was successful in getting participant input and feedback for the chapters on Estonia, Senegal, Turkey, and Vietnam. In these instances, the participants offered a variety of suggestions, such as rewording the excerpts provided (mostly for style and, in rare cases, for content), providing corrections on the contextual information provided and, in some cases, providing additional information about the topic at hand. Although it sometimes meant that I had to rework certain sections, I respected their wishes in terms of the changes requested. For the other contexts represented (Argentina, Egypt, and Ukraine), I was unable to contact the participants, and thus sought out other experts on that particular context for feedback.

The discussion in Chapter 1 provides a backdrop for the remaining chapters of this book, which highlight the stories of language instructors in seven different contexts: Senegal, Vietnam, Egypt, Argentina,

Turkey, Ukraine, and Estonia. Each context-specific chapter interweaves the theoretical considerations with the lived experiences of these teachers, including aspects of non-native speaker teacher status, enhanced by their multilingual identities in some cases, their dual identity of learner-teacher, and the implications of context on ideal teacher self-formation. The final chapter provides summative thoughts and commentary on the project as a whole and gives insights into future directions for further research on this topic. The context-specific chapters that follow will take you on a journey through the retrospective thoughts about self and language, as well as the relationship between these selves and context.

2 Senegal: 'We English teachers, we speak English'

Gaynaako paaɓi anndi keen laÿooru.
[It is the specialist who knows the in's and out's.]

A Senegalese (Pulaar) proverb

KEY POINTS

In this chapter, Ablaye:

(1) Believes that sharing a first language (L1) with students leads to an understanding of what they need.
(2) Has a positive attitude toward English and speaks it whenever he can.
(3) Expresses that English is needed to succeed in various aspects of life, such as jobs, diplomacy, and exams.
(4) Feels pride in speaking English well, even when it is not expected in a context like Senegal.
(5) Lives in a context where multiple languages coexist and are used according to the situation.

These aspects and others delineated in the chapter contribute to his ideal English teacher self.

Senegal, a country of approximately 76,000 square miles (about the size of Nebraska or South Dakota) on the western tip of Africa, has a complex linguistic past and present. According to Diallo (2009), in 2007, there were 14 national indigenous languages (Wolof, Serer, Pulaar, Jola, Mandinka, Soninke, Balant, Mancangne, Noon, Mandjai, Oniyan, Hassanya, Bedick, and Saafi-Saafi) with three waiting for a presidential decree (Laha, Bainuk, and Kanjack) and three at the codification stage (Dialonké, Ndut, and Bayale). Wolof, the most common L1 of Senegal, is the 'lingua franca of the country and is spoken by more than 80% of the population. It is spoken by 50% as their first language and 30% speak it as a second language' (Diallo, 2009: 197). However, despite the numerous indigenous languages of Senegal, French is the only official language of the country, as a result of the long colonial history that Senegal has with France. Although it is only spoken by about 1% of the population as an L1, it is used in education, the legal system, the media, and in other governmental administration (Diallo, 2009). Regarding the use of colonial languages for formal processes and interactions, there has been some criticism regarding education systems in Africa that use European languages as the primary language of schooling (Clegg, 2019), such as French in the context of Senegal.

The Senegalese first traded (mostly enslaved individuals) with Western Europe during the mid-15th century with the arrival of the Portuguese (Geller, 1995), although no attempts at colonization were made at that time. French commercial companies started trading on the Senegal River in the 17th century, and in 1659 St Louis, the first town established by the French, became the 'centre of French commercial activity on the west coast of Africa' (Crowder, 1967: 9). St Louis was the capital city of West African French colonies, meaning that it was the French center of commercial trade, as well as home to the French governor of West Africa. Additionally, in 1677, the French drove the Dutch from the Island of Gorée (Gellar, 1995). The French and the British were the two main colonial entities in Africa and often fought each other for colonies. Senegal's position at the western most point of Africa and its proximity to Europe made it a source of struggle between these two entities: 'British and French rivalry for empire and control over West African trade during the eighteenth century often pitted these two powers against each other in the Senegambian region' (Gellar, 1995: 5). During the Seven Years' War, the French lost St Louis to the British, but regained it in 1779. During the Napoleonic Wars, the British regained St Louis, ultimately returning it to the French with the Second Treaty of Paris in 1817 (Crowder, 1967). After that point and under the rule of King Louis XVIII of France, the French 'embarked on a policy of European colonization of Senegal' (Crowder, 1967: 11).

French colonization in West Africa began with the ideals of complete assimilation, or the idea that the French language, culture, and political and educational systems would annihilate the local traditions, even though 'While Europe was passing through the Middle ages, precolonial Senegal had already been organized into chiefdoms and larger political units patterned on the Sudanic state model, which flourished in West Africa during the ascendancy of the mighty Ghana and Mali empires' (Gellar, 1995: 2). However, 'Of all France's Black African colonies, Senegal was the only one where the policy of assimilation was applied in any significant measure. Indeed, it has become something of a showpiece from which other nations have tended to misconstrue the nature of French colonial policy' (Crowder, 1967: 7). Such was the assimilation that intermarriage became common, particularly in St Louis, where inter-racial marriages were recognized and mixed-race children could receive inheritances, something that was not common in other colonies (https://www.saintlouisdusenegal.com/les-signares/). However, the relationship of the colonizer versus the colonized was one of superiority versus inferiority. 'France defended its acquisition of colonies on the grounds of a "civilizing mission" that would bring peace, prosperity, and the benefits of French civilization to the "backward and primitive" peoples fortunate enough to come under French rule' (Gellar, 1995: 8). So extreme was the assimilation policy with Senegal that in the early 20th century 'with the advent of the Third Republic and political democracy in France, Africans born in the urban communes of Dakar, Gorée, Rufisque, and Saint Louis [Four Communes] were granted full French citizenship rights in Senegal' (Gellar, 1995: 8), and the Western-educated Senegalese who were active in the colony's politics in these Four Communes 'clearly identified with the egalitarian ideals embodied in the French Revolution and the Declaration of the Rights of Man' (Gellar, 1995: 10).

Senegal began negotiations with France in 1959 to officially regain its independence as a member of the Mali Federation (composed of Senegal and the former French Sudan). On April 4, 1960, the Mali Federation claimed independence from France. However, the Mali Federation was short-lived, because in September 1960, Senegal became independent with a constitution and a seat in the United Nations (Gellar, 1995). Despite being officially free from France as a colonizing power, its time spent as a 'privileged' West African French colony has left an enormous impact on the social, political, and educational scene in Senegal. 'The French connection is deeply rooted in modern Senegalese history... Senegal's privileged position within the French colonial system and the involvement of Senegalese intellectuals and politicians in metropolitan politics and culture during the colonial period have left cultural and emotional bonds that are not easily broken. Senegalese intellectuals still read *Le Monde*, and French opinion journals regularly and closely following French politics' (Geller, 1995: 84). Additionally, the official language of Senegal remains French, although Wolof is becoming more prevalent as the lingua franca of the country, as only those who are formally educated speak French.

To further elaborate on the role of multiple languages in Senegal, as well as on the realities of teaching English in this context, we turn to the discussion with Ablaye. Born in 1970, Ablaye received his MA degree in American literature and civilization. At the time of the discussion, he had been teaching English for nine years in a school in the town of Kaolack (population approximately 170,000), a city in the midwestern region of Senegal on the north bank of the Saloum River. Ablaye is a speaker of Serer, Pulaar, Wolof, French, and English; although his strongest teacher self is that of English, he has also taught French in elementary school, as well as Wolof literacy in a community language program. Throughout our conversation, we discussed the roles of the different languages in current-day Senegal, as well as the languages that he speaks on a regular basis. In terms of languages formally studied, Ablaye primarily focused on French and English, the two Western languages in competition, so to speak, in this context. From the conversation, it is clear that Ablaye has the most clearly conceptualized ideal English self.

Ablaye: Yes, [I'm] most interested in English. And whenever I see somebody speaking English, I don't speak French. I speak to him in English. In our country, it is what we are doing. We English teachers, we speak English.

The preference of English over French in Ablaye's case is perhaps surprising because of Senegal's strong connection to France and French, as a 'privileged' West African French colony. However, in spite of the strong French influence in Senegal, English is becoming an increasingly popular language to study, as is also indicated by the participants in Dyers and Abongdia's (2010) study in Cameroon. Like Senegal, Cameroon is a country where French is used in government and education, but where English is starting to be seen as having 'greater external power' (Wardhaugh, 1987: 173) than French in many sectors. For example, English is becoming necessary for jobs in the private sector: 'L'expérience professionnelle et les diplômes quels qu'ils soient ne suffisent plus pour obtenir un poste dans les entreprise. Il faut avoir en plus un bon niveau dans la langue de Shakespeare' [Professional experience and degrees are no longer enough to get a job. It's also necessary to speak the language of Shakespeare (English) well] – excerpt from *Jeune Afrique Economique* (cited in Mbaya, 2001: 68). English has also been very useful in negotiations within the Economic Community of West African States (ECOWAS) since its founding in 1973. 'Since the main goal pursued by ECOWAS is economic integration and cooperation among countries, the use of English-French or English-Portuguese bilingualism appears to be the most appropriate tool in order to increase communication among the member states' (Mbaya, 2001: 67). Additionally, English is important as the international language of tourism, making English translators a necessity, and in Senegal, English has also been spread by the music industry (Mbaya, 2001). As stated by Mbaya (2001: 65), most young people in Senegal would say, '"L'anglais est la langue de l'avenir; il nous rapproche des Etats-Unis" [English is the language of the future; it brings us closer to the United States]… It is a symbol of freedom, or development and of modernity'. As Ablaye explains:

Ablaye: In Senegal, French is a must. But if you want to study diplomacy, you have to master English. And nowadays, in many exams, in many competitions, if you want a job, they ask you whether you've mastered English or not.

In Ablaye's case, he is determined to speak English with whomever he sees. He also has a sense of pride in his English proficiency, indicating that he has developed an anti-ought-to self (i.e. Thompson, 2017a; Thompson & Vásquez, 2015) by gaining high English proficiency in a country where it is not necessarily expected. He describes a conversation he had with a group of journalists who were visiting his university during his teaching internship stage. In the course of the conversation, he told them that Senegal was a French-speaking country:

Ablaye: At the end, somebody said, 'You said that Senegal is a French-speaking country'. I said, 'Yes'. That person said, 'How did you learn English?' so I said 'Okay, we learn both English and French' (laughs). They expected me to speak French because it is a French-speaking country, but maybe they don't expect anybody from there [Senegal] to speak English at a certain level.

Related to Ablaye's comments on the language proficiency of English teachers in Senegal, Drame (n.d.) discusses a research survey in Senegal in which he investigates the lack of use of communicative language teaching (CLT) strategies in Senegalese classrooms. One of the most salient results is that it is not because of a lack of proficiency in the language. 'This seems to be a fair judgement when one bears in mind teachers' keenness on communicating in English when they meet a native speaker or when they engage in meetings, seminars, workshops, talking shops, etc.' (Drame, n.d.: 9), which is supported by Ablaye's description of the meetings he had with the journalists. Instead, the perceived lack of use of CLT in this context is likely due to logistical issues, such as class size (also see Destefano *et al.* [2009] for an overview of the Senegalese education system, and Gao and Xu [2014] and Guilloteaux [2013] for the implications of large class sizes):

Amy: What about the number of students typically that you have?
Ablaye: Okay. In my school, the average is 70.
Amy: Per class.
Ablaye: Per class. It means in some class you can have 65, the others 80, 82, 87, it depends. But the average is 70.

Ablaye, like anyone learning a foreign language, saw his motivation levels change over the course of the learning process. Indicating his fluctuation in motivation for language learning, Ablaye pointed out to me that he did not always like English. In asking him what his emotional attachment to English was, he responded:

Ablaye: With English? It's great. I love English so much. Yeah. I like it. But, you should know, I started liking it in twelfth grade.

Amy: Oh, before then you didn't like it.

Ablaye: Before that… I liked it the first year, but after that I had some teachers that I didn't appreciate. But I liked it most when I was at the university. Oh, it was wonderful – reading books, watching movies, studying novels, it was wonderful. I like it, I like English. And I chose to be a teacher of English.

As detailed above, at a pivotal point in his education, Ablaye describes how his ideal English language learning self transformed into an ideal English language teaching self. As Dörnyei (2009) describes, it was the effect of a role model in his university English instructors and the types of classroom activities that they employed that set him on his career path as an English teacher. Ablaye also talks about the role that being a non-native speaker has in terms of his language proficiency and teaching. Interestingly, he noted that when he met fellow teachers from British colonies, specifically mentioning India, Egypt, Ghana, Kenya, and Nigeria, he didn't notice a difference between his English and theirs:

Ablaye: But personally, when I meet teachers who… live in a country where English is the first language, I have seen that there is not much difference between my language and theirs.

He was also quick to describe his teaching situation and how native English speakers in the past have not been effective in teaching his students. This comment resonates with the literature regarding the advantages of those teachers who share an L1 and a cultural background with their students in terms of teaching effectiveness (i.e. Chun, 2014; Ma, 2012; Rao, 2010). I asked him how he thought I would fare teaching English in Senegal, and he said the following:

Ablaye: Yeah, it would be interesting. They will be very interested, but the problem may be that you may not know exactly what our students need. If you behave as if you are in front of American students, you will not be able to teach them. [**Amy:** I see.] Because you have to try to meet their needs. What do they need for English as a foreign language? … Two years there was somebody who came from the States. He lived here for 18 years. He tried to teach. He came to our classes, said he would like to teach some grammar, but it was very difficult for him. [**Amy:** I see, okay.] Yeah, because he tried to do something that the students could not grasp because it was too high for them. Maybe if you came to Senegal to teach, your challenge would be how to lower your level and meet them with their needs, but they would be very interested to have a native speaker. Because we are doing that sometimes. Each year we have somebody, an American, who comes in and we ask him to teach, to talk to the students. But they [the students] have problems to understand.

It is also the case that in Ablaye's school, there are no full-time native English speakers teaching English, so there is no point of comparison for the students, except for when a guest comes to visit the class. Drame (n.d.) also found that the students he surveyed stated that they learned more when listening to a Senegalese teacher, rather than a native speaker of the language in question. Tennant and Negash (2010: 23) support Ablaye's assertion that native speakers have not been very successful in interacting with Senegalese English language learners in the past: 'One very interesting point to consider in terms of communicative competence is the ability to consider the listener. There is an understanding that speakers often need to adjust their language to "accommodate" the listener. One interesting observation is that native speakers are much poorer at doing this than many non-native speakers'. In a later communication with Ablaye, he told me two main reasons that he believes that Senegalese students struggle to understand oral communications in English. The first reason, according to Ablaye, is the chosen teaching methodology, as many teachers focus on grammar points, structure, and reading comprehension, as opposed to activities to improve spoken language. He also notes that students do not have many opportunities to practice English outside of the classroom in Senegal.

Ablaye is confident not only in his language abilities, but also in his teaching abilities, stating that the problem is not the teaching itself because of their strong pedagogical training; the biggest challenge is trying to get the students interested in the language.

Ablaye: We don't have much problem to teach it. Because at the university, we study four years of English. Four years of intensive learning. And we have a special school where teachers are trained to teach English... Maybe the challenge is to get the students interested. This is our main challenge, to get the students interested in the language.

Although Ablaye was most interested in talking about English, I was also curious about his other language learning experiences. He also stated that he has positive attitudes toward French, but he stipulates that he likes it 'when it is spoken in an academic way', perhaps because of his early schooling in a private, French-medium school. Ablaye also discussed what he perceived to be the interaction between French and English; for example, he perceived English to be an easier language to learn than French. As he started learning French before he started learning English, I tried to understand if he thought the language itself was easier, or if the experience of learning French made the experience of learning English easier. As can be seen in the following excerpt, he perceived the English language itself to be easier than the French language:

Ablaye: I think English is easier than French.
Amy: English is easier? Because of studying French first or because it's an easier language than French?
Ablaye: It's an easier language... the English language itself is easier to learn than French. Because there are many grammar rules, many structures which exist in French that don't exist in English. And I know if I studied English and French at the same time, at the beginning, I would be more proficient in English than in French because English is a very simple language to learn. If you learn French, you will see French is very complicated. There are many grammar rules which don't exist in English.

Ablaye explains that students start learning French immediately on starting school at the age of six or seven, and then they start learning English in junior high school. According to a later communication with Ablaye, more recently some private schools in Senegal have taken the initiative to start teaching English earlier because of the perceived importance of the language. He also stated that students can add another language if they wish, specifically mentioning Arabic, Russian, Spanish, Portuguese, and German; however, none of the many languages native to Senegal are taught in schools. Ablaye explained that he formally learned to read and write Wolof at university so that he could help teach people who were not able to go to school to write in their native language; however, it's not a school subject for pupils growing up. Ablaye, like many Senegalese, did not learn Serer and Wolof in a formal way with a teacher in a classroom, as he grew up in a place where people use Serer and Wolof in daily interactions. This type of language use in multilingual contexts is described in Coetzee-Van Rooy's (2014, 2019) work, and it is quite different from how European languages are learned in this context. Curious about how he learned languages other than English and French, he explained to me the importance of the context in learning these languages. As he explained, Serer is his native language and Wolof is a close second language because of the environment where he grew up where people spoke both Serer and Wolof daily:

Ablaye: In the street when I talk to people and children. Yeah, but I learned Serer in my family. Everybody speaks Serer, and I learned Serer from them. I learned Wolof in the street meeting people. What this means is that I learned both languages at the same time. It means in my house, in my family, we speak Serer. Whenever you go out, everybody can't speak Serer, so it is Wolof. And I learned both languages at the same time, but I consider Serer to be my first language.

I was intrigued by the fact that Ablaye focused on talking to me about English, the language of his profession, and French, the language of his formal schooling. This is perhaps an indication of the importance placed on these European languages over the native Senegalese languages, an importance of economic value. Mastering French and English creates a path toward social well-being because of the increased opportunity for employment with these language skills, according to Ablaye. Languages such as Serer and Wolof are not options for study until university, although there are now community-supported literacy programs (see Samari and Métangmo-Tatou [2017] for a description of one such program in Cameroon). Ablaye also participated in teaching the national languages in these community-based programs.

Ablaye: I did the formal study of Wolof when I was at the university. And it was for teaching courses because in Senegal, for people who don't have the chance to go to school, we teach them their national languages. We teach them Wolof, or Serer, etc., so that they can read and write. Whenever they need it, they can write a letter in Wolof and send it to their parents... So, I learned how to teach Wolof.

Trudell and Klaas (2010) studied several of these language programs in this context and found a variety of motivations for participation in such programs. 'These motivations for integration and citizenship in national society can be seen in the data as a drive for legitimization, for parity with other cultural groups and for educational achievement. Paradoxically, they exist alongside equally strong motivations for cultural identity and distinctiveness' (Trudell & Klaas, 2010: 128). The seemingly necessary fact of interaction in multiple languages in Senegal is also support for Coetzee-Van Rooy's (2014) idea of developing language selves in multilingual African contexts where speaking these different languages is considered something that is needed to function in society. 'In the minds of people living in these types of environments there is an expectation that members learn many languages as part of their ordinary behaviour as integrated citizens that belong to the society... The "ought to language self" in a multilingual language mode society directs people to believe that if they are not multilingual in this society, they do not "fit in", because well-integrated citizens in this society are multilingual' (Coetzee-Van Rooy, 2014: 124). The pride Ablaye expressed when talking about his abilities in English and how he liked 'academic French' was juxtaposed by the perceived normalcy that he acquired Serer through socialization (i.e. speaking to his family) and Wolof 'in the street', as if it were nothing special. As Canagarajah (2007: 933) states, 'The multilingual speaker engages with the shifting and fluid situations in everyday life to learn strategies of negotiation and adaptation for meaning-making'.

His ideal English teacher self is also intertwined with the ought-to self. He not only loves English, but also needs it to make his living, as indicated by the following excerpt. It is also interesting to hear about his attitudes to the other languages he speaks, supporting Diallo's (2009: 196) statement: 'In a multilingual context like in Senegal, before formulating strategic language planning it is important to understand attitudes towards languages and speech communities with regard to language choice, status and acquisition planning'.

Amy: How do you think your feelings to French or English compare to your first languages that you learned at home before you went to school, emotionally speaking?

Ablaye: Yes. That is a tricky question. (laughs) Because I'm earning my life because of English. (laughs) Okay, I'm teaching English not only for interest but also because it is a way for me to earn my living, you see? So, this is very important. As far as my native language is concerned, I only use it when I am at home. Whenever I left the family, I no longer speak it. It means that English is very important for me. I don't know whether I would say it is more important, but I think it is very important.

His English ideal teacher self was formed via schooling, role models, and ultimately, his love of the language itself. When I asked him if he had a stronger emotional attachment to English or French, he indicated English and that he had to 'perform' it:

Ablaye: Yeah! I have attachment to English because I'm teaching it, and I need to perform it.

As Mbaya (2001: 63) cites, 'Between English and French, English is the language with "greater external power" in Africa' and is 'attracting more people and government in this continent'. As Ablaye indicates, it is the language that provides him with a career, and he prefers English to any of the other languages he speaks. It is predicted that the use of English will grow in this context: 'In a nutshell, the expansion of the English language is likely to [grow] within Senegalese society. Resistance on the part of French will depend on goodwill and much effort, especially in the non-formal sector where French is easily supplanted by English' (Mbaya, 2001: 73).

Upon subsequent communication with Ablaye, he told me about the increased focus of teaching national languages in Senegal. Today, in Senegal even if the importance of international languages such as English and French is acknowledged, there is also a tendency to promote national languages. In so doing, the government of Senegal has created bilingual classes in many elementary schools throughout the country. In those classes, students learn French and the most commonly used national language of the area. In addition to these bilingual classes, the government is currently implementing another program called 'Lecture Pour Tous' (*Reading For All*) funded by the United States Agency for International Development (USAID) (https://www.planusa.org/senegal-lecture-pour-tous), which started in 2016 and is funded through 2021. As a part of this program, students learn literacy skills in a national language (Wolof, Serer, or Pulaar) before learning literacy in French. This program is being implemented in six regions in Senegal: Diourbel, Kaffrine, Kaolack, Louga, Matam, and Saint Louis, indicating the nation's increasing perceived value regarding national languages.

Ablaye has created a strong ideal English teacher self during his career as an educator; included in this image is his status as a non-native speaker, which gives him teaching advantages in the classroom. His teacher self involves helping students succeed in their future careers because of English, and he also associates speaking English with his own survival, as it is his way of making a living. Initially, Ablaye was negatively influenced by his earlier English teachers, but he then found role models at the university level. His ideal self was formed around the pride he had in doing the unexpected in terms of learning English well in a predominantly French-speaking setting; his identity as an English teacher influences his desire to speak English whenever he can: 'We English teachers, we speak English'. He believes an ideal teacher should help their students become interested in the language, and he does this by 'performing English' when he teaches. In his ideal English teaching self creation, he has not forgotten the importance of promoting literacy in national languages and seems to embody Coetzee-Van Rooy's (2014) idea of a multilingual self. In Ablaye's words, 'At the political level, people are becoming aware that it is difficult to develop a country while ignoring the local languages'.

3 Vietnam: 'English is a privilege for me'

Đi một ngày đàng, học một sàng khôn.
[One day of travel will bring you a wealth of wisdom.]

Vietnamese proverb

KEY POINTS

In this chapter, Khiet

(1) Believes that the younger generation has more opportunities to learn English well.
(2) Grew to love English after first conceptualizing it as a tool.
(3) Expresses feelings about how politics influences attitudes toward English.
(4) Indicates that English is a 'passport' to a better life.
(5) Feels that language learning is cause for happiness.

These aspects and others delineated in the chapter contribute to his ideal English teacher self.

Vietnam's linguistic history, like its political history, is complex, and as Denham (1992: 61) states, 'Vietnam's linguistic history reflects its political history'. The linguistic history of this Southeast Asian country that stretches along the eastern edge of the Indo-China Peninsula was influenced by the various conquering nations and political allies; Vietnam is 'a saga of recurrent strife, turmoil, invasion, occupation and hardship' (Branigin, 1994: A22).

As Vietnam was under the control of China for almost 1000 years until the 10th century (Denham, 1992), the official language of the country during that period was Chinese with the Han script (Pham Minh Hac, 1991, 1994). In fact, 'For centuries, the neighbor to the north, China, had always considered Vietnam as its southern district' (Ngan Nguyen, 2012: 259). However, with 54 ethnic groups in Vietnam (the majority ethnic group being the Kinh), many languages are spoken in this country: 'Given the country's moderate size, the number of languages spoken and written in Vietnam is large' (Vasavakul, 2003: 219). In fact, Vietnam can be considered a 'multi-ethnic and multi-lingual country' (Buøi Khaùnh Theá, 2003: 1) where minority languages are protected. 'Minority languages are said to be the cultural property of the entire nation, and the government has recognized the right of ethnic minorities to use their spoken and written languages' (Vasavakul, 2003: 211), meaning that minority groups are bilingual or multilingual, speaking at a minimum their own language(s) as well as Vietnamese. That being said, Vietnam's linguistic history is turbulent, changing with the tide of political conflict.

French became the official language of Vietnam during French colonialism, a rule that lasted several decades, from the 1880s to the 1940s. 'When the French took Vietnam in the mid-19th century, they implemented a language policy that minimized Chinese influence. Vietnamese, the language spoken by the Kinh peoples, was recognized as *quoc ngu* ... However, French was also proclaimed an official language in the nation' (Ngan Nguyen, 2012: 260). With encouraging the learning and teaching of *quoc ngu* (Romanized Vietnamese), the French were mainly interested in pulling the nation away from Chinese cultural influences. They never had the intention of making *quoc ngu* the official language of Vietnam: 'The French promotion of *quoc ngu* was driven by two considerations. The first was to train Vietnamese collaborators to help administer local affairs. The second motivation was the French desire to sever Vietnam's cultural connections with China and to bring Vietnam into France's cultural orbit' (Vasavakul, 2003: 222). This Romanized Vietnamese was used as a bridge for the Vietnamese people to learn French, as the school and political systems revolved around French as a result of this colonialism.

Although Vietnam declared its independence from the French in 1945, the years 1945–1954 marked the Vietnamese resistance struggle, ending with the 1954 Geneva Accord. The Geneva Accord divided the country into two regions – North Vietnam and South Vietnam – each of which had opposite political orientations. This divide, along with the implications of the spread of communism, one of the great perceived threats to American democracy, was the catalyst for the Vietnam War, and thus, the influx of English into Vietnam, primarily in the South (Do Huy Thinh, 2006).

From the 1950s on, it was impossible to discuss language policy as a whole for Vietnam, as North Vietnam and South Vietnam had distinct attitudes and realities regarding foreign language instruction. Although Vietnamese was recognized as the official language after 1945, with the Ministry of Education stating that Vietnamese should be the official language of instruction in 1948 (Vasavakul, 2003), it was only in North Vietnam where Vietnamese was used regularly as the language of instruction;

South Vietnam maintained the French language curriculum for much longer. Although the use of Vietnamese in North Vietnam versus French in South Vietnam was vigorously debated starting in the 1950s, and some schools adopted the use of Vietnamese earlier than others, it wasn't until around 1975 (after reunification) that Vietnamese became the widespread language of instruction in both North and South Vietnam. There were several reasons why the French language retained its hold for longer in the South: 'First, the French political and economic cooperation and aid to the South continued. Second, French-educated people held strategic posts in the government' (Do Huy Thinh, 2006: 4).

After reunification in 1975, 'Russian was required to be the main foreign language at all educational levels in the whole country' (Do Huy Thinh, 2006: 5). In fact, the Institute for Educational Research 'set targets for foreign language study in Vietnamese high schools, aiming to have 60% study Russian, 25% study English, and 15% study French' (Denham, 1992: 62), although these targets were not maintained. The Soviet Union provided subsidized materials to Vietnam, making the study of Russian even easier to access. For a period of about 10 years after reunification, the economic decline resulted in many English teachers leaving the country for work elsewhere. It wasn't until the Sixth National Congress of the Vietnamese Communist Party (1986) that Vietnam 'decided to expand its relations with every country despite different political systems and to adopt a market-oriented economy' (Do Huy Thinh, 2006: 7) based on socialism.

After that point, although Russian still dominated the North in terms of foreign language study, more students throughout the country began to study English. Although there was an influx of English influence as a result of the Vietnam War, even to the extent of an English-only television channel and radio station (Do Huy Thinh, 2006), the population exhibited conflicting emotions about the language. With the difficulties created because of the Vietnam War, followed by the American trade embargo on Vietnam after the war ended, understandably there were some negative feelings associated with English. According to Ngan Nguyen (2012: 259), 'English did not become popular in Vietnam until the 1990s, after the collapse of the Soviet Union, the implementation of Doi Moi (economic reforms) and the normalization of US-Vietnam relations' and is now playing a role in the 'foreign cooperation, international integration, modernization and socioeconomic enhancement of the nation'. The Vietnamese governmental Decision No. 1400/QD-TTg issued in 2008 was meant to augment English learning by adopting it earlier in primary education and adopted the Common European Framework of Reference (CEFR) to measure language competency (Ngan Le Hai Phan, 2018). To illustrate these points further and to tell more about the current situation of English in Vietnam, additional discussion revolving around excerpts from Khiet's data is provided below. In our discussion, Khiet commented on topics such as his ought-to and ideal self development as a student and then as a teacher of English, attitudes toward English, the current role of English in Vietnam, and attitudes toward English teachers with an L1 other than English.

Khiet graduated from a university in South Vietnam in 1990 with a degree in English language teaching. He came to the United States to study for an MA degree and graduated from a large public university in the Northeast in 1999. At the time of the discussion, he was finishing his PhD in Applied Linguistics at a large Midwestern university, after which he would return to Vietnam to take up his previous position as a university-level language and content teacher. He had been an English teacher for around 25 years at the time of the discussion and had taught a variety of English language and linguistics/applied linguistics content courses at university level in Vietnam. In the American context, he also worked at the university writing center to support his PhD studies. As a first language (L1) Vietnamese speaker, Khiet focused on his experience with and the role of English in Vietnam; however, he did mention the role of other languages in this context. Specifically, he described how he first studied English with a textbook written in Russia. This example, along with others, indicates the complex nature of languages in the context of Vietnam.

In terms of his initial motivation to learn English, Khiet was encouraged by his parents at an early age to study English, despite the controversial nature of English for his generation. Living up to external expectations might have initially strengthened Khiet's ought-to self (Dörnyei, 2009); however, in hindsight, he agrees with his parents' encouragement.

Khiet: But my parents knew English would become the international language, and if I studied English, I might get a chance to study abroad or I might get a good job later. So, they advised me to study English, to become an English teacher. I think my parents were right.

Khiet's parents showed a lot of foresight with this decision, especially since up until 1986, the focus was on teaching Russian as a foreign language, as opposed to English. 'Formerly, Russian was the favorite choice. Children were selected for the Russian classes on the basis of their school grades, with the most able children being required to study the language' (Denham, 1992: 64). As discussed above, it wasn't until the Sixth National Congress of the Vietnamese Communist Party in 1986 that foreign languages other than Russian (and to a lesser extent, Chinese) were officially encouraged, and it wasn't until the 1990s that English became popular throughout all of Vietnam (Ngan Nguyen, 2012). As described above, French was still taught in some schools but was losing traction.

However, even during this transition when Russian was a common language taught in schools and, in many cases, required, English was still the language desired by many students and their families, particularly in South Vietnam.

Also complicating the role of English in Vietnam was an anti-American sentiment, one of the inevitable results of the Vietnam War: 'Amid the strongly heated anti-foreign, especially anti-American, echo, language policy slighted the study of these foreign languages' (Do Huy Thinh, 2006: 6). French and English books and other educational materials were publicly burned (Ngan Nguyen Long & Kemdall, 1981), and both English and French were considered 'remnants of the colonial and neo-colonial cultures and therefore were not embraced' (Ngan Nguyen, 2012: 261). In some cases, the sentiment was so strong that 'the fear of political discrimination made a great many people, especially those who got training in the United States and other capitalist nations, destroy even their foreign-granted certificates and degrees' (Do Huy Thinh, 2006: 6).

Khiet: Many years ago, when people studied English, anti-American people would think that it was very close to the US, so they would not like those who spoke or studied English. For example, when I took the university entrance exam in 1986, it seemed my class would be the last class who majored in English because they would ignore the learning of English in Vietnam. They [gave] more time and investment in teaching Russian.

Amy: Right in the 80s.

Khiet: So, it's very political. It's a political choice, too.

As Denham (1992: 64) states, 'because of its wartime associations, English was not initially regarded as politically neutral'; however, Khiet goes on to talk about how the conflict will, of course, be remembered, but that people should get past it and look toward the future. As Khiet indicates, English is a mechanism for learning information that will benefit Vietnam, as well as a tool to communicate with those who visit the country.

Khiet: I don't know whether I can say [this] on behalf of the Vietnamese people, but we tend to be generous. Of course, what happened between the US and Vietnam was very painful. And now we cannot forget it, but we should put it aside. So, we also welcome Americans to come to our country, and we also want to come here to learn the technologies and science and English so that we can contribute more to the building of the country. So, I think not many people have had hatred or hostility toward the US except the people, the old generation, and they are older.

In a subsequent discussion on this topic, Khiet clarified that those who were directly and indirectly involved in the war, thereby suffering losses, were of retirement age at the time of the data collection. It was also the case that those from the north of Vietnam had more negative effects befall them as a result of the war. Born in the late 1960s before the reunification of the country, Khiet is self-ascribed to be part of the 'older' generation who harbor some ill-will toward English because of the United States' involvement in the Vietnam War. However, he explained that he was too young to understand the political implications of language when he started studying English, which was the case for many of his peers. He always respects American people and culture; understandably, he does not agree with all decisions made by the US government. Peers from his generation are divided on this issue, as illustrated below.

Khiet: You can say maybe one-fourth of the people would hate the US. The other fourth would love the US. The other half have no idea. But I'm not sure. I have no statistics like that, but there are several groups like that. Some people hate, some people love, and some people do not care.

Despite some potentially negative culturally bound feelings toward English, English started to become more widespread because of the economic opportunities involved. As Do Huy Thinh (2006: 5) notes, 'Foreign companies and factories offered high salaries and recruited personnel with good English language competence' and 'The movement was strongly supported by a variety of jobs offered through foreign investments. English, the use of which was more popular in the South, tended to be a reason for more foreign investment there than in the North' (Do Huy Thinh, 2006: 8). Khiet reinforces this sentiment by illustrating the importance of English in Vietnam:

Khiet: And now English is so common and so English is becoming your passion... It is... all people should know English.
Amy: Is it a status symbol in some ways? If you know English, you're well-educated?
Khiet: Yeah. That's right. I think most jobs, most companies now also require those who speak English to work for them, so English is a kind of passport for you to have a better future, better job, good opportunities to go abroad. Yeah, there are so many reasons.

The idea of English as a passport is also mentioned in Ngan Nguyen (2012: 259): 'It [English] is the passport to advance not only in the intellectual world but also in many other walks of life'. In other words, there are external expectations to learn English, so students might form an ought-to self as they start to take English classes. In fact, in 1994, the

Vietnamese prime minister signed 'Instructions 422-TTg', which called for substantial foreign language improvement (especially English) for state administrators and officers, even allowing employees to attend English classes during working hours (Ngan Nguyen, 2012), so the environment was also conducive to learning this language. A few minutes later in the discussion, Khiet reiterates the external motivations of many Vietnamese people to study English:

Khiet: I think the main reason for learning English in Vietnam is first a chance to study abroad, second a high-paying job. You will get a high-paying job. Those are the reasons, yeah.

In fact, the need for English and English teachers increased rapidly, making English teaching itself a lucrative career: 'In the early 1990s, since the demand for English outstripped supply, those who had no official training also became teachers. In education, English teaching received the highest pay. An ordinary teacher with a teaching load of 35 hours per week can earn VN\$4–6 million or US\$400–600 per month. This [salary] was high as compared with the GNP per capita of US\$350 per annum' (Do Huy Thinh, 2006: 8). In other words, the demand for English in the business sector also affected the financial benefits and social status of being an English teacher. Many Russian teachers retrained to become English teachers (Hoang Van Van *et al.*, 2006) and Mydans (1995: para. 2) tells the story of Quoc Khoi, an English teacher in Vietnam who had previously studied French, Japanese, and Russian. Quoc Khoi is quoted as saying, 'Now I forget my Russian and my Japanese. Even French I almost forget. But English everybody in Vietnam must know because English is the language of commerce'. As we will see later in the chapter, what started as an ought-to self in terms of encouragement from his parents, gradually contributed to Khiet's development of his ideal English teacher self as he did indeed make this career choice.

As far as the opportunities that Khiet's students have to speak English outside of the classroom, he states that they come mostly from tourists. These tourists are a direct result of the free market-oriented economy that was adopted, which 'helped attract a considerable number of English-speaking visitors to Vietnam as tourists and business people' (Do Huy Thinh, 2006: 1). This was, of course, in sharp contrast to the recent past when most of the visitors were from the Soviet Union and Eastern Europe (Denham, 1992).

Khiet: Outside the classroom, those who are very active would find some foreign tourists to talk to. In my hometown there are not many tourists, but they can find some of them along the river because we have a very beautiful riverfront. So, that's the place where many foreign tourists come. Not only from the US but from many other countries, but most of them speak English. So, the students volunteer to work as tour guides. It's a good chance for them to practice speaking English with them.

Khiet's comment about his students practicing English not only with native English speakers, but also with speakers of other languages, further illustrates the global nature of English used as a mode of communication for those with a variety of language backgrounds (Dörnyei *et al.*, 2006) and is exemplified in the attitudes of Vietnamese English teachers toward English as an international language (Ngan Le Hai Phan, 2018). Other than interacting with tourists, Khiet also discusses the English-speaking club and the extra activities organized by British and American teachers in Vietnam, as well as speaking exchanges from teachers abroad:

Khiet: We have foreign volunteers, like, from Great Britain and from the US, and we have student exchanges. We have some activities for Vietnamese and US students to speak to each other... we also have some British and American teachers [in Vietnam]. At least two of them a year because we have some volunteer programs. So those American or British teachers come to provide more language practice with the classroom, in the classroom and outside the classroom because they organize some activities. But actually, I don't think we have many activities outside the classroom. But for the English-speaking club, we have it every month. It's a monthly event.

The conversation turned to Khiet's status as an L1 Vietnamese speaker teaching English in Vietnam. He stated that this was a common topic of discussion at the university where he worked in the south of Vietnam. The concept of what an English teacher should be like affected Khiet's development of his ideal teacher self, and how to negotiate that image with his current teacher self.

Khiet: We talked a lot about this problem. At first, we thought non-native teachers like me would not be able to teach English very well because we may speak more Vietnamese than English in the classroom. But now things change because the younger generations speak English better than I do.
Amy: The teachers who are younger.
Khiet: Yes. The younger teachers speak English better, so they use more English in the classroom, not like in my generation.

Khiet continues to talk about how the lower level of speaking had to do with the teaching methods used when he was a student, and the fact that

English students had little to no contact with English speakers or authentic texts. This sentiment is supported by Ngan Nguyen (2012: 263) (a summary in English of Hoang Van Van *et al.* [2006]): 'It was also found that many teachers were not used to the CLT (Communicative Language Teaching) approach, or did not know about the learner-centered approach. Many older teachers (age 45 up) did not even know about the CLT approach. Most of them had almost no opportunities to train abroad and extremely limited opportunities to communicate in English or to upgrade knowledge in the field'. On a similar topic, Ngan Le Hai Phan (2018) provides an overview of attitudes on various aspects of current English teaching practices and expectations in Vietnam. Khiet's experience, of course, is indicative of when he was a student, which was at a time when Soviet influence was prevalent. These Soviet influences, including the influx of subsidized Soviet language teaching materials, remained until the collapse of the Soviet Union.

Khiet: I think those who are under 35 [born in the late 1970s, early 1980s] will speak English more fluently because they were trained with the new textbook, the new teaching method. So, I think they will acquire English fast. But in my generation, we studied with the grammar-translation and audiolingual methods, so we could not speak after graduating from the undergrad program. We knew how to write, we knew how to read, but we could not speak it. We could not speak at that time. I think I could speak some English after studying in [the US], and now I think I speak English more fluently... but you cannot imagine an English teacher who couldn't speak English many years, 15 years, ago.

Amy: Were there a lot of teachers who could not speak English fifteen years ago?

Khiet: That's in the past. That thing is past. Of course, I say we could not speak English, it's not completely right. We could not speak English fluently. We could speak English, but the English we spoke in the classroom was the English we memorized in our lesson plan because we had to, we had to write our script for the lecture, and we just spoke exactly what the textbook said. [**Amy:** I see.] Yeah, so you are doing a presentation and you memorize what you rehearse, your ideas, and you speak. Nothing spontaneous.

Amy: I see. So that would be, what you were just describing would be a challenge of being a non-native speaker? The lack of fluency that you experienced with your generation of teachers?

Khiet: I think it's the biggest challenge for us because we... at that time we did not have any chance to have contact with any Americans or British people, so we just learned English from the textbook... And we sometimes had to study English with a Russian textbook. [**Amy:**

Wow. Okay.] It was an English textbook perhaps written by Russian experts. So, it was not authentic. [**Amy:** Not authentic, right.] Our English, our English speaking was not authentic, either.

Khiet's description of the lack of opportunity to speak and interact in the language classroom when he was a student was not just a phenomenon in Vietnam, but across the field of language teaching in general. Grammar-translation and audiolingualism in the 1960s and before, followed by the 'designer' methods of the 1970s gave way to communicative language teaching (CLT) in the United States in the mid-1980s, with varied implementation worldwide (Brown, 2007). According to Kieu Hang Kim Anh (2010), CLT was introduced into Vietnam in the 1990s, and several articles have been written about the integration of this method in the context of Vietnam. As Tin Tan Dang (2010: 5) states, the 'Communicative language teaching method and student-centered approach in second language training have not consistently been reported to be effective, given various situation problems such as big-size classes, a rigorous test-oriented system, and heavy learning workload. Therefore, several teaching practices derived from these "new" methods have not been widely accepted or appropriately implemented'. These large class sizes and the importance of test-taking are also emphasized by Khiet, who simultaneously underscores his success at effectively teaching grammar to his students in order to pass these important exams (see also Gao and Xu [2014] and Guilloteaux [2013] for implications of large class sizes):

Khiet: In my [grammar] class, there were about 60 to 70 students. Sometimes at the peak time, the students had to study for the exam, so they concentrated in my class up to 200 students. But, actually, I was supposed to take care of 50 students.

Amy: A grammar class up to 200 students?

Khiet: Yeah, but I'm talking about the basic English class. There were many big classrooms, so each of the teachers was supposed to take care of 50 students. But because they knew that I taught very basic English grammar, they just came to my class... they also attended the classes given by their teacher.

Amy: Like an extra class, uh-huh.

Khiet: To learn more or something like that. So, I think I gave them very basic systematic English grammar, so they found it helpful for them, especially for the exam. Because I'm not talking about acquisition, but they learned for the exam, I gave them very systematic grammar, so they were successful.

As Pham Hoa Khiet (2007) points out, 'it can be problematic to take a set of teaching methods developed in one part of the world and use it in another part… education is situated in a particular cultural environment, and within this environment, the definition of "good teaching" is socially constructed. In this way, assuming that what is appropriate in one particular educational setting will naturally be appropriate in another is to ignore the fact that ELT methodology is grounded in an Anglo-Saxon view of education'. However, Pham Hoa Khiet (2007: 196) continues with the argument of, 'Undoubtedly, CLT originates in the West, but to decide *a priori* that this teaching approach is inappropriate to a certain context is to ignore developments in language teaching, and this might lead to the de-skilling of teachers'. Phan Le Ha (2004: 56) also supports the idea of 'teaching' as a culturally influenced concept: 'The concept of being a teacher varies from one culture to another. What one culture values may not be valued by others' and advocates a 'harmonious combination of global and local pedagogies' (Phan Le Ha, 2004: 52). According to the foregoing excerpt, younger-generation English teachers were exposed to the 'new teaching method', which affected both their acquisition and teaching of English.

Also regarding the context of teaching English in Vietnam, according to Tin Tan Dang (2010: 5), 'Being strongly considered part of Eastern culture, the popular philosophy of educational practices in Vietnam is more associated with absorbing and memorizing than experimenting and producing knowledge' (but see also Kieu Hang Kim Anh [2010] for a counterargument). In relation to these learning expectations is the role of the teacher in Vietnam. The students are 'expected to *learn* the knowledge from their teachers and take it as the only one correct source' (Tin Tan Dang, 2010: 6). Perhaps because of these pressures, several times in the discussion, Khiet raises the notion that it is difficult for teachers in Vietnam to tell the students that they lack knowledge about a specific topic, which is a part of his ideal teacher self formation. Statements such as 'Vietnamese is a kind of tool that saves the teachers from being embarrassed by not being able to speak English well in the classroom' and 'It's so shameful to say "I don't know"' are found at different points in the discussion, with a more elaborate example as follows:

Khiet: If you say something wrong, you would feel very shameful. You would feel very ashamed in your mind and in your heart. And the student would not recognize that. But you would not feel comfortable at all. You don't feel comfortable with teaching with, for example, if you start the lesson and you say something wrong, the whole lesson will be a shame…

Amy: Disaster.

Khiet: Yeah, a disaster. You cannot make it as smooth as you can. Something like that. That's my feeling. Not being respected as a teacher or a professional. I want my students to respect me.

The concept of 'feeling ashamed' is not just related to linguistic knowledge; it also came up in the discussion regarding the cultural knowledge of L1 Vietnamese English as a foreign language (EFL) teachers, again, in the formation of Khiet's ideal teacher self.

Khiet: For example, many teachers complain that they do not have a chance to study abroad. So, when they explain the Statue of Liberty, they cannot make it more real because they just say what is right in the textbook, so they do not feel confident. So, some students are not good in asking the teachers, 'Have you been there? Have you been there, sir? Have you been there, miss?' They would be ashamed to say, 'I haven't been there'.

Also discussed in the literature about English language teaching in Vietnam is the idea that it is also the teachers' responsibility to teach the students respect and what it means to be polite, serving as a type of 'moral guide'. 'But as good Vietnamese teachers, they also need to perform their duty as "behaviour educators" or "moral guides". Put differently, they will tend to instigate forms of cultural performance, such as politeness, which is not the same as what the West expects' (Phan Le Ha, 2004: 55). In the discussion about the L1 English-speaking teachers who are teaching in present-day Vietnam (who, according to Khiet, are only assigned to speaking and listening classes), Khiet says the following:

Khiet: They can hang out, they can go to the coffee shop, they can go shopping together. So, their relationship can be more intimate, closer, but I don't think… some Vietnamese students are not respectful to the foreign teachers. You know why? Because when they speak Vietnamese, they call the foreign teachers with a title like their friend (Bạn). Not like Mr. Not like Mr. or Ms., but they call their name, and they call the teachers like friends, so Vietnamese teachers had to correct them many times. It's our culture. Our culture is different from American culture. American teachers may teach you that way, but you are not allowed to behave that way. That's how we want our students to behave. Yeah. We need to show respect because they spend a lot of time with you teaching you English, so you need to show respect for them.

In Vietnam, as in other countries, many native English-speaking EFL teachers may not have adequate training in the profession, and also might be quite young, perhaps teaching English to support their travels. In fact, there is a Vietnamese expression for such teachers: *tay ba lo*, which means 'Western backpacker' (Ngan Nguyen, 2012). Additionally, knowing the local language and culture (as illustrated above by Khiet) is essential for successful language teaching. As Phillipson (1992: 195) suggests, ideal EFL teachers are perhaps those who have a high level of English proficiency, yet 'come from the same linguistic and cultural background as the learners'.

Toward the end of the discussion, I brought up the topic of being emotionally attached to English. Khiet talks about the fact that for him, English is more of a tool rather than something emotional. He has found English to be important in his life, specifically in the context of acquiring knowledge and creating new personal relationships.

Khiet: I think at first it was a tool for me, but now I love it… I can communicate with people, and I think English is a tool, but using it as a tool, I can establish a lot of good relationships with not only American students, teachers, but also international students. [**Amy:** Right.] English is a privilege for me. Yeah. So, I love it.

At the end, Khiet says the following:

Khiet: And the most important thing is the happiness when you learn a language – when you learn a foreign language, and you can use it to talk to many people. Not only to your friends, but to people from other countries, too. It's so wonderful. Yeah. It's wonderful. You are expanding a circle of friends and you know more.

As can be seen throughout the chapter, Khiet's initial teacher self was more of an ought-to self, as he chose the profession with the encouragement of his parents. Through the excerpts presented, we see that the ideal self that Khiet envisions is not, in fact, a native speaker of English, but the younger generation of Vietnamese English teachers who learned via more communicative methods. He believes that an ideal teacher should be able to speak fluently; he is also proud of his knowledge of and ability to explain English grammar to students, so that they will succeed on the mandatory exams. We also explored Khiet's belief about the importance of both the linguistic and cultural knowledge needed to teach English effectively, how it is difficult for a Vietnamese teacher to say 'I don't know' to students, and how respect for teachers (both their knowledge and status) is an important part of Vietnamese culture. The lack of respect that students show toward L1 English-speaking teachers is, thus, perhaps part of the reason that Khiet does not use them as a role model in his ideal teacher self formation. Khiet views English as a tool, both for himself and for his students, and specifically indicates how it has helped him establish relationships with people from around the world.

Vietnam's relationship with English is complex and multifaceted, and not surprisingly, given the turbulent politics of the country during the past several hundred years: 'English was once considered the language of the enemy and lost its importance due to political prejudice' (Ngan

Nguyen, 2012: 263). Currently, however, English as a language of study is quite popular in Vietnam, as Kieu Hang Kim Anh (2010: 119) states: 'As a result of international integration, the demand for a skilled labor force having a good command of English has become increased and consequently, English has been the foreign language of first choice in the country'. In showing its dedication to English language instruction, the Vietnamese government has created a vision for English language learning and teaching called 'Teaching and Learning Foreign Languages in the National Education System, Period 2008–2020'. Under this project, by 2020, all English teachers in Vietnam will need to be at a B2 level (upper intermediate) of the CEFR. Additionally, all students will need to be at a B1 level (intermediate). There is a $450m budget for this project, 85% of which will be spent on teacher training, illustrating the importance that the government is currently placing on English language teaching in Vietnam (Ngan Nguyen, 2012; Parks, 2011). At least for now, English is maintaining its status as the most common foreign language taught in Vietnam.

4 Egypt: 'Why is he comparing her to a summer's day?'

من تعلم لغة قوم أمن مكرهم

[Those who learn another's language are safe from their cunning]

Arab proverb

> ## KEY POINTS
>
> **In this chapter, Hasani**
>
> (1) Believes that the most effective teaching involves sharing a first language (L1) with students.
> (2) Indicates that people tend to have a more positive attitude toward French than toward English.
> (3) Expresses that attitudes toward English are affected by the actions of the American president.
> (4) States that a person's education is often judged by their English level and that English is necessary in the globalized world.
> (5) Feels that people do not 'learn' a language but 'live' a language.
>
> These aspects and others delineated in the chapter contribute to his ideal English teacher self.

Egypt, like many places in Africa, has experienced identity and policy clashes with Western European colonizers, primarily the British and the French, whose influences remain today. In the case of Egypt, there is also discussion on the diglossic context in terms of the different varieties of Arabic used: Classical Arabic (CA), a high-prestige variety whose usage is associated with Arab heritage and Islamic religious values; Modern Standard Arabic (MSA), whose usage is associated with pan-Arabism ideologies and modernity, in part because there are fewer taboos surrounding the adoption of political and technological loanwords into the language; and Egyptian Arabic (EA), considered by speakers to be a marker of strong regional identity (Benkharafa, 2013). There are also many varieties of EA, depending on both geographic and social differences.

In brief, the European colonization of Egypt started with the French, led by Napoleon Bonaparte in 1798. The British arrived at the turn of the 19th century (1801), but were ejected by Muhammad Ali, who brought many reforms to the region. In 1882, the British again seized power and remained in power until 1922, following a string of violent protests. Although Egypt was granted independence from Britain at this time, the British military remained in Egypt until 1953 when Egypt officially became an independent republic (Jeffreys, 2016). While Mohamed Naguib briefly became president, he was soon forced to resign and was succeeded by Gamal Abdel Nasser, who became one of the most influential presidents in the Arab world, spreading socialist, pan-Arabist and Arab nationalist political ideologies. Under Nasser, efforts were made to make education more attainable for non-elite Egyptians, and the status of Arabic resurged, especially in relation to Arab nationalism (Abouelhassan & Meyer, 2016). However, the effects of French and subsequently British colonization lingered: 'Having previously been colonized by Western imperialism, the Arab world bequeathed the languages of the colonizers. Therefore, the mainstream through which the Arab countries reached the state of multilingualism can be accounted for by imperialism' (Benkharafa, 2013: 203). The colonial history continues to influence language policy and attitudes, particularly with regard to CA, a language that is not typically used in colloquial spoken language: 'Another more serious problem threatening Classical Arabic is bilingualism, namely French-Arabic bilingualism. Because of the attitudes associated with it, the Arabic language seems to lose weight in favor of foreign languages, namely French in the Maghreb and English in the Mashreq' (Benkharafa, 2013: 201). Both the French and the British had colonized a large part of Africa and created the Sykes–Picot Agreement in 1916 that divided most of the Arab world between France and Britain, with the exception of Saudi Arabia and North Yemen. 'France controlled the Mediterranean coast of North Africa and what is now Syria and Lebanon, while Britain controlled Iraq, Transjordan, Egypt and the Sudan' (Bassiouney, 2009: 210, see also Mansfield, 2003). The education systems were based on those of the colonial powers, the effects of which are still present today.

Over the last decade, there has been an increase in the use of English by Egyptians in the public sphere, particularly amid the political unrest of the Arab Spring and the Egyptian revolution of 2011. Throughout the 2011 protests in Egypt that led to the removal of pro-Western President Mubarak who had ruled Egypt for more than three decades, to the protests of the elected and then deposed Islamist President Morsi through the appointment of the military leader el-Sisi in 2014, English played a role in the communication of the protesters, both in the streets and on social media (Abouelhassan & Meyer, 2016). As Abouelhassan and

Meyer (2016: 147) describe: 'Behind the scenes, two forces have worked tirelessly in opposite directions: on one side, the Islamization process, begun after the collapse of the Ottoman Empire in 1924, which has been a source of nostalgia for many Islamist Egyptians; on the other side, secular efforts of modernization that started after the revolution of 1952'. Similar to Turkey, language use and policy in Egypt are heavily intertwined with these opposing forces (Abouelhassan & Meyer, 2016).

Hasani is the L1 Arabic Egyptian English teacher voice heard in this chapter, commenting on topics such as motivation to learn English, the aims of English versus French colonialism, attitudes toward English, and attitudes toward non-native speaker teachers of English. At the time of the discussion, he lived in Cairo and had been teaching English for about 16 years in different types of schools. He started learning English at age 12 and French at age 16, stating that he speaks 'a little bit' of French. Growing up, he lived in a rural area that did not have a designated English teacher; he also didn't have the chance to use English outside of the classroom. His son, however, who is being raised in Cairo, started learning English at age 4; as discussed later in the chapter, students living in Cairo have opportunities to interact with tourists outside of the classroom, which improves their speaking skills in English. Hasani has taught at both public and experimental schools in Egypt, and being an English teacher is a stable and relatively well-paid profession: 'Teaching English in Egypt is seen as a prestigious job that guarantees a relatively high income compared to other teaching professions' (Abouelhassan & Meyer, 2016: 148).

Hasani: I have been teaching English for sixteen years. I used to work in a public school in which students just learned very simple English language, but now, I am working in an experimental language school in which students study extra or advanced levels in English. They study, for example, English literature, novels, drama, poetry, something like that. I have been teaching in that school for ten years. Most students in Egypt can speak English fluently because they start studying English from the very beginning, from kindergarten. I think English is their favorite subject or their favorite language.

Hasani also explains the different systems of language education in Egypt, including the fact that in the public state schools, education is free, and the textbooks are provided. In what he calls experimental schools (private schools supervised by the government), where there is a greater focus on language learning, the students have access to the same free texts that all students have access to, but they pay for extra language texts.

Hasani: In Egypt, we have certain textbooks that must be taught, certain curriculum that must be bought. I like this way. I like our way because

> we give all the students in different classes with different teachers the
> same opportunity to learn the same material.

In these experimental schools, Hasani explains that the teachers receive
a higher salary. He also indicates that his students in the experimental
school where he works participate in an English club and put on plays,
such as Hamlet and Cinderella. Additionally, there are independent private schools that are run by foreign governments, where the curriculum
and language are based on the country of origin. Currently, the private
schools are mostly British or American (Bassiouney, 2009). With regard
to English education, Latif (2018) provides an overview of the trends in
English language teaching, as summarized by both published and non-
published studies from 2006 to 2015.

Even though French control of Egypt was relatively short (1798–
1801), French has had a lasting influence on Egypt. According to Francis-
Saad (1992: 130), French is considered a language that is spoken by the
elite, making them part of a sort of exclusive club, particularly because
most Egyptians speak English: 'Pour une bourgeoisie traditionnelle, le
français est signe d'appartenance à une élite sociale et marque certaine
d'une différence, - puisque la plupart des Egyptiens parlent l'anglais' [For
a traditional bourgeois individual, French represents a membership to an
elite social class that distinguishes that person, - since most Egyptians
speak English]. Upper-class females are particularly encouraged to learn
French from an early age, as it 'leur offrant un capital de raffinement'
[offers them the social capital of refinement] (Francis-Saad, 1992: 131);
in the past, French offered upper-class females a sort of social prestige
in terms of the refinement they would gain from knowing the language,
although this is less common today. Well into the 20th century, French
dominated language education in the private sector, whereas English
was more widely studied in public schools (Schaub, 2000). According to
Cochran (1986), between the world wars there were about 12,000 Egyptian students learning English in 152 British or American-run schools, in
contrast to the approximately 60,000 students in French (the most common), Italian, or Greek schools.

France has also been particularly active in the archeological aspects
of Egypt. For example, the Institut Français d'Archéologie was opened
in 1881 and remains active today (Imhoof, 1977), and 'from the time of
Mohammed Ali, promising young Egyptians had been sent to Europe
(primarily to the Egyptian School in Paris) to learn vital skills fitting
them for positions of responsibility that would lessen Egypt's reliance
on imported expertise' (Jeffreys, 2016: 10). Although the British also had
involvement in archeological initiatives in Egypt, the French were particularly strong in this area. These aspects and attitudes toward French
are perhaps what influences Hasani's idea that France's involvement in
Egypt was primarily a cultural (rather than a military) colonization.

Hasani: Yes, most Egyptians, I think, are affected by French. They have a positive feeling about French because, you know, Egypt was colonized by France. But the aim of that invasion or something like that... the aim of that was not a military one; it was a cultural one, okay? So, I think that the impact or the effect was positive. So, they just have a good impression about French. Yeah, we feel that they are peaceful. They are good, and they don't hate the Arabs.

The same feeling of cultural, rather than military, involvement cannot be said regarding the British and American relationships with Egypt. As the British had a much longer colonial history with Egypt, attitudes toward English are more complicated. Although English now affords many economic opportunities (e.g. Abouelhassan & Meyer, 2016), Hasani indicates that attitudes toward a language are greatly affected by the political connections toward a language. The example he gives is the attitude toward English during the Gulf War, indicating that British and American policy in this instance was 'the same'. He also talks specifically about how the president of the United States can affect general attitudes toward English, using the example of the positive attitude that people had toward President Barack Obama versus the attitude that people had toward 'the previous one' (i.e. President George W. Bush). As indicated in the excerpt, Hasani is hesitant about using the invasion of Iraq as an example, shown by his nervous laughter two times in this short excerpt. It can be assumed that the nervousness came from talking about the Iraq conflict with an American, but he is also clear that despite the political misgivings, he and others in Egypt have positive attitudes toward English because of the opportunities that the language provides.

Hasani: I have a good position, or a good impression, about English, but, because it is connected with, I don't want to, it is connected with policy, you know? It is connected with political [aspects]. It has something to do with the general policy of the governments. So, for example (nervous laughter) during the invasion of Iraq... It's difficult to support [someone] who is killing people, okay? I think it's very clear and evident. You know? So, the impression is always built upon the policy or politics. So, if, for example, if I like a certain government, policy, or way, of course, I like the language. I'll see the language in a good, or from a good perspective. But, the wars (nervous laughter) that you have gone through, affected the impression so much, I think.

Amy: Okay. Do you think that is also other people's image towards English? If I understand what you said, it's more linked with American culture rather than British culture.

Hasani: Well, I wanted to talk about that, too, because they were, both of them are together [during the invasion of Iraq]. They were connected together. So, there was no difference between the American and the British policy – they are the same. I told you that they have a good impression from the other side. The other side, which is to find a good job, to find something good, you have to manage the language. You have to be fluent in English. But, nowadays, I think most of the people in the Middle East are having a good impression about English. You know, because of Obama, because he has a good way, just in speaking. So, we, people always speak, so he speaks well. But, the previous one, the previous president is, of course, he's your president, but he showed some great, some sort of hatred.

Hasani again emphasizes the difference between attitudes toward the language and people who speak the language, and attitudes toward governmental entities. He particularly stresses that 'they' (i.e. Egyptians) know that Americans are very kind. As Imhoof (1977) indicates, as early as the 1970s, attitudes toward English in Egypt had moved from a necessary evil during British occupation to a vehicle of social mobility. Schaub (2000: 235) discusses how attitudes toward English are surprisingly positive in Egypt, considering the complicated past with both British and American governments: 'Given the long and often saddening history of Egypt as a colonized and occupied nation – the revolution in 1952, the Suez Canal War (in 1956) against their former colonizer Britain, and the anti-US sentiments in Egypt during the 1960s and early 1970s – it is indeed a surprise that there hasn't been resistance to the explosion of English within Egypt's borders. In fact, to the average speaker of English on a visit to Egypt, there seems to be a great love of the language, with people all over its cities and countryside eager to practice their English, to communicate in *il-Ingliizi*'.

Hasani: No, they don't have any negative feeling towards English. Sometimes, they used to have some negative feelings toward the American government, not the American people because of the policy... they know very well that the American people are very kind people.

The reality is that English is, indeed, a path to economic success in a variety of sectors in Egypt, although spreading English was not one of the objectives of British colonization (Cochran, 2008). 'Educational reforms undertaken by the British were not accessible to most Egyptians because the colonizers did not intend to educate all Egyptians... The British did not want to educate the majority of the people; they wanted to educate a small group who would work as obedient clerks. The British only invested in schooling to produce the government employees they needed' (Cochran, 2008: 149–150). As Egyptian colonization came after that of India, the British were wary of creating a situation in Egypt similar to what happened in India, where widespread British education ultimately led to dissatisfaction and rebellion (Reid, 1977).

Nonetheless, English use in Egypt has bourgeoned with higher education and jobs as a motivating factor. Elkhatib (1984) cites English-medium universities as a motivation for youth to learn English. More than this, however, is the 'promise of more money or better jobs that many Egyptians associate with the "commodity" of English' (Schaub, 2000: 228). This has been accelerated since the initiation of the open door economic policy by Sadat, which allowed an influx of foreign companies and banks into Egypt (Elkhatib, 1984). The economic benefits of knowing English were evident as early as the 1970s when 'a beginning secretary in a government position made £E70 a month, while an English-speaking secretary in a foreign company could start as high as £E350' (Cochran, 1986: 78). Other jobs, such as teaching positions, working in multinational companies, or interacting with tourists have motivated Egyptians to learn English (Abouelhassan & Meyer, 2016), and it is the case that 'nations around the world, especially Egypt, have known for some time that the study of English is increasingly important to their economic development, global political participation, and understanding of western cultural influences' (Abdul Monem *et al.*, 2001: 26). Indeed, Hasani talks about the economic opportunities that knowing English brings about, highlighting the importance of the ought-to self in terms of English language study.

Hasani: You know, there is a fact, which is that if you want your kids or your child to get a good job, he must learn English, not only learn English, he must be fluent in English. Either speaking or writing. It's a must now. So, everybody, okay, wants his kids to learn English very well, because, for example, they study, they have to study engineering in English. They have to study medicine in English. Okay? So, the good, or what we call the 'good faculties' or good jobs, depend mainly on English. Also, business is taught in English, banks. If they want to get a job in a bank, they have to learn English very well.

Amy: Why would it be necessary to speak English to work in a bank or a business?

Hasani: Because now, everything is globalized. Most banks in Egypt are directed from other banks either in the US or Britain or somewhere else. You know? So, most of them are dealing with English, with English people. They are connected with English, I don't know, shopping, selling, buying, or something.

Traditional jobs, such as working in banks, are not the only industries that require a command of English, and some might argue that even if English is not really necessary to do certain jobs, speaking English is a way to select for class. In the case of the tourism industry, English is a commodity, and many countries rely on tourism as a major source of national and personal revenue. Supporting this idea is the statement by Blommaert (2010: 148): 'Mass tourism is one of the agents of rapid change in many places in the world, and it has fascinating sociolinguistic effects'. Egypt, with its rich history of historical artifacts and sites, is one of those countries that rely on tourism. In what he refers to as 'grassroots Englishes', Schneider (2016: 3–4) discusses areas where people learn English with the sole purpose of working in the tourism industry: 'Speakers who have acquired English in this way mostly have an exceptionally high instrumental motivation'. Although Hasani's students also have the opportunity to go to school to study English, unlike the participants in Schneider's case studies (again, reflecting a class distinction), they are still affected by Egypt's tourist industry as a motivation to learn English.

As stated by Abouelhassan and Meyer (2016: 152), 'After realizing the necessity of tourism for economic development, the Ministry of Tourism was established in 1967 to promote tourist investment' and the Nasser government made deals with large international hotels, such as the Hilton and the Sheraton. The Ministry of Tourism saw the greatest expansion under Mubarak, who brought tourism to the beaches that were deserted due to colonization and the war with Israel. This was the first time that Egyptian tourism focused on sites other than monuments, such as the pyramids (Richter & Steiner, 2008). There are also four-year colleges in Egypt dedicated to the study of hospitality and tourism; as cited by Abdel Ghany and Abdel Latif (2012), over a period of 40 years, Egypt created 11 colleges and 14 higher institutes of tourism in Egypt. Although successful tourism students often learn languages other than English to distinguish themselves, English is one of the focus subjects and is considered crucial for the tourism industry. Hasani supports this assertion of the relevance of English when interacting with tourists who come to Egypt.

Hasani: In order to deal with any other nationality in the world, you can speak to them in English, and they will understand you. So, it's a must. It's a link. Also, all tourists who come to Egypt, whether they are from a native speaking country or not, okay, to communicate with them, you have to learn English. So, it's a must.

Hasani indicates that he sometimes takes his students to tourist sites to interact with foreigners and that his students also use English to chat with friends online. Recent research on language learning success has found that extramural language activities, or activities in which students engage outside of the classroom, are crucial for language learning success. Sundqvist and Sylvén (2016) provide a detailed overview of the importance of extramural language activity for language learning success, and Huensch and Thompson (2017) examine the connection between extramural language activities and the selves. For the latter, looking specifically at students enrolled in first and second semester classes, there were significant differences between the ideal and anti-ought-to selves between those students who participated in extramural language activities and those who did not. The most poignant difference was with the ideal self: 'Those learners in lower-level classes who did not participate in extramural language activities had a neutral to slightly positive ideal self ($M = 3.54$), while those who did participate in extramural language activities had a strong ideal self ($M = 4.79$)' (Huensch & Thompson, 2017: 421–422). In the case of Hasani's English language students in Egypt, interacting with tourists, as well as interacting online, increases in the instances of extramural language activities, giving the students the opportunity to strengthen their ideal English selves. Also, unlike the teachers in Gao and Xu's (2014) study, who were located in a rural context, both Hasani and his students have the resources that a large city like Cairo affords them in terms of resources to learn English.

Hasani: We have visits to the tourists sites. I, myself, used to take them to the pyramids and the Sphinx, and those places, and we used to talk to tourists there, just to give them the opportunity to practice the language because practicing the language in class is different from speaking to a foreigner or to a native speaking person. So, they usually enjoy these things very much. Of course, they have their own friends on the internet chatting and something like that. They have friends all over the world because I live in Cairo, and it is a capital, you know, and each student has his own laptop or computer or something like that. They are updated, and they know how to chat or to speak.

Hasani also sees the strong connection between language and culture, which he undoubtedly instills in his students as well. Emphasizing that a culture is more than politics, he stated that he talked about his ideas regarding language and culture in conjunction with the teacher exchange program in which he was participating during the time of the data collection. Purposefully creating opportunities for his students to interact with tourists in Egypt, Hasani is giving them an opportunity to interact with people from different countries without leaving Egypt.

Hasani: As I told some of my colleagues, because language is not only reading and writing; language is some sort of culture; language is a live thing, which we can live. I say, I'm telling them that we are living the language. Not, 'we are learning the language' because it's a culture.

In terms of Hasani's own motivation to learn English growing up, there were several people in his family with whom he could practice speaking. Although he has both English and French teachers in his family, he emphasized the fact that they speak English together. Although

Hasani does not explicitly state that his cousins were a kind of role model, this seems to have been the case. Having close friends or family members with whom to practice English is one of the aspects affecting the context, and thereby affecting Hasani's ideal language learning and language teaching self.

Hasani: My family, most of them are language teachers. [**Amy:** Oh, they are?] Either English or French.

Amy: Did you speak English or French with your parents, growing up?

Hasani: They can't speak, my parents can't speak English or French, but my cousins, I have three cousins who teach English and two who teach French... Yes, we speak English, I speak English with them... but not all the time, you know? Sometimes we speak just phrases or expressions or something like that but not all the time.

Hasani does not seem to have an emotional attachment to English, however. Even when directly asked, he circumvents the question, going back to how France supported language learning in Egypt more than the United States or the UK.

Amy: Okay. And what about your emotional attachment for English? I mean, what feelings do you have towards the language or the culture or anything?

Hasani: Okay. Of course, English, you know, I think France gives greater time and greater financial aid to spread the French language. They support the French language everywhere. But English, because, I think because, you know that is the widely spoken language, so, your care about spreading the language is less.

Rather than an emotional attachment to English *per se*, many Egyptians have formed a linguistic identity around the ability to casually switch from Arabic to English. In some cases, the ability to code-switch, or to change from one linguistic code to another, is a part of Egyptians' linguistic identity. Indeed, these new identities are enabled by this linguistic and cultural hybridity, as the act of code-switching has many functions. The common, and misinformed, perception is that code-switching occurs when a speaker has some sort of language deficiency and needs to fall back on another language. However, code-switching is often a purposeful occurrence, and the speaker might choose to switch codes for a variety of reasons (e.g. Zentella, 1997). In Egypt, code-switching used as a form of power came to the forefront in February 2011, the beginning of the Arab Spring that resulted in the abdication of Mubarak. The Egyptian media criticized the protestors in Tahrir Square for many reasons, one of which was the assertion that they were not 'true Egyptians' because of their use of English in chants and signage. As cited in Bassiouney (2012) and discussed further in Bassiouney (2013), the government-run media attempted to discredit the protesters because they 'are not "real Egyptians", and therefore do not represent what Egyptians want or demand' (Bassiouney, 2012: 112) because they 'use foreign languages, especially English, the language of past colonizers and American political hegemony' (Bassiouney, 2013: 98; see also Bassiouney, 2014).

However, English used in conjunction with the L1 is becoming increasingly common, as indicated by Nashef (2013: 313), 'With globalisation, the eradication of traditional borders, and the increasing influence of media, namely the internet and satellite television, the use of code switching and mixing have become more common globally, with English namely evolving as the dominant language'. Nashef (2013: 318) later asserts that 'with globalisation, and with Arab youth being exposed widely to American television shows and films, speaking colloquial American English has been the norm' and 'aid in the negotiation of one's identity vis-à-vis the recipients of one's utterance' (Nashef, 2013: 326). Hasani gives an example of how English is commonly used when speaking Arabic to show a certain level of education. In the following excerpt, he gives examples of how code-switching in Egypt can be used as a status symbol, particularly in the larger cities.

Hasani: B: A man's education is, we can say, somehow, is measured by how well he can speak English.... Instead of saying, '*shukran*', *shukran* is in Arabic, they can say, 'thanks' or 'thank you', you know, 'with pleasure', and something like that. They are substituting some expressions. Instead of saying them in Arabic, they say it, or they say them in English. But not everywhere. This is in the big cities and something like Cairo and Alexandria.

Supporting Hasani's assertion of using English to show social status, Trentman (2013) also gives examples of the common nature of English use in Egyptian society, in particular when interacting with foreigners. One of the Egyptian teachers interviewed for Trentman's (2013: 466) study indicates that Egyptians tend to use English with foreigners in order to 'complete a transaction quickly, to help the foreigner, or to show off their knowledge of English, a prestigious language important on the Egyptian job market'. Even though the foreigner in question might speak Arabic fluently, Egyptians still tend to speak English instead, even citing that speaking Arabic with a foreigner is somehow impossible: 'It's a psychological matter, it blocks my ability to speak with Emma in Arabic because she is American. No! An American, I just speak to her in English, you get what I mean?' (Trentman, 2013: 467).

In terms of ideal self formation and the non-native English-speaking status of English teachers in Egypt, Hasani explains the difference in job placements for L1 English speakers and L1 Arabic speakers who have learned English. Hasani indicates that there are 17 teachers in his current school, and that all of them are Egyptian. Hasani states that if someone is a native speaker of English, that person would work in a job that would pay more, such as in the international schools that serve wealthy students and where the salary is in dollars.

Hasani: If the teacher has the native accent, he won't, okay, he won't work in teaching in a [public or experimental] school. [**Amy:** Oh, really?] Yes, he will find another job, a better job, a better, more rewarding job than teaching. [**Amy:** Like what, for example?] Like what? For example, we have some international schools in Egypt. Now, there are so many international schools. They may pay you in dollars, you know? So, working in international schools is so profitable. You don't have to work for extra time or something like that, so, it's very nice, and easy, and, of course, your students will be rich ones, more respectable students, and something like that. If he is a native speaker, I think he is not going to work as a teacher of English in a public school or in an experimental language school.

Although the types of position possibilities might be different from L1 English speakers and L1 Arabic speakers, Hasani indicates that an Egyptian would be more effective in teaching English to Egyptian students because of a shared culture.

Hasani: I think I'll be effective more than you. Because I understand my own culture very well, and now I understand some, or a great deal of your culture, so I'm able to make that sort of link. But if anyone from another society, okay, is going to teach different kinds of students from a different culture, okay, he can teach some sort of language, but he can't create this sort of harmony between the two cultures. It's difficult for him. So, because sometimes I know how they think, okay? Without speaking or without listening to them, because I am the product or what we call the outcome of that culture, so I understand their point of view. And I can, I know how to change it. And I know how to make them see it from a different angle or a different perspective…. [for example] students, were asking, okay, 'why is he comparing her to a summer's day?' You know? In Egypt, a summer's day is not good at all. It's so difficult, you know?

Similar to the Turkish context, there seems to be discrepancies in compensation for those who speak English as an L1 and those who are L1 Arabic speakers. Despite this, Hasani believes that he, an L1 Arabic speaker, is a more 'effective' English teacher to his students, who share his L1, primarily because of the shared culture aspect.

The effectiveness in language teaching that comes from this shared culture is a strong part of Hasani's ideal teacher self formation, along with the concept that teaching is a respectable and secure career in his specific context. Growing up, he had role models in the form of cousins who were also teachers of both English and French, and these role models also helped guide him in his career choice. In terms of the characteristics of an ideal teacher, Hasani likes that he teaches a structured curriculum, as it gives everyone the same opportunities to learn and advance in English. He believes that his students enjoy learning English and that it is his job as a teacher to help prepare his students for their future careers. Hasani also conceptualizes his role as a teacher as integrating what he teaches in the classroom in authentic settings; as such, he finds opportunities for his students to use English to interact with tourists, giving them the chance to use English and to start to form their own ideal selves for English, which is possible because of the context in which he teaches. This contextualized language use connects to what is perhaps the most important part of his ideal teacher self – he believes that language is a living entity, ever evolving. As such, he helps his students live the language, rather than simply learn the language.

5 Argentina: 'Learning the language will never end'

Este mundo no va a cambiar a menos que estemos dispuestos a cambiar nosotros
mismos
[The world won't change unless we're willing to change ourselves]

Rigoberta Menchu

KEY POINTS

In this chapter, María and Carolina

(1) Feel that having also learned English makes them empathetic to their students' processes.

(2) Believe that it is the teacher's job to create a positive attitude toward English.

(3) Indicate that students express frustration at having to learn English when Americans aren't required to learn Spanish.

(4) Express that because of globalization, English is needed; however, wealthier students have more opportunities to learn English.

(5) Feel that 'learning the language will never end' and 'you have to love what you do'.

These aspects and others delineated in the chapter contribute to their ideal English teacher selves.

Like many of the chapters in this volume, Argentina has a complex relationship with English because of the sociopolitical realities with the UK and, in recent years, the United States. Spanish colonizers arrived in Argentina in the 16th century; Argentina was a Spanish colony until 1816 (Nielsen, 2003). Immigrants from a variety of countries came in the latter part of the 19th century, 70% of whom were Italian (Gallo, 1990). Starting in the 20th century, the immigrant population shifted to a majority of Spaniards (Luna, 1984), and Spanish became the lingua franca of

Argentina (Nielsen, 2003). The Amerindian languages spoken in Argentina are not emphasized as much as Spanish and English in the school system; the expectation is that the speakers of these languages learn Spanish for schooling and work. Araucanian (Mapudungun) is spoken by approximately 40,000 people living near the Chilean border. Near Bolivia and Peru, Quechua and Guaraní (known as Chiriguano in Argentina) are also spoken (Baker & Prys Jones, 1998). A more detailed description of indigenous languages in Argentina can be found in Hornberger (1994).

Although British immigrants were comparatively smaller in number than those from other countries in Europe, the British influence was strong because of the businesses they brought to Argentina, particularly the large-scale farming industry involving sheep, meat production, wood and tannin, and sugar, among others (Nielsen, 2003). By 1914, the Argentinian railway system was extensive with 80% of it owned and run by British companies (Write, 1974). This economic freedom that was advantageous to the British was the result of the Friendship, Commerce, and Navigation Treaty of 1825, which not only recognized Argentina's independence from Spain, but also gave Britain commercial freedom. The United States business investments in Argentina came in the 20th century and consisted primarily of automotive, oil, and mining foci. Unlike the British communities, the American communities never solidified in Argentina, and today, administrators of American companies are American-trained Argentinians (Nielsen, 2003). Even the British immigrants largely did not integrate with Argentinians, often treating the lower- and middle-class workers with contempt. Nonetheless, 'the English speaking community, though much smaller than the Spanish or Italian, has a social prestige and economic power that was incomparably superior' (Nielsen, 2003: 201).

According to Porto et al. (2016), English is taught in Argentina via a centrally organized system (where most students learn it), as well as through the school system of the British community. Private schools modeled after the bilingual structure of the British school became more prevalent in the early 20th century with approximately 25% of students attending these private schools, as 'Unfortunately, many Argentinians do not view the public education system as adequate and they are willing to pay for higher standards of instruction, especially when it comes to learning English' (Tocalli-Beller, 2007: 108). Additionally, students from middle-class and wealthy families often take private English lessons in addition to the mandatory English classes taught in school. As Banfi (2017: 15) indicates, 'In the years that preceded the 1990s it was those who could afford it who had access to foreign language tuition in the early years (be it private schools, extracurricular classes or private tuition)'. Until the 1990s, the role of English in public schools was limited. Federal mandates in the 1990s made English compulsory from Year 4 to Year 9, changing the status of English (Porto et al., 2016). Although English is not obligatory for post-secondary education, private universities typically require competency in English, as would studying at a university abroad (Nielsen, 2003). Recently, many state-funded universities have also started including an English requirement in their program of study. The New Federal Education Law of 1993 emphasizes the communicative value of language to be used in an international arena. However, according to Tocalli-Beller (2007), there have been some issues implementing communicative language teaching in some schools, largely because of the lack of resources and training, and also because of class sizes of 35–40 students (see also Snow *et al.* [1998] for further elaboration). Zappa-Hollman (2007: 624) also describes the problems of implementing the new federal law, going so far as to state, 'Argentina embarked on a controversial and overly ambitious plan that drove the country's education system down a dead-end road'. Although this is an extreme position, it is an illustration of what can happen when educational policy is formed without the buy-in of the primary stakeholders involved. Even in areas with relatively more resources, such as in Buenos Aires, disparities in class size, particularly in the less wealthy school districts, limit the effectiveness of English language instruction (Pozzi, 2017).

The focus of why and how English is being learned has, in many cases, shifted from focusing on a specific cultural context to the global and intercultural dimension of the language. According to Kamhi-Stein *et al.* (2017: 1), 'in the 2000s English began to be viewed as an instrument of empowerment and contestation of the current reality in the region and as a tool that contributed to the positioning of the different countries in the region vis-à-vis the rest of the world... English is currently being used as a cognitive *and* social tool that grants access to the world'. Valsecchi *et al.* (2017: 189) describe two main parameters for supporters of a more robust language learning program in Argentinian schools: 'On the one hand, there is a cognitive dimension, which supports the notion that learning an additional language helps students to reflect upon native language processes and optimize their use. On the other hand, there is an intercultural dimension, which considers that L2 learning enables students to become aware of the existence of other cultures and peoples, leading to a wider vision of the world and its diversity'. That being said, some students do not necessarily see this connection, as will be illustrated later in this chapter. Similarly, each English teacher has their own point of view of how language should be taught and what place English has in the world, and as Veciño (2017: 126) points out, 'The reality of public schooling in Argentina reflected and, to a large extent, continues to reflect, the sign of verticalist, hierarchical organizational models. High school classes are very often traditional, teacher centered, probably a reflection of long-established social hegemonic paradigms and structures', which is similar to the description of the social stratification described in Kormos and Kiddle (2013) in the context of Chile. It should also be remembered that larger cities, such as Buenos Aires, have more resources to implement language learning initiatives, such as *'Idiomas desde Primer Grado'* [languages from first grade] (Banfi, 2017). Pozzi (2017) describes another policy about providing computer and internet access to all teachers and students that, while not directly related to language learning, provides support for the process, as technology results in access to materials in English, which are needed for successful English language classrooms. However, as Veciño (2017) indicates, just being provided with these resources does not necessarily mean that they will be used effectively. Many smaller cities and less wealthy regions, however, do not necessarily have access to these resources.

The English teacher voices in this chapter are María and Carolina, Argentinian English teachers who speak Spanish as a first language (L1) and who are also both trained as translators. At the time of the discussion, María worked in Villa María, a town in the province of Córdoba, which is the heart of Argentina's agricultural region, and had been teaching for 21 years. From Argentina as well, Carolina was living in Chile at the time of the data collection and talked about several places where she had taught English in her 10 years of experience, including Argentina and as an exchange teacher in New Zealand. In addition to English, both teachers had also studied Italian, although neither had experience teaching it. María and Carolina discuss themes such as amotivation on the part of the students connected to negative attitudes toward the United States and the UK; motivation because of economic advantages; attitudes toward other languages, such as Italian; and attitudes toward non-native English-speaking teachers. Our discussion started with both Carolina and María describing their school and classroom settings in Argentina.

Carolina: I work for a privately run school with state funding. In that school I have approximately 30 students in my classes. They are sitting six rows, eight rows of students. It's usually the teacher standing at the front and all the students facing the teacher. And they have their own textbooks that they have to buy at the beginning of the year. [**Amy:** The students buy them?] The students buy them. So that kind of determines the kind of book I have to choose because I have to think of a book that is interesting but at the same time affordable because they will have to buy that book and many other books for other subjects... Sometimes I bring authentic material, I mean realia, to the classroom. It depends on what the topic is. And that's just to make them, I don't know, interested in what we are going to learn. And I usually have like half the class' attention. Not all of them. Some of them are just, I don't know, looking out of the window, so I usually interrupt my class to say, hey what are you doing? Did you hear this question? How would you answer this question? Do you agree with your classmate?

In the course of describing her work in the state-funded school, she alludes to the amotivation of some of the students as they are 'looking out of the window', and the results of Valsecchi *et al.* (2017) indicate that a majority (65%) of their 1522 participants admit to being difficult to motivate. Carolina contrasts her experience working in a state-funded school to that of working in a private language school. Both she and María also discuss the use of the target language, English, compared to the L1 of Spanish.

Carolina: On the other hand, I work in companies teaching English to business people or in a small language school with students that are over 20 years old. Most of them are university students or professionals who are learning English because they need it for professional development or to climb in their career ladders. So that is totally different. That's very communicative. The groups are usually of no more than eight to ten students. They're very participative. They ask lots of questions. Most of the class is done only in English. Except for starters; we could do like 6 months half English half Spanish but then we just try to get into English all the time. In that case we use computers, YouTube videos, authentic materials like newspaper articles, magazines. Sometimes we invite guests, native speakers, to the class, so they can talk to people who speak English, and sometimes we just change teachers so that they don't get used to just one accent, one way of talking, etc. So, it varies a lot.

Amy: Do you usually... what language is the language of instruction usually? Is it mostly Spanish or mostly English?

Carolina: I would say... at school? It's mostly Spanish. And... except for like classroom language then I can use English. And then at the private language school, it's mostly English.

María explains that she also works in a school similar to the one described by Carolina – the teacher salaries are paid by the state, but needed equipment and supplies are paid for by the students' families. She also discusses the use of English versus Spanish based on the level of the students she is teaching.

María: Okay the school. It's a school, the same as the one described by Carolina. It's half private, half public school. Why is this? Because the government pays the salary to the teachers and all the other expenditures or investments, as you want to see it, for maintenance or for more equipment, is paid by a fee from the students.

Amy: What is the language of instruction?

María: The language of instruction is in Spanish. It's mixed. In the group most trained, in fourth year, we generally speak English most of the time, but in the other group, no.

Motivation to learn a specific language often requires a positive attitude toward the culture where the language in question is spoken. In terms of forming an ideal self in the target language, it might be difficult to envision speaking the language if one has distain for the connected culture or cultures. In some cases, such as with English because of its status as an international language of communication, it is enough to be able to visualize speaking English with other international colleagues. As Kamhi-Stein *et al.* (2017: 2) state, 'In fact, the use of English in the region no longer requires adherence to an idealized mode of being and living associated exclusively with English-speaking countries'. In some cases, such as the following scenarios described by Carolina and María, the negative feelings toward the target cultures are too ingrained to overcome.

Carolina: They are not interested in English. It is difficult for them, and... my students usually relate English to the United States, and their idea of the United States as being a controller of the world and superior. So, they think, why do I have to study English? Do they study Spanish, for example? They have that feeling towards English because they associate it with the United States. That's when I try to explain to them that English is the language of communication. That's it's not only spoken here in the States, but also in many other countries, spoken by the whole world just to communicate. That it will be very useful for them when they finish school, when they want to travel... but this is another thing. Traveling is not part of their ambitions, and, yes, because of the money, but not just because of the money, because they don't even think about it.

However, María also indicates that part of her ideal teacher self is to be one who helps her students overcome negative attitudes toward English.

María: I wanted to add that the task of a teacher of English in Argentina is try to create a positive attitude towards learning English. Because, I mean, regarding, this, this has to do with the concept of globalization, too, because it is one of the languages that prevails, or is the one, the lingua franca so as to communicate with everybody, everywhere. And, apart from what Carolina said regarding the USA, we also have, the other part, the counterpart of England. We have had problems with England. Actually, nowadays, we are having some conflicts regarding petroleum, production, I don't know, exploitation, I don't know how to say it. So, it is difficult to create a positive attitude towards it.

Both Carolina and María describe conflictual feelings with English-speaking countries – England and the United States. Despite Carolina's attempts to motivate her students to be enthusiastic about English because of its usefulness worldwide, she describes her students as not considering using English to travel 'because they don't even think about it'. María adds the negative attitudes toward England regarding the exploitative practices of petroleum production in Argentina, although she does not elaborate further. As described in the first part of the chapter, following the implementation of the Friendship, Commerce, and Navigation Treaty of 1825, British businesses were given the freedom to operate in Argentina. Although immigrants from the UK often lived a relatively separate life from other Argentinians, the businesses brought jobs and the groups tolerated each other. In 1982, however, the Falklands War (the *Islas Malvinas*, in Spanish, see Reisman, 1983) broke out; it was a contentious war between the UK and Argentina. The UK won the war and feelings of ill-will remain. In this instance, it seems that negative attitudes impede the motivation to learn English. María also explains that her students' main contact with English is through music, as they do not need English to function in daily life. Because of the lack of a perceived need for English, as well as a lack of awareness of the prevalence of English in a variety of sectors, students might not develop a strong ought-to self in this context.

María: The only contact that the students have with the English language is through songs. Because they listen, they repeat them perfectly, even, some of the students sing because they like singing, and they demonstrate that they have very good listening capacity. But, other than songs, there is no other contact. They don't need it to buy things, to go to a certain shop, some of them, they can see many films, but they are subtitled.

Social status (i.e. context) also has an influence on the amount of English to which students are exposed. In addition to music in English, there are also English language newspapers, British and American cultural centers, and private English language institutes in Argentina (Nielsen, 2003). There is even the assertion that 'Either cable or satellite television is present in most homes, giving access to several English speaking news, sports and movie channels, some of which are not subtitled' (Nielsen, 2003: 205). However, as Carolina indicates, having access to these English pop culture resources does not mean that all (or even most) students engage with these cultural artifacts; there is a socioeconomic disparity that is also discussed in Kormos and Kiddle (2013). As in Gao and Xu (2014), many students in the Argentinian context do not have much contact with English outside of the classroom setting.

Carolina: I would say that the wealthier the students are, the more contact they have with English. [**Amy:** I see.] And because their likes are different, and their preferences are different. For example, they would tend to listen to more English music, and they would tend to see more Hollywood, probably, movies, whereas my students, who don't like English very much, they don't like English music either. Maybe in a group of 30 we have five students who usually listen to music in English. But all the rest listen to music in Spanish. They choose Spanish movies or dubbed movies. So, in some cases it's like English is not something they need until they reach a certain age, when they probably have to use it. And their parents probably don't have to use English, so…

Nonetheless, some students are indeed motivated to learn English because of the economic advantages involved. In Valsecchi *et al.* (2017), for example, 82% of their participants agree that learning English is beneficial to their futures. Even if they do not form an ideal self in English, the need for English to work and study in the contexts of their choosing helps to develop their ought-to-selves.

Carolina: Some of them really need English for communication in their jobs over Skype, through emails, business meetings, sometimes degrees, some of them are doing PhDs, and they need to read a lot of bibliographies in English, so it's kind of different reality.

In terms of her own emotional attachment to English, Carolina talks about learning English in relation to learning Italian. She has more of an emotional attachment to Italian because of her family heritage of Italian. María also indicates that there is more opportunity to speak Italian in her context because of the number of people from Italy.

Carolina: My grandfather was born there, and he immigrated to Argentina when he was 18, but all his family stayed in Italy.

María: But, there are many more opportunities of talking Italian with some grandparents because everywhere in Argentina, there are Italian immigrants… Many families have their grandparents, especially people from the farms in Argentina. Most of the farms were worked by Italian immigrants because the Argentineans didn't know how to. They were very handy with cattle, but not with agriculture, so there are many of those, but in Villa María there are many people who speak Italian because their parents or grandparents do.

When I specifically asked Carolina about her emotional attachment to English, she immediately turned to the description of Italian, indicating that it was initially her love of Italian that helped her grow to love all languages, including English (i.e. Thompson, 2017b).

Amy: Do you have a certain kind of emotional attachment or some type of personal relationship with English, do you think?

Carolina: Not really. It's really a mystery because I think I'm the only person who has studied English in my family. And I would say that I'm the only person who speaks English in the family. Italian would be more emotion-related, not English. I don't really know why I liked English. I don't know but I think it was question of language, culture learning because then I liked Italian, and I liked all languages, and I'm very interested in cultures and see and the possibility that languages give you to communicate first-hand. You don't have any, kind of, you don't need translation. You can say and understand what people say.

Both Carolina and María have strong identities about being non-native speakers of English, the language they teach. In fact, they find it to be more advantageous, and have incorporated this concept into the formation of their ideal English teaching selves. Carolina even indicates that as there are no native speaker teachers of English, no one even looks for that feature. In some contexts, having a teacher whose L1 is English is almost impossible; however, in bigger cities, although scarce, sometimes native speakers of English can be found in the classroom.

Carolina: Yes. I think that in our country, the possibility of having a native English teacher of English is zero... So it's not badly seen, I mean there's no cons for not being native... And as regards to the advantages of the non-native, is like you can use a little bit Spanish sometimes to help convey some difficult concepts, and having been through the process of learning itself makes it like... you can put yourself in the other person's shoes and see, okay, what could be difficult or easy for that person, and how you can just deliver that concept.

María relates her experience as a non-native speaker of English to her observation of a Spanish class when she was in the United States. In both cases, she observed the advantages of being able to connect to the students in a more efficient way, as do Ma (2012) and Chun (2014).

María: I was in a class of Spanish here the other day in high school. And they [students] really need their own language because they are English speakers and with a teacher of Spanish, they communicated... she was a native, both of them are native English speakers, and they need their own language to make some explanations easier, especially at the instructional point, you know? When you have to give the instructions of what to do with certain activity. The teacher spoke, and I saw myself reflected in that. And I said well, I think that for instructional language, a bit of the native language is necessary when you teach a foreign language.

Carolina contrasts teaching English to her students in Argentina with her experience of teaching English in New Zealand. Her opinion is that it is more logical to teach students with whom you share a native language. In expressing this, she also acknowledges the benefits of students working out the meaning of certain words or expressions by using context clues. Overall, however, Carolina thinks it is more beneficial for students and teachers to share a native language.

Carolina: Yes, so I was just thinking, in 2008, I lived for almost 8 months in New Zealand and, strangely, I got a job as an English teacher teaching English to Asian people. So we didn't share the language. And they were mainly Korean, Chinese, and Japanese, and two or three of them were Arabic [speakers]. At certain times, I felt why don't we talk the same language, so they just say the word and it's easier? Sometimes it took me like five minutes to explain an abstract concept, and I knew they got the concept when they'd enter the word in their dictionaries, and they saw it. Okay, but all the talking and the miming and the pictures that I had just done, it was useless. So sometimes for certain concepts it's, I don't know, I don't say it's essential, but it's really helpful if you share the language. It takes less time if you just say it quickly. Then there are some people who say, who argue that if you just say they will forget. If it takes them time to understand and they grasp the meaning, so they will remember. It depends. I mean, it depends on the students' learning styles and for some of them, I mean, just having the word and the translation it's easier and more effective, and for others it's more effective just to go through the process of discovering. So, I think you could do with or without native languages, sharing the same language.

Carolina also acknowledges that proficiency in the target language is needed to teach higher-level students. After talking about the proficiency needed for the more advanced levels, as was also discussed in Thompson and Fioramonte (2012), she circles back to the lack of metalinguistic knowledge that some native speakers might have when teaching. She gives an anecdote about an English for speakers of other languages (ESOL) teacher she was observing, saying that she herself would not necessarily be able to give grammar explanations in Spanish.

Carolina: I think in my school, we've never talked about that [the native versus non-native issue]. The thing is we're just two teachers, myself and another teacher, but then I'm thinking about this private language school where I teach, when we hire teachers, what do we look for in teachers? And sometimes, being non-native sometimes makes some teachers not be very fluent, and so if you want to have these teachers working with the upper intermediate or advanced class, they won't manage. They won't be able to work properly with the class. I had one teacher that was excellent. Her teaching approaches were perfect, but her accent was very Spanish, so her students talked to me and told me that they loved her, but they didn't feel comfortable with her because that was not a challenge, so they asked for a change. So, I think that in higher levels, it can be a disadvantage. Yeah? In lower levels it's usually... the students don't even notice the differences. Like, you speak English, that's great... So, on the other hand, once I was observing an American teacher, and she was teaching in a beginner level, and she was working with nouns, and they asked her why sometimes... explaining the −s in the simple present and the thing is that she couldn't explain why sometimes when you have playing, *plays*, you keep the *y*, but for cry, *cries*, you don't keep it. So, she was looking at the words and saying okay, this is the way it is, and she couldn't give an explanation. So, I think that in that case, all non-native English speakers would be able to answer that question because it's one of the first things we learn. So maybe that would happen the same with me in Spanish. I wouldn't be able to answer many questions in my own language.

Carolina and María have both developed a strong ideal teacher self in their identity as a non-native speaker teacher of English in a Spanish-speaking context, and it is clear that they love their chosen profession. They both indicate that it is important to keep learning, to be humble, and to know one's limitations. As Gregersen and MacIntyre (2015) indicate, one never really stops being a language student, even after becoming a language teacher.

Carolina: You have to keep trying and learning all the time. I mean, I think this is the same for all subjects. Math teachers must keep learning all the time, and the same with other teachers, but I think in our case it's more obvious. We need to keep track of what's going on.

María: Yes, and to be humble enough so as to know your limitations. Language, as we said, you never end learning. So, you have to be humble enough and conscientious enough so as to say I'm learning all the time, this will never end. Learning the language will never end, so you have to go on studying and studying and you will always find somebody who knows something that you don't know.

In the end, María indicates that you have to have passion for your profession, and with passion, anything is possible.

María: You have to love what you do. That's for me, because I have no other explanation for what I… as I told you, I don't know why I like it… you have to love it. And if you are passionate, you can go on.

The ideal teacher selves of María and Carolina revolve around several core characteristics. As was noted in an excerpt near the beginning of this chapter, María states that it is the duty of English teachers in Argentina to help students have a more positive attitude toward English, which is often a difficult task because of the conflicts between Argentina and both the UK and the United States. In the description of classroom activities, Carolina specifically states that the language of instruction in her classrooms is context dependent. In other words, which language to use in class is not a fixed part of her ideal teacher self but adjusts according to student need and the specific situation. Both María and Carolina indicate that they find sharing a language and culture with their students especially beneficial when teaching English; as such, the identity of being L1 Spanish speakers is a strong part of their ideal English teacher selves. They also comment on the learner–teacher duality, indicating that an ideal teacher will never stop learning, and will be humble, yet passionate, in their teaching. The formations of their ideal teacher selves depend on context and were formed based on their own social interactions and experiences.

The publications on teacher and/or learner motivation in the context of Argentina are in need of bolstering. In a 2007–2013 overview on English language teaching and learning, Porto *et al.* (2016) cite three chapters in the same conference proceeding (Mercaich Sartore *et al.*, 2012; Placci *et al.*, 2012; Tuero *et al.*, 2012), and Kamhi-Stein *et al.*'s (2017) edited volume on English language teaching in South America provides a systematic overview of the region; however, there are relatively few peer-reviewed articles on this topic. As can be seen from María's and Carolina's excerpts throughout this chapter, the context is ripe for exploration. Hopefully, the field will see more studies from this region, including those on ideal self formations of the L1 Spanish-speaking English teachers in the Argentinian context, as well as in the Latin American context more broadly.

6 Turkey: 'I'm better than these guys'

Milleti kurtaranlar yalnız ve ancak öğretmenlerdir
[Teachers are the one and only people who save nations]

Mustafa Kemal Atatürk

KEY POINTS

In this chapter, Barış and Musa

(1) Express concern over the hiring practices of native English speakers.
(2) Connect American politics to attitudes toward English.
(3) Indicate that some people perceive English as a threat to Turkish.
(4) Believe that English is needed to succeed in terms of universities and careers.
(5) Feel that English is a tool but can also create emotional attachments.

These aspects and others delineated in the chapter contribute to their ideal English teacher selves.

Turkey is located in a region of the world that has always been marked by cultural and linguistic diversity and is part of what is known as 'the cradle of civilization'. What is now modern-day Turkey is the centralized location of what was formerly the Ottoman Empire, and as stated by Selvi (2011: 184), 'The linguistic landscape in the Ottoman Empire was complex. Persian (the language of literature and science), and Arabic (the language of the Qur'an), had prestige and respect, whereas Turkish was not ascribed any particular status'. Additionally, the French influence was present in Ottoman times in terms of assistance in a variety of fields, including medicine, military schools, and later missionary schools (Alptekin & Tatar, 2011). This early French influence was the base of the reforms that Mustafa Kemal Atatürk made after 1923. This sentiment is supported by Yağmur (2001: 4): 'It was shown that the Ottoman Empire was a multi-ethnic and multilingual state'. Although a full description of the linguistic and cultural complexity of the Ottoman Empire is beyond the scope of this chapter, Lewis (1974) provides an excellent overview in English.

The multilingual and multicultural context of the Ottoman Empire was the foundation of modern-day Turkey. Immediately after being founded in 1923 by Mustafa Kemal (Atatürk – 'father of the Turks'), Turkey began to undergo linguistic and cultural reform: 'Language reform in Turkey is mostly associated with Atatürk and the beginning of the Turkish Republic in 1923' (Yağmur, 2001: 2). Atatürk's main objectives were to make Turkey unified and Westernized by means of secularism, language, and history (Aydıngün & Aydıngün, 2004). Although the reforms were multifaceted, including secularization and equal gender rights, this chapter's focus is the linguistic reforms that influenced the role that foreign languages, including English, have today in Turkey.

As Selvi (2011: 185) states, 'Each of these elements were manifested in educational reforms, and therefore played an integral part in the nation-building project, by forming Turkishness as a collective identity and social structure'. As part of the educational reforms, a Westernized alphabet was established by a language commission (*Dil Encümeni*) to encourage literacy among all people. This *Turkification* process was complex, as it involved the suppression of several minority languages, the most salient of which was Kurdish. These language policies were a result of a combination of linguistic and political ideologies. Some were highly critical of the Turkification process (i.e. Fernandes, 2012); however, others argue that without efforts to unify various ethnic groups in Turkey, the country could not have risen out of the shambles of the First World War and the fall of the Ottoman Empire to achieve the relative economic strength that it has today. As such, there are conflicting views on the educational policies implemented by Atatürk: 'What he achieved in the early 1920s is a "revolution" for many foreign and Turkish historians but a "tragedy" for many others. To be fair, however, Turkish reforms should be evaluated with respect to the circumstances and options available in the period immediately after the first World War' (Yağmur, 2001: 11).

What was the place for languages other than Turkish in this new, modernized Turkey? Atatürk, always looking toward the West for inspiration, encouraged the study of primarily European foreign languages in the educational system. Until the 1950s, French was the most popular foreign language studied, when it was surpassed by English. German ranks third on the list, followed by Arabic and Persian (Selvi, 2011). In the following excerpts, we will take a look at an introspective view of two English as a foreign language (EFL) teachers' (Barış and Musa) opinions on the role of English in Turkey today, with an emphasis on language learning and teaching, attitudes and emotional attachments toward English, as well as on their views of issues of non-nativeness in English teaching in Turkey. Both Musa and Barış grew up outside of the large metropolitan areas of Ankara and Istanbul: Barış grew up in Çankırı, a town in Central Anatolia, which is two hours north of the capital city, Ankara. Musa is from Kastamonu, a town four hours north of Ankara, in the Black Sea Region of Turkey. Both Musa and Barış are first language (L1) Turkish speakers and had several years of teaching experience at the time of the data collection, both in Turkey and in the United States. Although Musa studied 'a little bit' of French and Barış studied some French and German, our conversation was centered on issues involving English. Barış decided in high school that he wanted to be an English teacher. He studied 'like a horse' for the university entrance exam and was placed in one of the top schools in the country, Middle East Technical University (METU), where he stayed for his MA degree. Musa gained entrance into another top school for his BA degree, Boğaziçi University, subsequently going to METU for his MA degree. Both had teaching experience in a variety of settings, most notably private universities in Ankara while they were doing their MA degrees. Both came to the United States to pursue PhD degrees at a large midwestern institution, Musa in educational technology and Barış in applied linguistics.

There is no doubt that English has an important role in Turkey today: 'On an interpersonal level, it is used as a link language for international business and for tourism while also providing a code that symbolizes modernization and elitism to the educated middle classes and those in the upper strata of the socioeconomic ladder' (Doğançay-Aktuna, 1998: 37). However, the role of English in Turkey is not without controversy; this is perhaps not surprising given Turkey's complex linguistic history, especially considering the educational reforms that took place after 1923. In this era of globalization, English, although widespread as an international language (e.g. Sharifian, 2009), does not necessarily have a cultural attachment for many students who study English for instrumental purposes (Dörnyei *et al.*, 2006); nevertheless, sometimes specific cultures, or even specific aspects of a certain culture, play a role in attitudes toward a particular language. For example, in the case of Turkey, Barış explicitly states that the American president creates a frame by which many Turks view English, although it is certainly not the only factor regarding attitudes toward the language. He personally experienced such an attitude when doing his thesis on the topic of English language teaching:

Barış: It might be different now with Obama, but with Bush, when I did that thesis, it was the Bush government, and they were like ahhh, they were so dismissive about that. And politically that. Linguistically, English is thought of as attacking Turkish culture and everything you study. Turks are proud of being Turks and proud of their language. That's how they are taught. Because the Turkish language, it started as a nation-building approach and Atatürk had said that Turkish is the most beautiful language in the word, the best language in the world, exclusively. So, they are proud of their language. And they are against English medium education. Like why wouldn't you do things in Turkish? Why is it in English? Why are we learning science in English? Like that...

Musa: Not everyone, though. There is a group like that.

For some Turks, the representation of English by the president of the United States is perhaps not surprising, as Turkey has acted as a strategic ally for the United States and has 'enthusiastically co-operated with Washington in almost every possible way' (Selvi, 2011: 195). Barış' foregoing comment about a negative attitude toward English influenced by former President Bush is in the same vein as attitudes toward the Iraqi War, a war that led to a sharp decline in many Turks' attitudes regarding the United States (Selvi, 2011). Nonetheless, the popularity of English continues to grow, with many schools expanding their offerings and requirements for English.

The discussion continued on the topic of potential reasons behind the differing perspectives of the English language. Musa comments on the fact that since Turkey is a relatively young country with a 'Turkification' process that happened recently, it is not surprising that some people would be suspicious of outside influences. In fact, 'the prevailing present-day Turkish ideology aims at forming "one nation-one language" through the principle of *linguistic unitarianism* as seen in the case of France'[*] (Yağmur, 2001: 5). As presented in Önalan (2005), some scholars believe that the pervasiveness of English in Turkey may have a negative impact on the Turkish language and on Turkish identity, and that too much of an emphasis on the cultural aspects attached to English might have a negative effect on language learning. Similarly, participants in Karahan (2007) understand the economic value of English, but don't support the use of English for daily communication between Turks.

Musa: I think like Barış said, being a conservative would make you feel that it's [English] really obtrusive in the culture. I think most of the reaction is in terms of culture. Like, all the American movies are degenerating our youth. And they feel like... Turkey is considered to be a made country, like someone actually tried to make it. They changed the language, the alphabet, everything. So, there was like a huge Turkification process going on. So, obviously adding up new

---

[*] Atatürk was greatly influenced by France and French assimilation policies. See Chapter 2 on Senegal (this volume) for more details of linguistic imperialism brought about by these assimilation policies.

foreign words to this purified language would eventually get a reaction. But most people see that it's inevitable. Again, there are people who are offended by this, but then there are people who see knowing another language is a gift and a sign of progress, so...

Barış: I would agree. It depends on your orientation, political orientation, but most people, like my students, my participants in that research were all conservative, were all nationalist... And English, of course, is a pragmatic tool, but still associated with the American president.

Even though there is a sense of Turkish linguistic pride throughout the country, English is nonetheless becoming more widespread and, as Musa mentioned in the previous excerpt, is a sign of progress: 'The symbolic value attached to English-medium instruction among the general public is very high indeed, and concepts like *globalization*, *westernization*, and *modernization* contribute to the spread of English in Turkey' (Yağmur, 2001: 4). English-medium universities are common in Turkey, starting with the establishment of Ankara-based METU (Orta Doğu Teknik Üniversitesi) in 1956. Since that time, many other public and private universities offer either their content courses in English (i.e. engineering courses in English) or integrate English language courses into the curriculum in other ways. For those students who wish to attend English-medium universities but who don't pass the English language test, there is a one-year intensive English program (Selvi, 2011). Musa talks about the prestige of attending English-medium universities, a prestige that ostensibly comes from the ability to be able to disseminate one's research to an international audience. Additionally, the external validation of attending an English-medium university could also strengthen some students' ought-to selves, the self formed by adhering to external expectations (Dörnyei, 2009).

Musa: I mean, all the good universities in Turkey teach in English. So, I think it has... more prestige.

Additionally, Musa gave the example of some job advertisements being published in English, illustrating how English is becoming increasingly prevalent in Turkey, a statement that is supported by Doğançay-Aktuna's (1998) publication. In a survey that included 419 advertisements for 773 job vacancies in various sectors, 91 positions (22%) were printed only in English, and 426 positions (55.1%) required knowledge of a foreign language. Similarly, Doğançay-Aktuna and Kiziltepe (2005) emphasize the importance of English with regard to employment.

Musa: Yeah, the Hürriyet İK, they would have it in English. İK means some kind of human resources, and Hürriyet is the newspaper.

So, every Sunday they would issue this four-page HR paper. And it was in English.

Even though proficiency in English is becoming more important in the context of Turkish society, EFL students still have relatively little opportunity to interact in English outside of the classroom (i.e. Aslan, 2017). The one exception is with English in the online modality, such as with movies, music, and video games. Although no research in the context of Turkey discusses the effects of this 'extramural English', there has been research in other contexts. In the Swedish context, for example, several studies point to the positive correlation between extramural English and EFL proficiency (e.g. Sundqvist, 2009; Sylvén, 2004; Sylvén & Sundqvist, 2012). The results indicate that the more extramural English in which a student partakes, the better their overall proficiency in English will be, and that active engagement, for instance in the form of digital gaming, is more conducive to language learning than passive engagement, such as listening to music and watching films. This sentiment is supported by Musa, who observed that the students who play video games or take the time to interact with other media sources in English have generally better proficiency in English, perhaps creating an ideal self, the language learning self that an individual would like to become (Dörnyei, 2009), connected to gaming and cultural artifacts, rather than to a specific target culture.

Musa: I did have a couple of really motivated students who would [learn] mostly through games... I'm not saying because it's my personal interest, but the students who would play games would have a really different understanding in terms of the language. They would actually see its communicative purpose. And the students who would watch lots of movies and would surf on the internet a lot, listen to foreign music. So, those students would have a different level of English. They would conceptualize the whole thing better than students who were just straight out of high school, prepared for the exam, and did nothing else.

Turkey is similar to many countries that have a standardized English language test for university entrance. Because of this, students are not necessarily motivated to learn to use English communicatively, but they are motivated to learn how to pass the English language test. With the onset of communicative language teaching (CLT), the theory by which many English teachers in Turkey are trained, real, task-based communication in the English classroom is encouraged. However, there is a disconnect with this teaching method and what the students feel is important, as Musa indicates, which is supported by Alagözlü (2012: 1759), 'although the authorities seem to be aware of the novel developments in the field of language teaching, it has been observed that [the] Grammar-Translation method is the most common way to teach English in Turkey'.

Musa: They got more motivated when we do some tests. 'Okay we're going to do some tests, then'. 'Oh, okay!' So, when it's a game, it's time wasting for them, like, let's play a language game. They don't want to do that.

Perhaps it is the conflict of learning English and the need to preserve the Turkish language and culture, coupled with the lack of opportunity to speak English outside of the classroom that makes the majority of students feel that it is 'unreal' as Barış states, or have some sort of lack of emotional connection to English. As some scholars would argue, forming an identity, or an ideal self, in the language is a pivotal point to learning the language effectively. It would seem that Musa's students had a more strongly formed ought-to self, as they were more motivated by external evaluation (tests), rather than taking part in communicative activities.

Barış: They feel unreal. They don't feel an identity in that second language, but those who come to the USA for a summer or so, they do better. They feel a presence in a second language.

Along with the role of English in Turkey with regard to maintaining the Turkish language and culture, one of the most discussed topics in this data was the stratification of the L1 Turkish-speaking English teachers, and the non-Turkish-speaking English teachers. Perhaps surprisingly, there was not necessarily a divide between native and non-native speakers, but instead between those who look Turkish and those who do not look Turkish. However, the concept of physical appearance and L1 status has been discussed by other scholars in the field. Amin (1997: 580) reported on participants' beliefs that 'Only White people can be native speakers of English' and Inbar-Lourie (2006) discusses the fact that self-identity might not be the same ascribed identity of others (i.e. students). Statements such as 'Though I was born in the Ukraine, the students in my school think I come from England' (Inbar-Lourie, 2006: 274, also see Ruecker & Ives, 2015) parallel the situation that Musa describes below. Although his comments do not directly refer to student opinions, he describes Russian teachers who were hired as 'native English speakers' in Turkey.

Musa: The [speaking] teachers are always native [English] speakers or speakers who are Russian (laugh) or African... who can't speak Turkish. So, we have a different definition for speaking teachers. Teachers who don't have to speak English natively but don't, can't speak Turkish (laugh).

...

Musa: They don't look Turkish. They don't even look American, like, they are ohhh they're blonde, they can go American. But they don't look Turkish, that's the point.

Barış and Musa discuss the fact that, in most cases when comparing Turks versus non-Turks in the EFL teaching context in Turkey, Turkish teachers were more qualified to teach English. As Barış observed about the non-Turkish teachers, 'they weren't even ELT majors'. Despite this, in Barış's and Musa's experience, the Turkish teachers received a considerably lower salary than the non-Turkish teachers. Their experience is supported by Çelik (2006: 372) who states that Turkish EFL teachers 'even face discrimination in hiring or promotion practices' and that 'schools [are] paying native speaker teachers much more than what their non-native speaker counterparts get paid'.

Barış: So, our salary was about $500.00, which is low in Turkey standards. We were paying almost $300.00, $400.00 for the rent. So barely living with any money. Just because we were Turkish... At the same time, there were two or three people from the States, in the primary school. There was a girl from Australia, I think. But none of them were ELT graduates, TESOL graduates. I think one of them was a biology teacher. There was a rumor that one of the old guys was a shop owner back in England. So yeah, they would do the speaking lessons, speaking and listening lessons, which was again considered as the easy part because you just like push the button and make them listen... So those guys were making about $2,000.00, and they were also given a rent allowance. Yeah, like $500.00 a month. And if they didn't want the money, they would give them a furnished apartment. So, graduating from college, we had to struggle finding an apartment, we just got out of the dorm, right? All that trouble we went through, those guys were enjoying the city.

Intrigued by this conversation, I was curious to see how such a salary discrepancy affected the morale of the Turkish teachers. In Barış's case, the answer surprised me, as he stated it motivated him to be a better teacher, reminiscent of Thompson's (2017a) anti-ought-to self concept, in which people are motivated by a challenging situation, or a misguided external expectation that the individual wants to reject.

Barış: I think it pushed me. It was a motivation for me. I'm like, I'm better than these guys, I can teach them stuff. And I always tried to... I mean, you can't necessarily prove yourself with English because it's their native tongue, but with the knowledge and the liking of the students, it also created... I did sense the separation between the native teachers. They would have this corner of the room for themselves.

This excerpt also brings to light another point of discussion. Along with the salary discrepancy, there was also a kind of social stratification between the Turkish teachers and the non-Turkish teachers. In our conversation, both Musa and Barış indicated how the educational system is quite compartmentalized. The central government has relatively tight control over the curriculum, and various 'units' are responsible for different tasks. So much so that Musa even states, 'I never developed a handout' when he was asked about who developed materials for his students. One of the results of this sort of social stratification was that all of the non-Turkish teachers were grouped together in a 'speaking unit', which further separated them from the Turkish teachers.

Barış: Yeah it was a big room, right, like this big. And they would pick the corner, and it was their corner – four or five of them hanging out together. Turks were the... we were the rest. There were one or two really nice guys who were really open-minded. They were trying to learn Turkish and all that. So, we were really good friends with them, but apart from that, everyone was aware of this, like, separation from the others.

Musa adds the following:

Musa: I think they were isolated. They had their own room, the speaking units. They were also a unit. We are so 'unitarian', like everyone was a unit.

Barış and Musa continued to discuss the relationships they had with the non-Turkish teachers, reflecting on the idea that the isolation could have been two-sided, and that in some cases, friendships were forged.

Musa: We never hung out, I didn't do anything social with them, not even a single lunch. Did you ever have lunch with them?
Barış: I don't think so, actually, but there was that British guy, David. He would speak Turkish just like really fine, so we would hang out with him but like that was it.
Musa: I never hung out with any of them.
Amy: Why was that? Was that your choice, their choice?

Barış: All their choice. Like they used to hang out with each other. Russians with Russians. As if they were a family and they are away, like they were abroad somewhere.

Musa: It could have been our mistake, too. First of all, I should add that at the primary school, the native speakers were closer in terms of age to us. I ended up going to a couple of parties with them, so I did see like that side of like their lives.

After more discussion, Barış states:

Barış: I should say that I never really felt really close with them. Most of it has to do with me feeling that I can do the same job if not better than them and making less money in every equation. In university too, they were making money in dollars, in US dollars, and we were making Turkish liras, and they would make at least like 50% more than me. We do the same job if not much more. I would teach 15, 18 hours a week, they would teach speaking lessons like 12 hours a week. Really easy stuff... I teach grammar and reading, and I have a speaking teacher from the speaking department which would be one of those guys. And when you, I feel like I own the class and they would be like the visitors. Like three hours a week – they don't really care. I would see the [lack of] motivation in their eyes. They wouldn't really care about my students. And I was like, all right those guys can't do it; I should probably teach that too myself. So, I would go over whatever they covered in my class.

A theme that was also brought up in the discussion, one that is also often discussed in the literature, is the idea of the different strengths of both native and non-native speakers (traditionally researched as the advantages and disadvantages of being a native versus a non-native speaker of English) when teaching English in an EFL setting (i.e. Medgyes, 2017). For Musa and Barış, the Turkish teachers were able to be more successful in the Turkish context, a sentiment that other publications have supported (e.g. Ling & Braine, 2007). Seidlhofer (1999: 235) discusses the fact that non-native speaker teachers in EFL contexts serve as 'double agents' 'facilitating learning by mediating between the different languages and cultures through appropriate pedagogy'. Via the excerpts, it is clear that both Musa and Barış have formed a strong ideal teacher self couched in their identity as Turkish-speaking non-native speakers of English. Mediating language and culture specifically for the Turkish context is the example of the English language placement test for English-medium universities. One advantage that Musa discusses is that the Turkish teachers knew the system (Turkish educational culture) and were also able to teach the discrete grammar points in Turkish. Although the ultimate advantage of having English classes in Turkish is debatable, there is no doubt that this method helps with regard to the testing structure in this context.

Musa: Yeah for me, a Turkish person in Turkey teaching English would find it really easy to teach and help the students. But again, I'm talking about a grammar-driven curriculum where the test is grammar. So, while maintaining your Turkish instruction, you teach everything in Turkish. You teach English grammar in Turkish. The students can actually be really quite successful in their exam. [**Amy:** I see.] So, for grammar teaching purposes, being able to use Turkish was an advantage over the native speakers [of English].

Barış adds that being Turkish and teaching Turkish students also helps with the student–teacher rapport. In his opinion, many of the Turkish students treat the non-Turkish teachers too casually, even bordering on disrespect. This could partially have to do with the fact that many of the non-Turkish EFL teachers do not speak Turkish very well and, according to Devrim and Bayyurt (2010: 16), students believe that non-Turkish teachers 'should be able to speak Turkish, be familiar with cultures in Turkey, [and] be familiar with "target language culture"'.

Barış: I now realize that being a non-native [English] speaker, you can establish more rapport with students. The native speakers, students were even making fun of them. They had some situations where students were swearing at them in Turkish... the way they respect them, and [how they] they respect Turkish teachers is totally different. They feel more relaxed with the native speakers to the extent that they are disrespectful.

Toward the end of the discussion, I inquired about their relationship with the English language or, more precisely, if they had any sort of emotional attachment to English. Barış said that for him, English represented a 'sort of success'. He also mentioned the fact that his wife is an English speaker, so there is an emotional attachment in that way. Thus, in addition to his ideal teacher self formed around his knowledge of English and his status as a Turkish speaker, he has also formed an ideal English self based on his relationship with his English-speaking wife, as well as with his English-speaking social group.

Barış: To me, English is sort of success. I was never as good at in physics, in physics examinations, I don't have any success stories. But for English, I have that national exam that I did in two hours, and I have a whole college degree and masters and PhD in this. So, it has positive things career-wise. I have had many successes in English. Success stories in English. And in Turkish. I... I don't have any award in Turkish!

They all came after English. And the emotional attachment, with my wife. With my wife, I speak English. And with some of my friends, with the people that I love here, I speak English.

For Musa, his relationship to English was more on a practical level. He is glad to be able to use English as a tool and to be able to disseminate his thoughts and knowledge in English. This sentiment is supported in Dörnyei *et al.*'s (2006: 105) discussion about the role of 'Global English': 'the relationship between motivation and the choice of Global English is losing its strength because people tend to take up the study of English increasingly as a self-evident part of education rather than driven by a motivational decision'. For Musa, English is important for communication and the dissemination of ideas, as stated in Selvi (2011: 182): 'English is increasingly used for intra-national as well as international communication with the rest of the world'.

Musa: For me, I… emotional attachment, I mean, I don't necessarily love a language. I don't think I'm that kind of a person. But yeah, I mean, I don't think I necessarily would have a special sort of feeling in a tangible way to a language. So, I mean, I use English, I feel really lucky that I can use it as a tool. And I'm trying to get better at it. I do know passively my vocabulary is better than the active stuff I can use, so I'm always trying to improve my English. And I see the value in being able to read, write, and speak in English because you are reaching a wider audience. It's really great, it's just… English is a really nice tool that I can use. Language, languages are tools for me.

Amy: Reaching a wider audience… can you elaborate on that for me a little more?

Musa: In the educational technology department, we have student blogs, and so we write, we propose about educational matters on this ideaplay.org if you go there. So, people read it, comment on stuff, English is just a medium for that. I use it to convey my feelings about educational matters. My papers I write for my classes, it's again like a wide audience if the thing I write is successful in the end, if I get to publish that stuff. So, I think there is a bigger community following English written and spoken stuff than other languages.

For Musa, learning English is highly practical for academic communication. Barış also discussed the reality that there are more job openings for English teachers than for teachers of other languages. The demand for English teachers is a reflection of the popularity of the language. According to Genç (1999), about 98% of the student population studies English at the primary level, whereas only about 2% of students study French and German (the second and third most popular languages to study in

Turkey); thus, 'English carries the instrumental function of being the most studied foreign language' (Selvi, 2011: 186) in Turkey.

Barış: First of all, universities offer English teaching positions. Let's say they have openings of 500 people every year. German and French teaching, they have openings for ten people. Same for job situations. Openings for German teachers, two people, openings for English teachers, 3,000. English is always doing better.

As can be seen in the previous excerpts, Barış's ideal teacher self is built upon his successes in English, as well as the support he provides to his students, all of which is mitigated by an ideal self as an English user strengthened by his relationship with his wife and other close friendships formed through English. He has also formed an anti-ought-to, or rebellious, self, to be the best English teacher he can be to show others that he is as qualified as (or more qualified than) the native English-speaking teachers, who are paid more. For Musa, his ideal teacher self is also that of a Turkish speaker, with his ideal self as an English language user based on the practicality of the language. As for many users of English, English is a tool that helps them accomplish the goals that they have set out to accomplish. Both Musa and Barış associate speaking English with being part of a more liberal mindset, and they both feel that it is their job as a teacher to make English 'real' for their students.

The role of English in Turkey is that of economic development, although the use of English in this context is not without controversy. Although the opinion on American foreign policy might fluctuate, 'the symbolic power [of] the English language was considered to be more powerful than unfavorable US foreign policies' (Selvi, 2011: 196), and several studies have shown Turkish students' desire to learn English (i.e. Thompson & Aslan, 2015). Even though some people are opposed to the widespread use of English, most realize that it is currently a necessity for economic development on an international scale. Despite the recent linguistic unification efforts by Atatürk to promote the use of Turkish in all sectors, 'the linguistic landscape of Turkey has always included a foreign language other than Turkish' (Selvi, 2011: 196). The Turkish linguistic landscape is increasingly multilingual as the suppression of the use of minority languages has substantially reduced, and language instruction (especially English) is becoming increasingly integrated into educational and business sectors.

7 Ukraine: 'I know how my people think'

Людина без книги, як риба без води
[A person without a book is like a fish without water]

Ukrainian proverb

KEY POINTS

In this chapter, Lavra and Olexandra

(1) Feel that knowing how their students think makes them more effective teachers.
(2) Believe that it is the teacher's job to create a positive English-speaking classroom environment.
(3) Comment on the shift from using Russian to using Ukrainian.
(4) Express that English will open doors and is a mechanism for understanding people.
(5) Indicate that each language learned is an easier process than the last.

These aspects and others delineated in the chapter contribute to their ideal English teacher selves.

Like many other nations in the region, language policy in Ukraine was greatly influenced by the rise and fall of the Soviet Union. Although there was and still is tension in ex-Soviet countries, Ukraine has seen some of the most dynamic fluctuations in legislation involving the use of Russian, and the titular language, Ukrainian, in the public sphere since the last years of the Soviet Union, as well as since Ukraine's independence in 1991. There have been many recent policy changes regarding the use of Russian and Ukrainian, perhaps because of the prominence of Russian in Ukraine, even toward the end of Soviet times: 'in the last Soviet years, the majority of the pupils in eleven of the republics were enrolled in titular medium schools. The only exceptions were Belarus, Kazakhstan, and Ukraine, where urban titulars often shifted to L1 Russian and most pupils attended Russian-medium schools' (Pavlenko, 2013: 265). As such, recent events and policies are likely to further promote changes in attitudes and language use in this nation. Pavlenko (2013: 262) comments on the dynamic, and sometimes violent, public discussions regarding language policy in Ukraine: 'As I am working on this article, I keep one eye on breaking news from Ukraine, where the new language law first led to a fistfight in the parliament and then to clashes between protesters and police. Nothing new, really – just another chapter in the ongoing saga of "language wars" in the post-Soviet space, where every new language law may lead to heated emotional exchanges, public strife, and even military conflicts and secession'.

A detailed discussion of language policy in Ukraine is beyond the scope of the current chapter; however, a brief overview to situate the participants' comments is needed. One of the most recent publications on the topic of language policy in Ukraine at the time of writing this chapter is Reznik (2018: 171), who explains the shift in language policy in the following way: 'In the light of its direct correlation with major political milestones, independent Ukraine's language policy can be divided into three chronological periods: the early independence years and the 1990s; pre- and post-Orange Revolution Ukraine; and post-Euromaidan Ukraine, from 2014 onwards'. In the late 1980s, toward the end of the Soviet Union, there was a push for the reintegration of the Ukrainian language, described in Reznik (2018: 173): 'The Ukrainization campaign was seen as a successful precedent, making Ukrainian not only the main language of political, social and cultural life, but also turning it into a tool of social change and civic education', which resulted in a 1989 language law making Ukrainian the only state language. However, even though 'the symbolic role of the 1989 language law can hardly be overestimated', the language law was not enforced and 'In practice, the dominance of Russian in all spheres of public life remained unchallenged' (Reznik, 2018: 174).

For the second phase of the language policy shift, the epicenter was the Orange Revolution (late November 2004 to January 2005) with the events leading up to and in the aftermath of this revolution. Reznik (2018: 175) calls this period a 'sociolinguistic paradox' because of the language policy in place supporting the role of Ukrainian in every aspect of the public sphere alongside the economic realities and the pro-Russian political scene, which made enforcing the pro-Ukrainian policies difficult. Although a variety of measures were taken in an attempt to strengthen the role of Ukrainian, the lack of governmental support and the dominance of Russian in the public sphere stymied these efforts. As an example, only 7% of publications were in Ukrainian in 2002 (Reznik, 2018: 176). The 2004 election of Viktor Yushchenko was marred with controversy, particularly spurred by his opponent, Viktor Yanukovych, a staunch supporter of the Russian language in Ukraine. Yushchenko's predecessor and supporter of Yanukovych, 'warned that the October 2004 elections would be Ukraine's dirtiest, a prophecy that proved to be accurate. The attempted poisoning of Yushchenko during the campaign shows how far his opponents were willing to go to stop his election. Western medical tests concluded that Yushchenko's blood-dioxin level was more than 6,000 times higher than normal' (Kuzio, 2005: 30). Seeking to reverse the pro-Ukrainian law of 1989, Yanukovych's platform promoted Russian to a state language, giving it equal legal status with Ukrainian, meaning that, 'the Ukrainian state would also become bilingual in the symbolic sphere, a victory that pro-Russian parties looked forward to' (Reznik, 2018: 177), although language policies themselves were not one of the top voter concerns in 2004 (Kuzio, 2005: 35). However, the 2004 election and the Orange Revolution (peaceful protests and demonstrations) were a milestone in Ukrainian history, as ostensibly they 'completed Ukraine's transition from a post-Soviet state to a European state' (Kuzio, 2005: 29) and 'represented the second and final stage in the Ukrainian revolution that began toward the end of the Soviet era' (Kuzio, 2005: 42; see Kuzio [2005] for details about the election and the Orange Revolution). Although pro-Ukrainian Yushchenko won the election, his time as president was difficult for a variety of reasons, and he lost re-election in 2010 to Yanukovych.

As previously mentioned, Yanukovych was pro-Russian, and his agenda was prioritized after the 2010 election when he became president. In a perversion of the intent of the policy envisioned to promote language rights for all first languages (L1s) in Ukraine, in reality, Russian was the primary language promoted using this policy, and as Moser (2015: 179) states, it was 'particularly at the expense of Ukrainian'. The Law on the Principles of the State Language Policy [*Zakon pro zasady derzhavnoi movnoi polityky*], adopted in July 2012, further strengthened Russian's role in Ukraine. This controversial law, which favored Russian and undermined efforts for Ukrainian language education and use, contributed to the overall political shift toward cooperating with Russia, rather than the European Union. This shift resulted in the Euromaidan Revolution (also known as the Ukrainian Revolution) in February 2014 (Reznik, 2018). Unlike the Orange Revolution, the Euromaidan Revolution resulted in violence. After this revolution, Yanukovych fled to Russia.

Now, in post-Euromaidan Ukraine, 'The Euromaidan revolution and the war have brought about dramatic transformations in Ukrainian society, most importantly, in the renewed sense of national identity and the resurgence of the Ukrainian political nation' (Reznik, 2018: 181). Kulyk (2016: 602) explains that even though there are tensions between ethnic Russians and ethnic Ukrainians, these attitudes do not necessarily translate into attitudes toward the two languages, with one focus group participant stating: 'It is not the language we are at war with'. Additionally,

Kulyk (2016: 607) states that 'people in various parts of Ukraine are reluctant to give up their accustomed reliance on the Russian language, although they recognise the special role of the titular language as a national attribute'. The past few years have seen a number of policies enacted to strengthen the role of Ukrainian (Ukrainization or de-Russification), including the renaming of Soviet place names and having higher quotas of pop culture output broadcasted in Ukrainian (Reznik, 2018).

The two teacher voices in this chapter are Lavra and Olexandra. Both are from southern Ukraine – Lavra from Odesa and Olexandra from Zaporizhia. According to Kuzio (2005: 38), southern Ukraine 'is more rural but includes cosmopolitan cities like Odesa'. Zaporizhia is located on the Dnipro River, and is also an important city in southern Ukraine (sometimes also categorized as eastern Ukraine), as it is a busy railroad junction and river port. At the time of the data collection, Lavra had over 20 years of teaching experience, whereas Olexandra had 12 years in the classroom. Lavra worked at a gymnasium, which is a university preparatory, post-secondary school, meaning that there is a strong focus on languages: 'we study English a bit more profoundly than on average… three or four hours in elementary school [per week]', and she emphatically stated that the language of instruction in her classroom is English. Olexandra also taught at a gymnasium at the time of the data collection, but she specialized not only in English, but also in German and French. Both teachers indicated Russian as an L1, but Olexandra also stated that Ukrainian was an L1. As is discussed in this chapter, there was, and still is, a complex dynamic between the Russian and Ukrainian languages in Ukraine.

Amy: Did you study Russian?
Oleksandra: Ah yes, Russian. Ukrainian is our official language, and for our lessons and when writing some documents, we use Ukrainian. But Russian is the language which we use in our everyday communication, and we studied it at school.

Even with the concentrated efforts to reinstate Ukrainian as the main language of communication, the use of Russian outside of school has been a common practice in Ukraine. Although there are few studies documenting classroom language learning practices after the collapse of the Soviet Union, Friedman has a series of studies based on data from a longitudinal project in the country. Particularly relevant to this chapter is her 2009 article on corrective feedback in a Ukrainian fifth-grade classroom in an attempt to teach the students to use a more pure form of Ukrainian: 'Taking the position that standards of linguistic correctness are socially constructed (Bourdieu, 1991; Silverstein, 1996), I analyze these feedback practices as a manifestation of an ideology of "pure language" (čysta mova) that originated in response to the historical position of Ukrainian as subordinate to Russian and the perceived need to establish it as a distinct language suitable for representing a distinct nation' (Friedman, 2009: 347). In terms of Russian use outside of the classroom, despite that in slightly over half of the households both parents identify as Ukrainian in this study, Friedman (2009: 354) noted that '80 per cent routinely used Russian outside of school'. In this study, the fifth-grade participants had both Ukrainian language and literature classes: four language and two literature classes of 45-minutes each per week with two additional hours of Russian weekly. One of the teachers in the study 'agreed that Ukrainian-medium schooling had given the current group of fifth graders better command of the language than what he had observed in earlier generations of students. However, he also expressed concern about the dominance of Russian in many children's lives' (Friedman, 2009: 355). As Oleksandra comments, Ukrainian is now the emphasis of language study at school, and the emphasis on Russian is perhaps changing.

Amy: Is that the same for younger generations as well, or is it changing?
Oleksandra: Yes, it's changing because now, for example, my daughter is in the first grade and they don't have Russian language lessons in this grade. They will study it later, but they won't even have marks for this lesson. So, they are aimed at teaching more Ukrainian than Russian. But they speak Russian, and it's very difficult for them, and they mix Russian and Ukrainian words.

This 'mixing' of Russian and Ukrainian has been documented in terms of the Russian influence on Ukrainian. The term *suržyk* is the linguistic term for a sort of hybridization of Russian and Ukrainian throughout the entire language system (e.g. Flier, 1998), and some Ukrainians use the term to describe using Russian in Ukrainian speech (e.g. Bilaniuk, 2005). As Friedman (2009: 350) describes, 'Critics of *suržyk* characterize it as an unnatural product of centuries of linguistic oppression and cite its existence as a threat to Ukrainian national consciousness'. In Friedman's 2009 article, she illustrates the corrective feedback provided in the classroom by both the teacher and the other students. As Friedman (2009: 356) describes, most of the corrections centered around Russian vocabulary, Russian pronunciation of words existing in both languages, and words in Ukrainian that originated in Russian. In Friedman (2016), she uses the original classroom observations along with interviews conducted four years later to focus the topic on language socialization. As she explains, her interest was piqued by the use of '*ridna mova* [native language or mother tongue] to refer to Ukrainian, often in conjunction with first-person plural forms such as *my* [we] or *naša* [our]' (Friedman, 2016: 168). In English, the term 'native language' refers to the language learned first, whereas this is not the case in this Ukrainian context. Instead, *ridna mova* refers to a language to which they most closely identify, even if their proficiency level is low (Arel, 2002; Bilaniuk & Melnyk, 2008). In interviewing her participants, 'they unanimously agreed that all Ukrainians should know the Ukrainian language and by a large margin rejected the proposal that Russian should become a second state language on the grounds that it was a "foreign language" or *ne naša* [not ours] or *ne ridna nam* [not native to us]. In addition, many identified Ukrainian as their own *ridna mova* [native language]' (Friedman, 2016: 172). Despite this identification with Ukrainian, many of the students expressed linguistic insecurity when it came to Ukrainian, and indicated that they spoke Russian, or Ukrainian mixed with Russian, outside of the classroom. The students, however, could see the linguistic landscape shifting, as one of them states, '"my children my grandchildren will speak only Ukrainian", indicating that a Ukrainian community that speaks "only Ukrainian" is not only imagined but imaginary, at least for his generation' (Friedman, 2016: 175). The students' feelings in Friedman's studies are echoed in Lavra's comments regarding her feelings toward Russian.

Amy: Do you have specific feelings toward the culture of the languages you've studied?

Lavra: In Ukraine there is a paradox situation, I should say. Because the official language is Ukrainian, and half of the country speaks Ukrainian as their first dia… language, and half of the country speaks Russian as their first or mother tongue. Because of the traditions, and because of the history, of course, the situation. I don't feel bad about that situation, actually. I'm one of those who believes that the more languages that you know, the better. And so, I don't feel bad either about knowing English, knowing Russian as the first language or knowing Ukrainian, as long as you are tolerant of the other language. So, I feel absolutely good. I feel absolutely fine. I'm quite happy. And I don't like these, you know, biases… I don't believe in that.

Lavra is happy to have a range of languages at her disposal, specifically mentioning not only Russian and Ukrainian, but also English. Oleksandra feels the language/culture connection, and comments as such.

Oleksandra: [about languages in general] It's interesting, and when you study the language, you can feel this culture, and it's very interesting.

Both Oleksandra and Lavra have had experience studying languages to varying degrees of proficiency. Lavra comments on how knowing one language can help learn subsequent ones, a comment very much related to the concept of perceived positive language interaction (PPLI, e.g. Thompson, 2016).

Amy: Have either of you seen any interactions between the languages you've learned?

Lavra: Oh yes, definitely. Definitely. Since English vocabulary consists of 75% of the roots which are similar to the French roots, it's obvious that you can find *difficult, difficile, facilitate* and things like that. So, lots of things which are like connections between English and French. And then when I was trying to study German, I tried to find the roots or some things in grammar which would be similar. And then when you know some French, well it's just a piece of cake to know some words in Italian. So, with every next language it becomes more interesting and easier.

Now turning the focus on English language learning and teaching, English language learning has recently bourgeoned in Ukraine. One reason is because of immigration to other nations in search of work, a trend that started in the early 1990s. Soon after the fall of the Soviet Union, there was 'a whole new class of businessmen striving to establish ties with foreign partners' as well as the 'intentions of many people to travel to developed Western countries or even to try settle there for good' (Tarnopolsky, 1996). The trend continued into the early 2000s, according to Prybytkova (2009), who reports that tens of thousands of Ukrainians with college degrees left Ukraine to look for jobs, primarily in the United States (Kozlovets, 2008). As for international business, Smotrova (2009: 728–729) states, 'A second major reason for English's growing importance is the need for skilled English users among businesses trying to develop global partnerships'. With an updated report on his 1996 data, Tarnopolsky (2015: 16) reinforces this notion with the idea that many adults are learning English because of the international business opportunities and that 'hundreds of thousands of people are learning English for improving their life prospects'. The desire to move abroad or the job prospects in Ukraine as a motivation to learn English indicates that many English language learners have a strong ought-to self (i.e. Dörnyei, 2009) when it comes to English language study. In our discussion, Lavra encourages this type of ought-to self motivation with both her students and colleagues, telling them that English will open doors for them in terms of study and travel.

Lavra: I always say to my colleagues and my pupils that English together with math will open some doors for you... They can survive if they know some English, so it's just objective reality, and whether we like it or not, English is widely spoken... So I would say that English is quite important, it's seen as, well, if not a survival skill, it's a skill which is important if you want to have a career, become a professional, and it may open some ways to develop their professional knowledge to meet other people, maybe to go somewhere abroad to study, to work. So, it's seen as a vehicle of development, of personal development.

Lavra's comment is supported by data presented in Salakhyan (2015: 37): 'English is no longer seen by Slavic speakers as belonging to the English-speaking countries and communities, nations and cultures', a concept that is also stated in motivation research (Dörnyei *et al.*, 2006). One of the comments by a Ukrainian participant in Salakhyan (2015: 37) reinforces this idea: 'I can't say that English is language for me. If I speak Italian I speak only with Italians, yes, only with native speakers. And if to say about English I spoke English very often with people who are not native speakers that is why I have more feeling that it's just the language for the world'. Lavra also emphasizes that language learning isn't just about learning the language itself, but achieving cultural competence is also an important part of the language learning process. This concept is supported by the American Council on the Teaching of Foreign Languages' (ACTFL) global competence position statement: 'Global competence is vital to successful interactions among diverse groups of people locally, nationally, and internationally. This diversity continues to grow as people move from city to city and country to country. The need to communicate with someone of a different language or culture may arise at any time; knowing more than one language prepares one to know how, when, and why to say what to whom' (https://www.actfl.org/list/position-statement/global-competence-position-statement).

Lavra: We all understand that English is important, and nobody argues about that. But more and more we begin to understand that it's the way to understand people. It's the way to understand cultures, and that's the way to open their eyes to the world, which is even more important than being grammatically correct, and so on. So, if they learn a language, then they learn the culture. We don't think that everyone who finishes our school and who are quite good at English, they will all go to study in America or in Europe, where they will have to use English. But we all believe that through English, we teach them culture and understanding. So it's all part of culture, which is very big. We feel like a family of European cultures, world cultures. And this is very, very important, that makes them more of, I don't know, aware of other things which there are in the world, and it opens their horizons. It makes them different people. So that's what is very important.

Starting with a 1994 regulation of the Ukraine Ministry of Education, foreign languages became a required and state-regulated subject in state schools with efforts to incorporate communication as a main student learning outcome. However, because of the lack of opportunity to use English outside of the classroom, as well as limited state resources, the result was poor learning outcomes for many students. Tarnopolsky (1996: 618) provides the results of 300 students he interviewed in Dnipro-petrovsk, 79% of whom 'asserted that they had acquired absolutely no communicative competence in English after 8–9 years of study'. Recently, the Ministry of Education and Science of Ukraine (MESU) has proposed a variety of initiatives to improve English language education, one being a standardized syllabus for primary and secondary education, which was approved in 2004. The standardized syllabus means that teachers have to abide by national recommendations, even when it comes to choosing books for their classes, as well as teaching methods. At the beginning of the discussion, Lavra indicates that the teachers try to integrate Brit-ish textbooks when possible, but that it sometimes requires parental resources to do so. As for Ukrainian texts, the government has a say.

Lavra: Our minister of education sends us a list of recommended books. And from that, we can choose.

Later in the discussion, Lavra also talks about the required teaching methodology, communicative language teaching, and how it is difficult for some teachers to align with this method, despite the requirement to do so.

Lavra: It's the state requirement that all the teachers try to know as much as they can about this methodology [communicative language teaching]... There may be some teachers who are, well, who have their teaching beliefs, which stick to the past, but it's their problem. So now it's not possible for us to stick only to those methods. It's in our national curriculum... we have to do our best to provide learning of English as a means of communication. So, they need, even after two classes of English, they need to be able to explain themselves, to introduce themselves, to ask about the things that they need to know, to have, and so on. And not only just to know what present perfect or past continuous is, which used to be, like ten years ago.

Olexandra reinforces the idea of how teaching methods have changed since the time she started learning English at age 10. At that time, the focus was not on communication, but on rote learning:

Olexandra: Ten. There were not many interactive techniques at that time, and we just read, translated, and wrote some letters or some-thing like that at my school. And when I decided to enter the univer-sity to learn Eng... uh, foreign languages, I had some private lessons, and I understood that I knew nothing. And for one year, I had to learn so many things. I had a very good teacher, and she helped me very much, and only with her help it was possible for me to enter the university.

Lavra concurs with Olexandra on the older methods used when she was learning English:

Lavra: And in those days, there were different methods, right? So, they were very much not aimed at communication, but more focused on correctness and things like that. Vocabulary and so on. Reading. When I began teaching, times changed, and it was intended to be more communicative and it meant more authentic materials.

The new syllabus proposed by MESU was created in collaboration with a variety of entities including the British Council, the cultural section of the United States embassy, and the Peace Corps, and it 'marks official recognition of the move toward communicative approaches sparked by globalization' (Smotrova, 2009: 729). However, Smotrova (2009: 730) indicates that the public education sector suffers from 'large class sizes, relatively few hours of instruction, low student motivation owing to overly formal teaching methods and lack of elective courses, and low quality textbooks for most of the 91% of students who attend nonspecialized secondary schools'.

Teaching methods and student motivation are constantly improving in this context, however. Tarnopolsky (2015: 18) also discusses the results of a multi-year study at a private language school, which indicate that students are interested in learning English for communication but that they also feel that 'focusing on language forms is indispensable' (Tarnopolsky, 2015: 19). Thus, communicative language teaching (communicative activities with a purposeful focus on form, e.g. Savignon, 2001) is the method that is attractive to these adult learners. It is also the case that parents push for their children to have more opportunities with English, emphasizing the importance of the ought-to self in this context. The students also realize that English can help them in the future, as Olexandra explains:

Olexandra: They [parents] want their children have more lessons with the teacher to be taught more. And, our senior pupils also want to take part in different programs. For example, many of my students, they take part in different exchange programs for students, and they want to study, for example, here. There is some program where they can study for a year in the USA. It's very interesting for them, and they know that it can help them in their studies and in their future careers.

One of the results of the revised communicative syllabus in Ukraine was the integration of native speakers into the classroom in order to expose learners to 'authentic language', so to speak. In conjunction with a government-funded program from the United States, English language fellows are sometimes placed in Ukraine (Selec & Abramicheva, 2012), as are Peace Corps volunteers (Smotrova, 2009). While placement of native speakers in Ukrainian classrooms is well-intentioned, 'classroom culture shock almost inevitably occurs when a teacher moves to a different country' (Selec & Abramicheva, 2012: 21). As stated in Smotrova (2009: 731), 'It is widely believed that Peace Corps volunteers serving as EFL teachers succeed where many Ukrainian teachers do not by emphasizing communication strategies and trial-and-error learning versus the traditional focus on rote production of accurate language. Peace Corps teachers are also thought to make EFL more enjoyable, and to possess the sociocultural competence the current syllabus requires'. However, as has been documented in other cases as well, sometimes the integration of a native English speaker, who might or might not be familiar with the L1 culture and context, is not the idealized language instruction that outsiders seem to think. As Oleksandra indicates, sometimes Peace Corps volunteers have trouble teaching in this context:

Oleksandra: We have this native speaker in our school. She is from the Peace Corps volunteers. And sometimes, she has more difficulties with our students because they can't understand her.

Lavra reinforces this idea, strongly advocating for Ukrainians as English teachers, as she feels that they are more suited to help students.

Lavra: Well, I think that I have a lot of advantages as a teacher of English as a non-native speaker. I know how my people think. And so, I can predict, and I can anticipate some of the difficulties. I can understand why they don't get the point when, for example, we explain some grammar... So I know how my children think, and I know not only how they think but the way they feel... I can cushion some of the difficulties and I can predict them, and I can eliminate them before actually they begin. And there are some cultural questions which may be really a challenge if there is a non-native, a native English-speaker who comes, for example, to Ukraine, and they begin to teach. And we have those people in language schools which are private language schools and they invite native speakers, and sometimes I just laugh to myself when people advertise all our teachers are native speakers! Which must automatically mean that all the leavers of this school will speak like native speakers. But this is an illusion, actually, because they may have more difficulty in getting the message across than non-native English speakers, actually the locals, the aborigines, so to speak, who will teach English to the Ukrainian people... I can help them more. I mean, my people.

Both of these teachers work hard to create a positive learning environment for their students, for which using English is imperative. Creating an English-speaking atmosphere, as Lavra explains, is crucial to their success in teaching, and is part of the formation of their ideal teacher selves:

Lavra: You are not part of the English-speaking environment, and that makes it more difficult for you that you are responsible to find all those materials. You have to try to create this English-speaking atmosphere in your lesson, and you have to make them feel that they have to speak naturally in the lesson, so that they would respond naturally to what you are saying. So, this takes time to establish, but all of the teachers who make it a point to happen, then it happens.

As both Lavra and Oleksandra indicate, sharing the language and culture of their English language students plays a strong role in both of their ideal teacher selves, as does the belief that they can teach their students more effectively than native English speakers. Their dedication to their students and the English language in general is admirable, a trait observed by an English language fellow placed in Sevastopol National Technical University: 'I have nothing but admiration for Ukrainian teachers of English and their dedication to their subject' (Selec & Abramicheva, 2012: 21). Oleksandra and Lavra have both developed their ideal teacher selves including the notion of a language–culture connection, emphasizing the global competence needed to succeed in jobs in the current world economy. Oleksandra, specifically, talked about an English teacher role model that affected her own ideal English teacher self. They also visualize themselves as teachers who use communicative activities, teaching in English as much as possible, without forgetting the context in which they are situated in terms of student goals and parent expectations. As both of them indicated Russian as an L1 in a Ukrainian context, it is clear that the context in which they are situated plays a role in their generally flexible language attitudes.

As Smotrova (2009: 731–732) states, 'Ukraine has favorable conditions for developing EFL education, including generally increased learner motivation owing to socioeconomic change and growing contact with English-speaking countries, increased exposure to English outside the classroom, and strong government support'. There is a bright future ahead for Ukrainian language learning and teaching of English.

8 Estonia: 'Teachers speak better'

Mida Juku ei õpi, seda Juhan ei tea
[Literal translation: What Juku doesn't learn, Juhan doesn't know]
(Figurative translation: What you don't learn as a child, you won't know as an adult)

Estonian proverb

KEY POINTS

In this chapter, Mia and Darja

(1) Feel confident in their and their students' English abilities, which are noticed by people abroad.
(2) Believe that sharing a first language (L1) with the students helps them know the specific difficulties that might arise.
(3) Express strong positive attitudes toward English.
(4) Describe the complicated relationship with Russian in Estonia.
(5) Indicate that language learning in Estonia is crucial because of the relative size of and opportunities in Estonia.

These aspects and others delineated in the chapter contribute to their ideal English teacher selves.

The Estonian state was founded on February 24, 1918, at the end of the First World War and after the Russian Revolution (Red October) in 1917, having previously been ruled by the Russians, Germans, Danes, Poles, and Swedes. Independent statehood was short-lived, as Estonia was incorporated into the Soviet Union on August 6, 1940 (Rannut, 2004); however, the period between 1919 and 1940 'was not only an era of development for the Estonian State but also for its national language, which became the language of government at all levels and the primary medium of instruction throughout the education system' (Taylor, 2002: 319–320). Verschik (2005: 285) noted that during this first independent period for Estonia, 'the languages of the former elites (Russian and

German) lost their dominant position and became equal in status to other minority languages'.

The language status of Estonian shifted again with the annexation of Estonia by the Soviet Union in 1940 and resulted in the displacement of Estonian as the societal language, incorporating Russian into all parts of the political, educational, and cultural systems. Other than a short interlude during the Second World War and German occupation, the Russification of Estonia, and indeed other Soviet states, continued until the collapse of the Soviet Union in 1991 (Mälksoo, 2003; Rannut, 2004). Pavlenko (2013), citing Besters-Dilger (2009) and Taranenko (2007: 264), explains that 'Sociolinguists commonly use "russification" as a trope referring to consistent and long-lasting attempts to forcibly make Russians out of non-Russians'. Both Pavlenko (2013) and Rannut (2004) point out that this 'Russification' was not equally applied to all language and ethnic groups.

Many of the current generation of language teachers in Estonia learned English during Soviet occupation, and thus, did not have the opportunity to travel during the early part of their studies, nor did they have teachers who had traveled during their studies. This is not the reality for those who studied English after the fall of the Iron Curtain, as many people, both teachers and non-teachers, regularly travel abroad now. Darja and Mia are two Estonian English teachers with over 30 years of teaching experience each at the time this chapter was written. Both have MA degrees: Mia in education sciences and Darja in English as a foreign language. Darja lives and works in Estonia's second-largest city, Tartu; Mia lives and works in the smaller town of Võru. Both speak Estonian as an L1, and although English is the language that is the focus of their teaching and learning selves, both Mia and Darja talk about the importance of learning multiple languages in the context of Estonia. Situating her English language learning experience, Darja describes what it was like to learn English during Soviet rule of Estonia, particularly when it came to teacher experience and materials:

Darja: When I think back to my student days, our lecturers or tutors at the university, they hadn't been to a foreign country. We lived behind the iron curtain, so to say. But, I highly appreciate the work our teachers at school and lecturers at the university did because the only access to the English-speaking world was through some shaky radio waves, BBC or Voice of America. You can imagine that, when in 1991, Estonia became independent, we had the possibility to travel again. I graduated from the university in 1985, and my first visit to, for example, the UK was in 1992.

　　　...

Mia:　No, we didn't have any TV. It was through books, through very old tapes, which were read, recorded, and, actually, the man who read was Estonian who had lived in England. And, it was the thing that happened there when we went to school with no authentic texts.

As is always the case when one language is suddenly imposed upon a society, there are controversies over the learning and use of that specific language. During the Soviet period in this region, there was mass migration of Russians, which encouraged the spread of the Russian language (Pavlenko, 2008; Smagulova, 2008). Russian immigrants to Estonia clustered together in urban centers and worked in Soviet-created jobs. As a result, they never had any reason to interact with Estonians or learn the language (Rannut, 2004: 4). The issue was that while native Estonians were obliged to learn Russian during this period for economic advancement and job security, the Russians who migrated to these occupied Soviet territories were not obliged to learn the titular languages, or the former official language, of the country: 'This approach to language management enabled high levels of monolingualism among native speakers of Russian and high levels of bilingualism and titular language maintenance among most titulars' (Pavlenko, 2013: 265). Estonians, on the other hand, were faced with the destruction of their formerly multilingual society as Russian was imposed as the language of the public sphere, dominating such realms as academic instruction and commerce (Fonzari, 1999; Rannut, 2004).

Learning Russian was obligatory in school, and it was introduced quite early – earlier than the other languages people learned. According to Mia, Russian was introduced in Grade 2 when they were students. As can be expected, attitudes toward the Russian language were mixed. On the one hand, it was readily available, making learning the language easier. On the other hand, there was a sense of separation between Russian speakers and Estonian speakers, as indicated by Zabrodskaja (2015: 224): 'Generally, Russian-speakers did not learn titular languages in Soviet times because Russian was the language of inter-ethnic communication (язык межнационального общения)'. This sentiment was also felt by Mia.

Mia: I can speak Russian to some extent. We studied it at school, actually, and it was, we can say, we had authentic material as we had authentic teacher, who was Russian. And it was easier at that time because Russian was everywhere: on television, in the streets.

Amy: What about your emotional attachment to Russian?

Mia: I don't like it very much.

Amy: You don't. Okay.

Mia: I don't feel very comfortable because I have forgotten a lot of it. But, at school, it was technically something we rejected, and we didn't like.

Amy: Ah, do you think that you rejected it because of the political situation?

Mia: Yes. Yes. Yeah.

Amy: So, it's something you were forced to do but...

Mia: It was forced, and the attitude was, 'this Russian and those Russians', so, at least it was in my school, in my class where I went, it was somehow quite negative attitude towards Russian.

As Zabrodskaja (2015) notes, there is often an 'us versus them' attitude, which is illustrated by Mia's description. However, Darja has a different feeling toward the language. Although she was not happy about the political situation, she remained impartial to the language as such:

Darja: I started studying Russian, I think it must be in, in grade two. I was eight then. I can say that my experience was neutral because I can't think of myself having any sort of political biases. I appreciate the language, the culture, the literature. But all the political aspects, that's entirely another topic.

Among the Baltic nations, Estonia has the second-largest Russian-speaking community. A number of large-scale quantitative studies have indicated that 'in general, in Estonia, the segregation of the Russian community is likely to continue' (Zabrodskaja, 2015: 225).

Some scholars, such as Ozolins (2002), have supported the use of the term 'colonizers' when it comes to the relationship of Russian and countries such as Estonia. Others, such as Pavlenko (2011), argue against using that term, stating that Russians did not have a more privileged status than L1 speakers of other languages. It is the case, however, that L1 speakers did have an advantage in terms of knowing the language that was needed to succeed in work, school, and society in general. 'What is clear is that Russian has not retained as powerful a position in the Baltic countries as, for example, French and English have retained in much of present-day Africa, India and other typical post-colonial settings' (Zabrodskaja, 2015: 224).

The fall of the Soviet Union in 1991 brought about radical change in terms of language use in countries such as Estonia, as legislation that restored Estonian to its former position in society and its prestige was introduced. According to Pavlenko (2013), in terms of languages in use in various sectors, there is no clear data for this time period in this region. After the fall of the Soviet Union, there was a lack of fieldwork by applied linguists, as most of the work carried out on post-Soviet language reforms was done by political scientists. Although general trends can be seen, details about situational-specific language use are missing from the literature. 'To say it simply, we have never learned who in the early 1990s stopped using what language or started using another language with whom and when' (Pavlenko, 2013: 263). She also discusses the difficulties encountered depending on who was engaged in the research. For example, outsiders who came in, 'rarely had full understanding of the local languages and contexts' whereas 'local sociolinguists had the understanding of the local languages but little familiarity with contemporary theories and methodologies and no funding to undertake comprehensive fieldwork' (Pavlenko, 2013: 263).

What is known, however, is the promotion of Estonian as the language of focus: 'legislative acts and strategic documents were adopted by the parliaments of the three Baltic countries (the *Riigikogu* in Estonia, the *Saeima* in Latvia and the *Seimas* in Lithuania) concerning the status of titular and the other languages used in the republics: their status, teaching and use within the educational system, as well as in society at large' (Zabrodskaja, 2015: 263). Pavlenko (2008) further explains the use of Russian, or lack thereof, in countries such as Estonia, as the country reinstated Estonian as the sole language of the state. De-Russification was a natural course of action post-occupation, Estonia thereby 'replacing Russian with titular languages in the public sphere, and in particular in government, administration, legislation, official documentation, secondary and higher education, science, technology, and the media. The laws also required that employees of state institutions, organizations, and businesses that have contact with the general public must know and use the official language' (Pavlenko, 2008: 65). As Estonia has one of the largest L1 Russian-speaking populations in this region, this large monolingual Russian population caused problems for nation-building efforts. When a large portion of the population suddenly finds themselves without the language skills for gainful employment or other ways of being integrated into society, problems are likely to arise: 'these Russian speakers woke up one morning to a political and linguistic reality not of their doing and found themselves involuntary and at times unwelcome migrants in countries, where their native language was no longer sufficient for employment and education' (Pavlenko, 2013: 266). This sentiment was especially difficult, as there were varying levels of Russian integration into Estonian society, as described in Zabrodskaja (2015). Some Estonian Russian speakers felt a sense of being in the middle of two cultures: 'I cannot refer to myself as either part of Russian culture or of Estonian. I am stuck in the middle' (Zabrodskaja, 2015: 232). However, there is a sense that L1 Russian speakers living in Estonia should indeed learn Estonian. The fact that there are many who have chosen not to do so has been perceived as a 'lack of appreciation of Estonia as a separate country and of Estonians as a different nation' (Lauristin & Vihalemm, 1997: 118).

The language planning that took place after the fall of the Soviet Union has made Estonian the primary language of educational instruction, as well as the language used in most other public realms. Policy changes included a change in the language used in the media, schooling, and Russian place names/other lexical items, among others. As can be noted, there are multiple perspectives on the use of Russian versus Estonian in the public sphere. What is clear, however, is how the shift back to using Estonian for education and political purposes motivated the surge in English language learning and teaching. In an attempt to avoid using Russian as the language of communication, the lingua franca of the region became English. One of the most relevant outcomes of these policy changes was 'to increase levels of competence in English as an alternative to the former lingua franca Russian' (Pavlenko, 2013: 266). Although there are Estonians who learn Russian and vice versa, Fonzari (1999: 40) also discusses the notion of the rationale for the uptick in English use, as well as the sense of freedom that communication in English brought to many people in Estonia: 'In Estonia, the fifty years of Soviet power have associated English with the language of freedom, the word *freedom* being used here in the broad sense of trading and communicating on a much wider scale with no political interference, and have determined a situation in which the majority of the Estonian ethnic group, reluctant to learn Russian, and the resident Russians, hurt in their pride and therefore reluctant to use Estonian, have taken up English as their language of communication'. As Darja explains, with Mia emphatically agreeing with her, English is now commonplace in Estonian society, which gives students more access and more opportunities to learn and practice.

Darja: We have foreign languages, including English, all around us: television, internet, printed press. But it's a global thing, I think. And, logically, it also comes into our classrooms and [**Mia:** Yeah. Yeah.] and homes and so, it's the normal state of things.

Both Darja and Mia also talk about why learning a language other than Estonian is important.

Darja: I think, for Estonians, learning a foreign language is really very important because we are a small nation in number. The population of Estonia is 1.3 million, and less than 1 million among them are Estonians. So, this is essential, that we have to know foreign languages.
Amy: Who else, besides Estonians, are there?
Darja: Russians, Belarussians, Ukrainians, Finns, Germans, many nationalities. I think English is the first foreign language [**Mia:** Yeah, almost everywhere]. Also, German, French, Finnish, maybe Spanish.
Mia: Russian.
Darja: Russian, definitely, as we are neighbors, so we have to know the language. [**Amy:** Right.] Young people understand that it's really necessary. It opens the doors, so very many young people, when they learn English in high school, very many continue their education in UK, USA. Australia is also very popular at the moment.

Fonzari (1999) provides a statement from the Ministry of Culture and Education, which supports Darja's concept of the need for foreign language study in Estonia: 'In Estonia, the necessity of foreign languages is acknowledged by the Ministry of Culture and Education: "In such a small country like Estonia with a small population the knowledge of foreign languages is extremely important" (in Ministry of Culture and Education of the Estonian Republic, 1995: 3). Pupils learn the first foreign language in grade 3 and the second foreign language in grade 6' (Ministry of Culture and Education of the Estonian Republic, 1995: 41). Darja's statement also supports Fonzari's assertion that English is 'a window on the Western world for Estonia' (Ministry of Culture and Education of the Estonian Republic, 1995: 40), as it provides a chance for an education abroad. Fonzari's study is one of the few to discuss language learning motivation in Estonia, and the findings indicate that the students are motivated by an internal desire to learn English (ideal self, Dörnyei, 2009), as well as the economic opportunities English affords (ought-to self). Mia also provides evidence that parents are quite supportive of English study in Estonia, and some even provide some sort of external motivation, like a trip, which perhaps enhances students' ought-to self. It is also the context of the town itself; there seems to be the expectation that children will learn English, so parents push them to do so at a very early age. This generation of students also has an ideal self that includes technology and spends time 'immersed' in the language; thus, these students have already had exposure to the language even before attending their first class. This is a situation that is quite different from English language exposure during the time of the Soviet Union.

Mia: And, it's also, somehow, parents are very supportive of studying English... I know that parents put their children in kindergarten already to start learning English. And, those young people, they are so much at their computers, and they [are] just immersed in English. I don't know. They come to first class, second class; they are great. They know English. They now have got, picked up some words, and, they can manage. And, they are interested. Of course, for some, it might be some kind of external motivation that moms have promised to do: 'Okay, you study well, I'll take you to London on a trip'. It might also be that, but it isn't most, mostly not the case. They just feel that it is something they need in their daily life.

Mia, unlike her feelings toward Russian, feels a strong attachment to English, which undoubtedly plays into her ideal English teaching self.

Amy: What about your emotional attachment to English?
Mia: I like it. I love it! (Laughter)
Darja: You love it. (Laughter)
Mia: I love English! (Laughter)
Mia: I really love it.

Amy: Why, do you think? Is it the culture attached to it? Is it the language itself? Or...

Mia: It's the language, the culture, everything, the books. I like everything about it. My kids at school sometimes say that, 'You're more English than Estonian'. (Laughter)

Opportunities today are also different from when Estonia was part of the Soviet Union, both in terms of the students as well as of the teachers. In terms of the teachers, travel and exposure to the target languages and cultures in question undoubtedly added to the formation of their ideal teacher selves.

Darja: Today, it's different because young people have so many opportunities to travel, and teachers have opportunities to go here and there and take all sorts of language courses. We have a very active teacher organization in Estonia. It's the Association of English Teachers. We have annual conferences and seminars and guest performers from UK and other countries.

Indeed, there is a dynamic association for these teachers, The Estonian Association of Teachers of English (EATE), or *Eesti Inglise Keele Õpetajate Selts*, maintains an active website and a variety of activities and teacher development activities. At the time of writing, there were 260 members from all levels of English teaching (http://www.eate.ee/), and researchers, such as Oder (2008), postulate that the political shift has created the need to redefine the characteristics and roles of language teachers.

Some aspects of these participants' ideal teacher selves formed even before the Iron Curtain had been lifted. One part of their English language teacher identity had to do with the amount of English (versus Estonian) used in the language classroom. I asked about this during our conversation, and Darja indicated that 80–90% of her classes are conducted in English. To encourage them to speak English, she talked about how she would give her students extra tasks if they didn't speak English in class. The student would speak English to avoid the extra work, but Darja thought it helped them develop more effectively.

Darja: they don't want to have this extra task. But it makes them think in English, actually.

Mia also indicated that she mostly used English in her classroom and why this was not problematic for her students:

Amy: What about the language that you use in your classroom? Is everything in English?

Mia: Yes, we try to stick to English as a working language.

Amy: Okay. What might be times when you would switch to Estonian?
Mia: So, maybe some aspects in grammar, some that are maybe complicated to explain. But we start using English as a working language at an early age, so it's usually not a problem.

Another part of the formation of their ideal teacher self identity is both of their statuses as L1 Estonian speakers who teach English. Mia discusses the fact that she can understand the language issues that cause problems for her students and compares her English teaching to an L1 Russian speaker who taught her Russian.

Mia: I can understand what are specific problems of our students. I remember I had a Russian teacher who was native Russian, and she couldn't understand why we couldn't understand the problems in Russian. But, she couldn't understand it because it was her mother tongue, first language, and she taught it through Russian. She didn't know any Estonian. And so, it was a problem, and that's why I think it is, it is our advantage that we know what might be the tricky problems, tricky things for our students.

Darja adds that there are some difficult aspects of not having English as an L1, such as idioms, and Mia also indicates that sometimes pronunciation (i.e. Thompson & Fioramonte, 2012; Wolff & de Costa, 2017) and grammatical aspects can also be tricky for L1 Estonian teachers of English.

Mia: The advantage would be that I know what the special difficulties are of my language learners. I think it's one of those things. But disadvantages, we're not always very sure about the grammar because, in Estonia, we try to be very precise about those things [**Amy:** I see.] and about pronunciation. We pay attention to those things, too.
Darja: You really must be very, very well informed about different aspects, because the students can ask all sorts of tricky things. Teaching idiomatic expressions can sometimes also be tricky.

As Darja indicates, however, their ideal teacher selves are not created in comparing themselves to L1-speaking teachers of English, not only because of the lack of English-speaking teachers found in this context, but also because she does not find the comparison a logical one. At the time of the data collection, there were few native English speaker teachers in Estonia, although this situation has changed rapidly in recent years.

Darja: Well, I think this [comparisons to L1 English-speaking teachers] is not so much an issue in Estonia because we don't have native speaker teachers.

Darja goes on to explain that the requirements for becoming a teacher are stringent in Estonia, and that it's not possible to have different salaries for people from different backgrounds.

Darja: We do have some native speakers every now and then, but it's not on regular basis. Getting a teacher's position in Estonia depends on meeting the requirements for teachers which are the same for everybody. [**Amy:** Okay.]

Mia: Yeah.

Amy: Okay. So, you think the level should be the same.

Mia: Yeah. To get paid, you have to meet certain requirements, and then it is the same salary for everybody.

Before Estonia joined the European Union, most Estonians very rarely came into contact with native English speakers and usually interacted with the language via media and the internet, as Verschik (2005) notes. However, even in the late 1990s, in a survey of Estonian schoolchildren, Fonzari (1999: 46) found that only 25.2% had 'never communicated with English speakers in a real life situation', meaning that the majority of students had done so. Before joining the European Union, Fonzari also posits that Estonians used English in order to consume pop culture, a consumption that indicates that Estonians are moving toward a more Western aesthetic, and are actively using English to advance politically, economically, and technologically within the country. After Estonia joined the European Union in 2004 and then the Schengen area in 2007, movement by other Europeans into Estonia, and movement of Estonians to other European countries became exponentially easier. The Estonian Ministry of Foreign Affairs states, 'According to the results of last year's Eurobarometer survey, the residents of Estonia consider the most positive result of the European Union the free movement of persons, goods and services' (https://vm.ee/en/estonia-5-years-european-union). As such, interactions with English speakers from a variety of contexts are rapidly changing in the Estonian context.

Both Mia and Darja indicate pride in their English language abilities, which plays a role in their ideal teacher self identities. They also give the example that L1 English speakers are frequently impressed with the English levels of their students. If the students have a high proficiency in English, then that of their teachers must be even higher.

Mia: I just had an experience, well, let's see, it was the beginning of January. We were just going out on a youth project with people from England, from Yorkshire, and they were just talking to me as to natives. And then, some just, 'Oh, you're not English-speaking people!' So, it means that they didn't even think about it. [**Amy:** Oh, I see.] It means teachers manage well. So, it is a very positive attitude.

[**Amy:** Right] They are always surprised that our children speak so well whenever they go abroad. And, it means teachers also have to speak well. Teachers speak better.

Darja: When our students go on study trips to, for example, the UK and when the British learn that the Estonian school children know at least two foreign languages, [**Mia:** Yeah.] there is usually a 'Wow!' moment. [**Mia:** Yeah]

Amy: Okay. So, people have generally been very pleased with your...

Mia: Yeah. Yeah. There's a positive attitude.

Darja: Positive! Yes, positive.

Amy: Okay.

At the end of the discussion, when I asked if they had anything else to add, Mia stated that English 'has really opened doors'. Darja also added that although they have personally benefited a lot, it is also important for them that their former students have become successful. Evidence shows that the success of former students also plays a role in creating the ideal teacher selves, as it did with Alex in Thompson (2017a: 44), who states that the success of his students is part of his identity as an educator: 'Now, I guess I am reliving this process vicariously through my students. I got the same high when we were [at a Chinese language competition] and the judges stopped the competition to tell me that heritage learners were not eligible after our student delivered his speech in Chinese. I get that sense of validation, which is highly motivating for me'.

Darja: We have benefited a lot. I think our students are lucky, but also very hardworking. A really good command of the English language has helped our former students, for example, to enroll in top universities also in the English-speaking world.

Viewed through the eyes of Darja and Mia, this chapter on Estonia illustrates the dynamics in the usage of Russian and English, largely due to the rise and fall of the Soviet Union. Indeed, the formation of their ideal English language selves, which transitioned to an ideal English teacher self, was at least partly due to a juxtaposition of English and Russian. Evident in both the literature on Estonia and the discussion with Darja and Mia is the idea that Russian is the symbol of oppression, whereas English symbolizes relative freedom, which inevitably affected both Mia's and Darja's attitudes toward the languages.

For both Darja and Mia, the circumstances of learning English and becoming an English teacher took place when travel outside of Estonia was impossible and having access to authentic language materials was difficult; as such, their own English teachers were their role models and helped with their own ideal teacher self formation. Their demand for their students to use the English language in the classroom was one aspect of both of their ideal teacher selves, as was their status as L1 Estonian speakers and their confidence in and love of the English language. As Darja stated, comparing themselves to native English-speaking teachers is not a useful exercise and does not interact with the formation of their own identities as English teachers. The availability of resources to learn English has changed drastically in recent years (after the late 1980s and then again after 2004), and English language use is much more prevalent in society today; English language use was 'chosen by the self-liberated population as their medium of communication with the outer world' (Fonzari, 1999: 40) and as 'a stepping stone in the economic transition and the integration of Estonia into Europe' in the 1990s (Fonzari, 1999: 41). As Estonia is now part of the European Union, English has become a more neutral lingua franca in this context, where it is an important language of economic advancement. Both Darja and Mia have a strong sense of English teacher identity and feel that an ideal teacher should bring English as it is used in the world into their classrooms. Perhaps most crucially, their ideal self is connected to the English level and successes of their former students. As proof of their English teaching prowess, if their students speak well, the 'Teachers speak better'.

9 Final Thoughts

Education without morals is like a ship without a compass, merely wandering nowhere.

Martin Luther King, Jr

In the context-specific chapters, we discovered the learning and teaching endeavors of several English teachers, along with the sociopolitical contexts that shaped their teaching experiences and ideal English teacher self formations: Ablaye from Senegal, Khiet from Vietnam, Hasani from Egypt, Carolina and María from Argentina, Barış and Musa from Turkey, Oleksandra and Lavra from Ukraine, and Mia and Darja from Estonia. As was delineated in the first part of the book, it should be understood that context is not monolithic (Mercer, 2016) and is the subjective reality of those who live it (van Dijk, 2009). There are multiple contextual elements that the learners shape and that shape the learners (Ushioda, 2015), and the construction of self concept cannot be separated from context (Mercer & Williams, 2014a). These language teachers have all experienced the teacher–student duality in terms of language learning and teaching during their own paths to proficiency (Gregersen & MacIntyre, 2015), and their experiences in and with the actors in their specific contexts have shaped what they perceive the ideal English teacher to be.

Through the conversations about their language learning and teaching journeys, all of the teachers discussed issues of teaching English as a second language (L2) user of English, attitudes toward English in their specific context, the idea of English as a global language, and commented on language learning in general. Many of the teachers also discussed the complexities surrounding attitudes toward languages other than English (LOTEs) (both theirs and others'), the pride they have in their own and their students' English levels, and the role models that helped them reach their current position. Through these discussions, the teachers' visions of their ideal teacher selves emerged through the understanding of what it meant for them to teach English in their specific sociopolitical environments.

Teaching a Language That Is Not an L1

This topic is controversial, as outlined in Chapter 1 of this book. As can been seen in the literature, as well as in the narratives presented in the context-specific chapters, the formation of the ideal teacher self relates to the non-native status of the teachers in question. Several scholars have recently disputed the term 'non-native' (Cook, 1999; Dewaele, 2018; Ortega, 2013), offering suggestions for more neutral terms (L2 user, LX user, etc.). Some scholars have argued that a monolingual teacher is, in fact, the antithesis of what is needed to prepare students to succeed in a multilingual, multicultural world (Kramsch, 2014), and others have argued that there should be no labels at all (Aneja, 2016) because students do not perceive a difference when labels are not imposed (Aslan & Thompson, 2017). Nonetheless, teachers who teach a language that is not their first language (L1), whether it be English or a LOTE, are often positioned, or position themselves, as non-native, which raises a multitude of complex issues and interactions.

An unexpected theme throughout the narratives was that of the confidence and competence of these teachers in their language proficiency, as well as in their teaching abilities. This was most explicitly relevant with Ablaye from Senegal and Mia and Darja from Estonia. Ablaye discusses how he enjoys surprising people with his English ability, which is unexpected in the Senegalese context. Mia and Darja indicate that when they travel abroad with their students, there is often a 'wow' moment when people realize that English is not their L1. They also feel pride in their students' levels because if the students speak well, 'teachers speak better'. Unequivocally, the teachers expressed that they were able to do a better job teaching their students than would an L1 speaker of English. Ablaye from Senegal says, 'You may not know exactly what our students need' and Khiet from Vietnam talks with pride about how students all crowd into his grammar class before exam periods. Hasani from Egypt indicates that he would have a more accurate understanding of his students' beliefs and experiences than would a native speaker (Ma, 2012), bringing up the classic Shakespeare piece of comparing a woman to a summer's day. María and Carolina from Argentina discuss the importance of being able to convey difficult concepts because of having to learn those same concepts themselves (Rao, 2010); they also indicate the helpfulness of sharing the students' L1 of Spanish (Yoo, 2014). Both Lavra and Olexandra from Ukraine and Mia and Darja from Estonia raise the concern of students having trouble understanding L1 English speakers (Chun, 2014), and Musa and Barış from Turkey and Khiet from Vietnam explain the issue of the lack of respect that students sometimes have for L1 English-speaking teachers in the classroom, either because of a lack of a shared L1, or because of the casual comportment that the native speakers sometimes bring to the classroom in their contexts.

In the literature about L2 users of English, the data suggests that many of these teachers are not satisfied with their own proficiency levels (Hiver, 2013; Solano-Campos, 2014; Thompson & Fioramonte, 2012; Valmori & de Costa, 2016). For the most part, this was not a common theme found in this data, with the exceptions being Mia and Darja from Estonia and Khiet from Vietnam. Mia and Darja indicate that some teachers might sometimes feel insecure about pronunciation and grammar, as Estonians like to be 'precise' about those things; they might also struggle with idioms. Khiet talks in several different places about his own English fluency and that of others of his generation, explaining that the younger generation of teachers is much more fluent. Interestingly, in both cases, these teachers learned English at a time when there was little opportunity for contact with English outside of the classroom, and even their own classroom resources were described as substandard. Khiet, for example, talks about having to learn English from a Russian textbook, and Mia and Darja talk about the great respect they have for their own English teachers who taught them well despite only having access to a few resources such as the BBC on 'shaky radio waves'.

The teachers who wanted to talk the most about the native/non-native divide were Barış and Musa from Turkey, where there seemed to be the greatest influx of L1 English speakers into the teaching context. Barış and Musa talked about the hierarchy in terms of English language education (the Turkish teachers had this background, but the L1 English speakers often did not), which made the discrepancy in salary even more preposterous. The L1 English-speaking teachers made four to five times the salaries of the Turkish teachers, despite their lower working hours and lack of training. Unexpectedly, this seemed to motivate Barış in particular to be better: 'I'm better than these guys, I can teach them stuff' (anti-ought-to self, Thompson, 2017a). This teacher dyad was also the only group that brought up race and nativeness in terms of who was considered to be a 'native English speaker'. Many of those labeled as 'native' were actually Russian or African, according to the narrative, but 'they don't look Turkish, that's the point'. There has been relatively little work on race and English language teaching, but several scholars (Charles, 2019; Holliday & Aboshiha, 2009; Jenkins, 2017; Ruecker & Ives, 2015; Todd & Pojanapunya, 2009) have documented issues around language ownership and the operationalization of 'native speaker' in other contexts.

English as a Global Language

The juxtaposition of the negative attitudes toward English due to political conflicts with the number of people worldwide studying English is striking. The reason, perhaps, is what Dörnyei *et al.* (2006) postulate – English is no longer perceived as being tied to a specific cultural context or discourse community. This concept was one of the catalysts for the development of the L2 Motivational Self System (L2MSS) (see Dörnyei & Ushioda, 2009) which questions the limits of integration motivation, or motivation to learn a language primarily to feel connected to a specific cultural group (Gardner, 1985). In the course of the conversations with the English teachers highlighted in this book, all of them specifically mentioned the global nature of English. María, for example, states that it is the lingua franca to 'communicate with everybody, everywhere'. Hasani notes that 'In order to deal with any other nationality in the world, you can speak to them in English, and they will understand you. So, it's a must. It's a link'. Darja talks about the accessibility of English in the Estonian context in current times, something that was not possible previously: 'We have foreign languages, including English, all around us: television, internet, printed press. But it's a global thing, I think'.

Several of the participants noted that English was a tool in a global sense, for both them and their students. Musa states, 'It's really great, it's just... English is a really nice tool that I can use. Language, languages are tools for me'. Khiet, in Vietnam, also used the word 'tool' to describe his relationship to English, but he went on to explain how this feeling changed over time as he realized the global importance of the language: 'I think at first it was a tool for me, but now I love it... I can communicate with people, and I think English is a tool, but using it as a tool, I can establish a lot of good relationships with not only American students, teachers, but also international students... English is a privilege for me. Yeah. So, I love it'. In the Senegalese setting, Ablaye notes that English is needed to study diplomacy, as well as other opportunities. 'If you want a job, they ask you whether you've mastered English or not'. Lavra, in the Ukrainian context, tells me that English 'is important if you want to have a career, become a professional', a sentiment that is also echoed by Khiet: 'I think the main reason for learning English in Vietnam is first a chance to study abroad, second a high-paying job'. In the Estonian context, the sentiment is similar, as Darja states: 'Young people understand that it's really necessary'. She goes on to say that after learning English in high school, some students continue their education abroad in an Anglophone setting, a sentiment that is echoed by Olexandra in the Ukrainian setting: 'There is a program where they can study for a year in the USA'. All of these instances show the external expectation of learning English, or the ought-to self (Dörnyei, 2009), which relates to the global nature of the language; however, as Khiet illustrates, what starts as an ought-to self can morph into an ideal self as the learning process progresses. He learned to love the language that first served as a tool for him.

Contextual factors for negative attitudes toward English, specifically the connection between English and politics, were mentioned in almost every discussion. Several of the teachers talked about how attitudes toward English were influenced by the governmental policies of the

United States or the UK. In the Argentinian context, Carolina states that her students resist English because it is perceived to be the language of the United States, 'a controller of the world and superior'. Her students questioned the rationale for them to learn English when Americans are not expected to learn another language, such as Spanish, to the same extent. María also reminds us of the conflictual relationship with another Anglophone country: 'We have had problems with England'. Hasani from Egypt, however, states that there are no negative feelings toward English, *per se*, but toward American governmental policies. In the Turkish context, Barış reminds us: 'English, of course, is a pragmatic tool, but still associated with the American president'. Similarly, in Vietnam, Khiet states that although the situation is changing, 'Many years ago, when people studied English, anti-American people would think that it was very close to the US, so they would not like those who spoke or studied English'. Peers from his generation have started to shift, 'You can say maybe one-fourth of the people would hate the US. The other fourth would love the US. The other half had no idea'. With the current generation, he indicates that there are even fewer negative feelings toward the United States, with the focus more on the benefits that learning English can provide 'to learn the technologies and science and English so that we can contribute more to the building of the country'.

What is fascinating is how the teachers were able to separate the need for English as a tool to succeed and their feelings about the political situations of Anglophone countries (Dörnyei *et al.*, 2006). Lavra expounded upon English used as a mechanism for general cultural competence in her Ukrainian context: 'We all understand that English is important, and nobody argues about that. But more and more we begin to understand that it's the way to understand people. It's the way to understand cultures, and that's the way to open their eyes to the world, which is even more important than being grammatically correct, and so on'. Similarly, and also related to the role of English as a global language for communication, Khiet ends the discussion by reminding us how English helps him to interact with people from all over the world: 'And the most important thing is the happiness when you learn a language – when you learn a foreign language, and you can use it to talk to many people. Not only to your friends, but to people from other countries, too. It's so wonderful. Yeah. It's wonderful. You are expanding a circle of friends and you know more'.

Attitudes toward English as Compared to LOTEs

In addition to the political affiliations of English, the teachers all indicated some sort of emotional attachment to English, and almost all of the teachers whose stories are detailed in these chapters have experience with learning a language (or languages) other than English. The learning experiences for these languages differed based on the context; of course, as these individuals chose the path of becoming English teachers as their careers, it is understandable that their attachment to English is overall greater than to that of other languages. Several of the teachers expressed their 'love' for English (Ablaye, Khiet, Mia); Barış talks about how English is his connection to his wife; Hasani equates English with education; and María and Lavra indicate that it is the teacher's job to create positive attitudes toward English. As these teachers, for the most part, have a multitude of language learning experiences, some of them brought up attitudes toward English versus LOTEs. For example, Carolina says that she feels a stronger attachment to Italian because of the context; Italian is spoken by friends and family more than English. Hasani talks about the money spent teaching French versus teaching English in Egypt, indicating that the French government allocates more resources to the effort than do Anglophone governments. Certainly, in all of the contexts highlighted in the book, the interactions of attitudes toward specific languages and colonialism and/or political conflicts cannot be overlooked.

There are two contexts, however, where the comparison of attitudes toward English and LOTEs was the most salient: Estonia and Senegal. In the Estonian context, Darja and Mia discussed learning English in comparison to learning Russian. Because of the history between the Soviet Union and Estonia, Russian was a necessary language to learn, as Darja states: 'Russian, definitely, as we are neighbors, so we have to know the language'. In terms of her feelings toward Russian, Darja indicates, 'I appreciate the language, the culture, the literature. But all the political aspects, that's entirely another topic'. At the same time, when asked about her attachment to Russian, Mia states, 'I don't like it very much'. Compared to English, when she states, 'I love English! I really love it'. Mia explained that English has 'opened doors' for her and was a language that she valued for personal and professional reasons. Whereas Russian was the language needed to thrive in Estonia in the past, the language for advancement in Estonia has shifted to English, even more so after 2004 when Estonia joined the European Union.

In the case of Ablaye in Senegal, he also states that he is 'most interested in English' and that he speaks English to anyone he can. In our conversation, he indicates that he is not the only English teacher who has such an attitude: 'In our country, it is what we are doing. We English teachers, we speak English'. Ablaye also seems to have developed an anti-ought-to self (Thompson, 2017a), when he laughs and says, 'They expected me to speak French because it is a French-speaking country, but maybe they don't expect anyone from there [Senegal] to speak English at a certain level'. Also interested in how Ablaye viewed English compared to his native languages Serer and Wolof, he answered, 'I'm earning my life because of English... I don't know whether I would say it is more important, but I think it is very important'. In a subsequent communication with Ablaye, he also stressed how more efforts for literacy in the local languages are unfolding. In his words: 'At the political level, people are becoming aware that it is difficult to develop a country while ignoring the local languages'. As excerpts from these two contexts illustrate, learning English is necessary to succeed because of its status globally, but learning English should not be at the expense of other languages.

Indeed, it was the case that many of the teachers also talked about a general fondness for languages and language learning in general, indicating a cosmopolitan outlook. Ablaye, much like the participants in Coetzee-Van Rooy's (2014; 2019) studies, lives with different languages in different spaces; however, he chooses English whenever he can. Lavra expresses her opinion that learning each subsequent language is easier because of previous experience (Thompson, 2016, 2020), and she, as well as Hasani, discuss the language–culture connection. Hasani also talks about languages as being alive: 'Language is a live thing... we are living the language'. Specifically in the Estonian context, Darja expresses the idea that it is important to learn other languages in Estonia because of the small Estonian population. Language learning is a necessity in this context. Many of these teachers may have what Henry (2017) describes as an ideal multilingual self (a self that perceives learning multiple languages to be an ideal) with English at the forefront. Additionally, one potential reason for these teachers' high level of confidence in their English ability, unlike much of the literature on non-native speaker teachers, is what Ellis (2013: 457) describes as the more confident and positive attitudes that plurilinguals have toward language learning in general: 'challenging but possible', which is a sharp contrast to the monolingual mindset. To illustrate this point, in a 'flipping the script' blog post to highlight the deficit model used to describe multilingual K-12 students in the context of the United States, educationallinguist (2015: para. 2) points out that monolinguals are the ones who have failed to assimilate into the multilingual norm worldwide: 'The major cause of this language gap is the failure of monolingual White communities to successfully assimilate into the multilingual and multidialectal mainstream'. Indeed, the normative expectations of the necessity of a standard variety of English in any given context undermine and devalue the rich linguistic repertoires of those who have multiple language systems at their disposals.

Ideal Teacher Selves

All of the English teachers spotlighted in this volume have developed ideal teacher selves in concordance with their interpretations of their own specific contexts (van Dijk, 2009); another teacher in the same context might have a different interpretation (Mercer, 2016). Nonetheless, all of the teachers in this book embody the learner–teacher duality as discussed in Gregersen and MacIntyre (2015), positioning themselves as lifelong learners, as well as teachers. In the Argentinean context, Carolina and María have formed their ideal teacher selves on the pretext of a humble attitude and the desire to continue learning. Hasani in Egypt envisions the ideal teacher to be someone who shares the L1 and cultural background of their students; he also sees his profession as a respectable and secure career. Darja and Mia are confident and secure in their abilities and have formed ideal teacher selves in conjunction with the future success of their Estonian English students. Like Hasani, Ablaye thinks that he is more effective than an L1 English-speaking teacher; his ideal teacher self is formed on this concept, as well as on the solid economic standing his profession has given him, including the use of his pedagogical acumen to promote literacy in Senegal's national languages. In the Turkish context, Barış's ideal teacher self is constructed on the successes he has had in English and is strengthened by his personal relationships in English. For Musa, his ideal English teacher self relates to his identity as a Turkish speaker and the practicality of the English language. Both Lavra and Oleksandra in Ukraine developed their ideal English teaching selves to include the notion of a language–culture connection. They also envision an ideal teacher in their context as one who uses communicative activities, keeping in mind the needs and goals of their students. Finally, Khiet's initial English teacher self was more of the ought-to self variety, as his parents were the ones who encouraged him to choose this profession. Khiet's image of an ideal English teacher is not connected to native speakers, but instead to the younger generation of Vietnamese teachers, adding to the growing body of literature illustrating the importance of the linguistic diversity found in varieties of English from contexts other than those in the inner circle (Nuske, 2018; Schreiber, 2019). Having linguistic and cultural knowledge, as well as being respected as a teacher, is how Khiet describes his ideal teacher self.

Concluding Thoughts and Future Directions

As can be seen from the narrative analysis in the context-specific chapters of this book, all of the ideal teacher selves of these individuals have a symbiotic relationship between context and self (Mercer & Williams, 2014b; Ushioda, 2015). The concept that L1 English speakers would be more effective teachers was not part of any of their constructions of their ideal teacher selves; on the contrary, they all felt that teachers who share a linguistic and cultural background with their students would be the ones to excel in the classroom. Evidence such as this further supports the need to empower teachers based on training and experience, not based on their L1. This perspective is not to denigrate the experience and expertise of native English-speaking teachers. However, as the non-native English-speaking teachers are often the ones who have less social capital, the teacher narratives in this project serve as a reminder that the diverse backgrounds and expertise of these teachers should be celebrated, not disparaged (Canagarajah, 2007) in order to facilitate a more inclusive pedagogy in the field of English language teaching (Ramezanzadeh & Rezaei, 2019; Subtirelu, 2019; Tsang, 2019). After all, as illustrated in Aslan and Thompson (2017), when not primed to think about potential differences between native versus non-native-speaking teachers, the distinction is often irrelevant to students.

As Dörnyei (2019) suggests, future research needs to focus on the less frequently analyzed aspect of the L2MSS – the learning experience. As proposed in Thompson (2017b), an effective way to do this is to more explicitly connect the learner and the sociopolitical context. Another aspect that needs to be further explored in future research is that which Gregersen and MacIntyre (2015) discuss: the interplay of self when a language learner and a language teacher are embodied in the same person. Particularly relevant for those who teach a language other than their L1, such as the teachers in this project, language learning is a lifelong journey. Other teachers have expressed this duality, such as the participant in Mercer (2015b), who indicated that a teacher self seemed to be embedded in her overall English as a foreign language (EFL) self. In this project, María from Argentina expresses the notion that 'learning the language will never end', which is an expression of her learning/teaching self duality; to some extent, all of the teachers expressed the desire to continue learning. Focusing on this aspect of L2 teacher profiles for those who teach either English or LOTEs will help the language learning and teaching community better conceptualize ideal self formation and all that it might entail.

Finally, as was salient in all of the conversations with these English language teachers, multilingual identity should be at the forefront of pedagogical discussions. In that regard, emphasis should be placed on understanding the complex and dynamic relationships among language systems, as well as attitudes toward the different languages in a multilingual speaker's and/or teacher's repertoire. While all of these teachers acknowledged the importance of English for them on both personal and professional levels, this was inevitably done within the manifestation of their bi-/multilingual identities.

References

Abdel Ghany, S.Y. and Abdel Latif, M.M. (2012) English language preparation of tourism and hospitality undergraduates in Egypt: Does it meet their future workplace requirements? *Journal of Hospitality, Leisure, Sport and Tourism Education* 11 (2), 93–100. https://doi.org/10.1016/j.jhlste.2012.05.001.

Abdul Monem, D., El-Sokkary, W., Haddaway, C. and Bickel, B. (2001) English language teaching in Egypt: At the crossroads of global communication. *ESL Magazine* 4 (6), 26–28.

Abouelhassan, R.S.M. and Meyer, L.M. (2016) Economy, modernity, Islam, and English in Egypt. *World Englishes* 35 (1), 147–159. https://doi.org/10.1111/weng.12171.

Alagözlü, N. (2012) English as a foreign language cul-de-sac in Turkey. *Procedia – Social and Behavioral Sciences* 47, 1757–1761. https://doi.org/10.1016/j.sbspro.2012.06.896.

Al-Murtadha, M. (2019) Enhancing EFL learners' willingness to communicate with visualization and goal-setting activities. *TESOL Quarterly* 53 (1), 133–157. https://doi.org/10.1002/tesq.474.

Alptekin, C. and Tatar, S. (2011) Research on foreign language teaching and learning in Turkey (2005–2009). *Language Teaching* 44 (3), 328–353. https://doi.org/10.1017/S026144481100005X.

Amin, N. (1997) Race and the identity of the non-native ESL teacher. *TESOL Quarterly* 31 (3), 580–583. https://doi.org/10.2307/3587841.

Aneja, G.A. (2016) (Non)native speakered: Rethinking (non)nativeness and teacher identity in TESOL teacher education. *TESOL Quarterly* 50 (3), 572–596. https://doi.org/10.1002/tesq.315.

Arel, D. (2002) Interpreting 'nationality' and 'language' in the 2001 Ukrainian census. *Post-Soviet Affairs* 18 (3), 213–249. https://doi.org/10.2747/1060-586X.18.3.213.

Aslan, E. (2017) Doing away with the 'native speaker': A complex adaptive systems approach to L2 phonological attainment. *Language Learning Journal* 45 (4), 447–465. https://doi.org/10.1080/09571736.2014.934271.

Aslan, E. and Thompson, A.S. (2017) Are they really 'two different species'? Implicitly elicited student perceptions about NESTs and NNESTs. *TESOL Journal* 8 (2), 277–294. https://doi.org/10.1002/tesj.268.

Aydıngün, A. and Aydıngün, I. (2004) The role of language in the formation of Turkish national identity and Turkishness. *Nationalism and Ethnic Politics* 10 (3), 415–432. https://doi.org/10.1080/13537110490518264.

Baker, C. and Prys Jones, S. (1998) *Encyclopedia of Bilingualism and Bilingual Education.* Clevedon: Multilingual Matters.

Baleghizadeh, S. and Gordani, Y. (2012) Motivation and quality of work life among secondary school EFL teachers. *Australian Journal of Teacher Education* 37 (7), 30–42. https://doi.org/10.14221/ajte.2012v37n7.8.

Banegas, D.L., Roberts, G., Colucci, R. and Sarsa, B.A. (2020) Authenticity and motivation: A writing for publication experience. *ELT Journal* 74 (1), 29–39. https://doi.org/10.1093/elt/ccz056.

Banfi, C. (2017) English language teaching expansion in South America: Challenges and opportunities. In L.D. Kamhi-Stein, G.D. Maggioli and L.C. de Oliveira (eds) *English Language Teaching in South America: Policy, Preparation and Practices* (pp. 13–30). Bristol: Multilingual Matters.

Bassiouney, R. (2009) *Arabic Sociolinguistics*. Edinburgh: Edinburgh University Press.

Bassiouney, R. (2012) Politicizing identity: Code choice and stance-taking during the Egyptian revolution. *Discourse and Society* 23 (2), 107–126. https://doi.org/10.1177/0957926511431514.

Bassiouney, R. (2013) Language and revolution in Egypt. *Telos* 2013 (163), 85–110. https://doi.org/10.3817/0613163085.

Bassiouney, R. (2014) *Language and Identity in Modern Egypt*. Edinburgh: Edinburgh University Press.

Benkharafa, M. (2013) The present situation of the Arabic language and the Arab world commitment to arabization. *Theory and Practice in Language Studies* 3 (2), 201–208.

Benson, P. (2019) Ways of seeing: The individual and the social in applied linguistics research methodologies. *Language Teaching* 52 (1), 60–70. https://doi.org/10.1017/S0261444817000234.

Bernaus, M. (2020) Teachers' and learners' motivation in multilingual classrooms. In A.H. Al-Hoorie and P.D. MacIntyre (eds) *Contemporary Language Motivation Theory: 60 Years since Gardner and Lambert (1959)* (pp. 40–56). Bristol: Multilingual Matters.

Besters-Dilger, J. (2009) *Language Policy and Language Situation in Ukraine: Analysis and Recommendations*. Frankfurt am Main: Peter Lang.

Bilaniuk, L. (2005) *Contested Tongues: Language Politics and Cultural Correction in Ukraine*. Ithaca, NY: Cornell University Press.

Bilaniuk, D.L. and Melnyk, D.S. (2008) A tense and shifting balance: Bilingualism and education in Ukraine. *International Journal of Bilingual Education and Bilingualism* 11 (3–4), 340–372. https://doi.org/10.1080/13670050802148731.

Block, D. (2003) *The Social Turn in Second Language Acquisition*. Washington, DC: Georgetown University Press.

Blommaert, J. (2010) *The Sociolinguistics of Globalization*. Cambridge: Cambridge University Press.

Boo, Z., Dörnyei, Z. and Ryan, S. (2015) L2 motivation research 2005–2014: Understanding a publication surge and a changing landscape. *System* 55, 145–157. https://doi.org/10.1016/j.system.2015.10.006.

Bourdieu, P. (1991) The production and reproduction of legitimate language. In J.B. Thompson (ed.) *Language and Symbolic Power* (pp. 43–65). Cambridge, MA: Harvard University Press.

Brandão, A.C. de L. (2018) Visualizing EFL teacher identity (re)construction in materials design and implementation. *Applied Linguistics Review* 9 (2–3), 249–271. https://doi.org/10.1515/applirev-2016-1060.

Branigin, W. (1994) As trade opens, a war closes. *The Washington Post* February 6, A22.

Brown, H.D. (2007) *Teaching by Principles: An Interactive Approach to Language Pedagogy* (3rd edn). New York: Pearson.

Buôi Khaùnh Theá (2003, November 6) Multilingual education in the community of minority peoples of Vietnam. Paper presented at the Language Development, Language Revitalization and Multilingual Education in Minority Communities in Asia, Bangkok, Thailand. See https://www.sil.org/resources/archives/65413 (accessed 20 November 2020).

Burri, M. (2018) Empowering nonnative-English-speaking teachers in primary school contexts: An ethnographic case study. *TESOL Journal* 9 (1), 185–202. https://doi.org/10.1002/tesj.316.

Busse, V. (2017) Plurilingualism in Europe: Exploring attitudes toward English and other European languages among adolescents in Bulgaria, Germany, the Netherlands, and Spain. *The Modern Language Journal* 101 (3), 566–582. https://doi.org/10.1111/modl.12415.

Canagarajah, S. (2007) Lingua franca English, multilingual communities, and language acquisition. *The Modern Language Journal* 91 (s1), 923–939. https://doi.org/10.1111/j.1540-4781.2007.00678.x.

Carolan, B.V. (2013) *Social Network Analysis and Education: Theory, Methods & Applications*. Thousand Oaks, CA: Sage.

Castro, E. (2018) Complex adaptive systems, language advising, and motivation: A longitudinal case study with a Brazilian student of English. *System* 74, 138–148. https://doi.org/10.1016/j.system.2018.03.004.

Çelik, S. (2006) A concise examination of the artificial battle between native and non-native speaker teachers of English in Turkey. *Gazi University Kastamonu Education Journal* 14 (2), 371–376.

Charles, Q.D. (2019) Black teachers of English in South Korea: Constructing identities as a native English speaker and English language teaching professional. *TESOL Journal* 10 (4), e478. https://doi.org/10.1002/tesj.478.

Cheung, M. and Sung, C. (2016) Does accent matter? Investigating the relationship between accent and identity in English as a lingua franca communication. *System* 60, 55–65. https://doi.org/10.1016/j.system.2016.06.002.

Chun, S.Y. (2014) EFL learners' beliefs about native and non-native English-speaking teachers: Perceived strengths, weaknesses, and preferences. *Journal of Multilingual and Multicultural Development* 35 (6), 563–579. https://doi.org/10.1080/01434632.2014.889141.

Claro, J. (2020) Identification with external and internal referents: Integrativeness and the ideal L2 self. In A.H. Al-Hoorie and P.D. MacIntyre (eds) *Contemporary Language Motivation Theory: 60 Years since Gardner and Lambert (1959)* (pp. 233–261). Bristol: Multilingual Matters.

Clegg, J. (2019) How English depresses school achievement in Africa. *ELT Journal* 73 (1), 89–91. https://doi.org/10.1093/elt/ccy053.

Clément, R. (1980) Ethnicity, contact and communicative competence in a second language. In P.R. Giles and P. Smith (eds) *Social Psychology and Language* (pp. 147–159). Oxford: Pergamon Press.

Clément, R. (1986) Second language proficiency and acculturation: An investigation of the effects of language status and individual characteristics. *Journal of Language and Social Psychology* 5 (4), 271–290. https://doi.org/10.1177/0261927X8600500403.

Clement, R. and Noels, K.A. (1992) Towards a situated approach to ethnolinguistic identity: The effects of status on individuals and groups. *Journal of Language and Social Psychology* 11 (4), 203–232. https://doi.org/10.1177/0261927X92114002.

Cochran, J. (1986) *Education in Egypt (RLE Egypt)*. Abingdon: Routledge.

Cochran, J. (2008) *Educational Roots of Political Crisis in Egypt*. Lanham, MD: Lexington Books.

Coetzee-Van Rooy, S. (2014) Explaining the ordinary magic of stable African multilingualism in the Vaal Triangle region in South Africa. *Journal of Multilingual and Multicultural Development* 35 (2), 121–138. https://doi.org/10.1080/01434632.2013.818678.

Coetzee-Van Rooy, S. (2019) Motivation and multilingualism in South Africa. In M. Lamb, K. Csizér, A. Henry and S. Ryan (eds) *The Palgrave Handbook of Motivation for Language Learning* (pp. 471–494). Cham: Palgrave MacMillan.

Cook, V. (1999) Going beyond the native speaker in language teaching. *TESOL Quarterly* 33 (2), 185–209. https://doi.org/10.2307/3587717.

Copland, F., Mann, S. and Garton, S. (2020) Native-English-speaking teachers: Disconnections between theory, research, and practice. *TESOL Quarterly* 54 (2), 348–374. https://doi.org/10.1002/tesq.548.

Crowder, M. (1967) *Senegal: A Study of French Assimilation Policy*. London: Methuen & Co.

Csizér, K. and Lukács, G. (2010) The comparative analysis of motivation, attitudes and selves: The case of English and German in Hungary. *System* 38 (1), 1–13. https://doi.org/10.1016/j.system.2009.12.001.

Csizér, K. and Tankó, G. (2017) English majors' self-regulatory control strategy use in academic writing and its relation to L2 motivation. *Applied Linguistics* 38 (3), 386–404. https://doi.org/10.1093/applin/amv033.

Csizér, K., Kormos, J. and Sarkadi, Á. (2010) The dynamics of language learning attitudes and motivation: Lessons from an interview study of dyslexic language learners. *The Modern Language Journal* 94 (3), 470–487. https://doi.org/10.1111/j.1540-4781.2010.01054.x.

Denham, P.A. (1992) English in Vietnam. *World Englishes* 11 (1), 61–69. https://doi.org/10.1111/j.1467-971X.1992.tb00047.x.

Destefano, J., Lynd, M. and Thornton, B. (2009) *The Quality of Basic Education in Senegal, A Review: Final Report*. Senegal: USAID.

Devrim, D.Y. and Bayyurt, Y. (2010) Students' understandings and preferences of the role and place of 'culture' in English language teaching. A focus in an EFL context. *TESOL International Journal* 2, 4–23.

Dewaele, J.-M. (2010) 'Christ fucking shit merde!' Language peferences for swearing among maximally proficient multilinguals. *Sociolinguistic Studies* 4 (3), 595–614. https://doi.org/10.1558/sols.v4i3.595.

Dewaele, J.-M. (2018) Why the dichotomy 'L1 versus LX user' is better than 'native versus non-native speaker'. *Applied Linguistics* 39 (2), 236–240. https://doi.org/10.1093/applin/amw055.

Dewaele, J.-M. and Mercer, S. (2018) Variation in ESL/EFL teachers' attitudes towards their students. In S. Mercer and A. Kostoulas (eds) *Language Teacher Psychology* (pp. 178–195). Bristol: Multilingual Matters.

Diallo, I. (2009) Attitudes toward speech communities in Senegal: A cross-sectional study. *Nordic Journal of African Studies* 18 (3), 196–214.

DiAngelo, R. (2018) *White Fragility: Why it's So Hard for White People to Talk about Racism*. Boston, MA: Beacon Press.

Dikilitaş, K. and Mumford, S.E. (2020) Preschool English teachers gaining bilingual competencies in a monolingual context. *System* 91, 102264. https://doi.org/10.1016/j.system.2020.102264.

Do Huy Thinh (2006) The Role of English in Vietnam's Foreign Language Policy: A Brief History. Paper presented at the 19th Annual EA Education Conference, Australia. See https://www.worldwide.rs/en/role-english-vietnams-foreign-language-policy-brief-history/ (accessed 20 November 2020).

Doğançay-Aktuna, S. (1998) The spread of English in Turkey and its current sociolinguistic profile. *Journal of Multilingual and Multicultural Development* 19 (1), 24–39. https://doi.org/10.1080/01434639808666340.

Doğançay-Aktuna, S. and Kiziltepe, Z. (2005) English in Turkey. *World Englishes* 24 (2), 253–265. https://doi.org/10.1111/j.1467-971X.2005.00408.x.

Dörnyei, Z. (2005) *The Psychology of the Language Learner*. New York, NY: Routledge.

Dörnyei, Z. (2009) The L2 motivational self system. In Z. Dörnyei and E. Ushioda (eds) *Motivation, Language Identity and the L2 Self* (pp. 9–42). Bristol: Multilingual Matters.

Dörnyei, Z. (2019) Towards a better understanding of the L2 learning experience, the Cinderella of the L2 motivational self system. *Studies in Second Language Learning and Teaching* 9 (1), 19–30. http://doi.org/10.14746/ssllt.2019.9.1.2.

Dörnyei, Z. and Ushioda, E. (2009) *Motivation, Language Identity and the L2 Self*. Bristol: Multilingual Matters.

Dörnyei, Z. and Chan, L. (2013) Motivation and vision: An analysis of future L2 self images, sensory styles, and imagery capacity across two target languages. *Language Learning* 63 (3), 437–462. https://doi.org/10.1111/lang.12005.

Dörnyei, Z., Csizér, K. and Németh, N. (2006) *Motivation, Language Attitudes and Globalisation: A Hungarian Perspective.* Clevedon: Multilingual Matters.

Drame, M. (n.d.) Resistance to communicative language teaching in a foreign language context: A Senegalese case study, 1–18. See http://fastef.ucad.sn/LIEN12/drame.pdf (accessed 20 October 2020).

Dweck, C.S. and Yeager, D.S. (2019) Mindsets: A view from two eras. *Perspectives on Psychological Science* 14 (3), 481–496. https://doi.org/10.1177/1745691618804166.

Dyers, C. and Abongdia, J.-F. (2010) An exploration of the relationship between language attitudes and ideologies in a study of Francophone students of English in Cameroon. *Journal of Multilingual and Multicultural Development* 31 (2), 119–134. https://doi.org/10.1080/01434630903470837.

educationallinguist (2015) What if we talked about monolingual White children the way we talk about low-income children of color? *The Educational Linguist.* See https://educationallinguist.wordpress.com/2015/07/06/what-if-we-talked-about-monolingual-white-children-the-way-we-talk-about-low-income-children-of-color/ (accessed 20 October 2020).

Elkhatib, A. (1984) Case studies of four Egyptian college freshman writers majoring in English. Unpublished PhD dissertation, Columbia University.

Ellis, E.M. (2013) The ESL teacher as plurilingual: An Australian perspective. *TESOL Quarterly* 47 (3), 446–471. https://doi.org/10.1002/tesq.120.

Ellis, E.M. (2016) 'I may be a native speaker but I'm not monolingual': Reimagining all teachers' linguistic identities in TESOL. *TESOL Quarterly* 50 (3), 597–630. https://doi.org/10.1002/tesq.314.

Erdil-Moody, Z. and Thompson, A.S. (2020) Exploring motivational strategies in higher education: Student and instructor perceptions. *Eurasian Journal of Applied Linguistics* 6 (3), 387–413. https://doi.org/10.32601/ejal.834670.

Fan, F. and de Jong, E.J. (2019) Exploring professional identities of nonnative-English-speaking teachers in the United States: A narrative case study. *TESOL Journal* 10 (4), e495. https://doi.org/10.1002/tesj.495.

Fernandes, D. (2012) Modernity and the linguistic genocide of Kurds in Turkey. *IJSL* 2012 (217), 75–98. https://doi.org/10.1515/ijsl-2012-0050.

Flier, M.S. (1998) Surzhyk: The rules of engagement. *Harvard Ukrainian Studies* 22, 113–136. http://www.jstor.com/stable/41036734.

Fonzari, L. (1999) English in the Estonian multicultural society. *World Englishes* 18 (1), 39–48. https://doi.org/10.1111/1467-971X.00120.

Francis-Saad, M. (1992) Caractère social du français en Egypte. Bilinguisme et interférences. *Etudes de Linguistique Appliquée; Paris* 88, 130–137.

Friedman, D.A. (2009) Speaking correctly: Error correction as a language socialization practice in a Ukrainian classroom. *Applied Linguistics* 31 (3), 346–367. https://doi.org/10.1093/applin/amp037.

Friedman, D.A. (2016) Our language: (Re)imagining communities in Ukrainian language classrooms. *Journal of Language, Identity and Education* 15 (3), 165–179. https://doi.org/10.1080/15348458.2016.1166432.

Gallo, E. (1990) La gran expansión económica y la consolidación del régimen conservador liberal 1875–1890 [The great economic expansión and the cosolidation of the conservative-liberal regime 1875–1980]. *Historia Argentina: La República Conservadora* 5, 19–91.

Gao, F. (2010) Learning Korean language in China: Motivations and strategies of non-Koreans. *International Journal of Bilingual Education and Bilingualism* 13 (3), 273–284. https://doi.org/10.1080/13670050903006929.

Gao, X. and Xu, H. (2014) The dilemma of being English language teachers: Interpreting teachers' motivation to teach, and professional commitment in China's hinterland regions. *Language Teaching Research* 18 (2), 152–168. https://doi.org/10.1177/1362168813505938.

Gardner, R. (1985) *Social Psychology and Second Language Learning: The Role of Attitudes and Motivation*. London: Edward Arnold.

Gardner, R. (2010) *Motivation and Second Language Acquisition: The Socio-Educational Model*. New York: Peter Lang.

Gardner, R.C. and Clément, R. (1990) Social psychological perspectives on second language acquisition. In H. Giles and P. Robinson (eds) *Handbook of Language and Social Psychology* (pp. 295–517). Chichester: John Wiley & Sons.

Geller, S. (1995) *Senegal: An African Nation between Islam and the West* (2nd edn). Boulder, CO: Westview Press.

Genç, A. (1999) Ilköğretimde yabanci dil [Foreign language in primary education]. *Buca Eğitim Fakültesi Dergisi* 10, 299–307.

Gkonou, C. and Mercer, S. (2018) The relational beliefs and practices of highly socio-emotionally compenent language teachers. In S. Mercer and A. Kostoulas (eds) *Language Teacher Psychology* (pp. 158–177). Bristol: Multilingual Matters.

Golombek, P. and Doran, M. (2014) Unifying cognition, emotion, and activity in language teacher professional development. *Teaching and Teacher Education* 39 (1), 102–111.

Gregersen, T. and MacIntyre, P.D. (2015) 'I can see a little bit of you on myself': A dynamic systems approach to the inner dialogue between teacher and learner selves. In Z. Dörnyei, P.D. MacIntyre and A. Henry (eds) *Motivational Dynamics in Language Learning* (pp. 260–284). Bristol: Multilingual Matters.

Guilloteaux, M.-J. (2013) Motivational strategies for the language classroom: Perceptions of Korean secondary school English teachers. *System* 41 (1), 3–14. https://doi.org/10.1016/j.system.2012.12.002.

Hajar, A. (2018) Motivated by visions: A tale of a rural learner of English. *Language Learning Journal* 46 (4), 415–429. https://doi.org/10.1080/09571736.2016.1146914.

Harwood, J. (2010) The contact space: A novel framework for intergroup contact research. *Journal of Language and Social Psychology* 29 (2), 147–177. https://doi.org/10.1177/0261927X09359520.

Hayes, D. (2009) Non-native English-speaking teachers, context and English language teaching. *System* 37 (1), 1–11. https://doi.org/10.1016/j.system.2008.06.001.

Henry, A. (2017) L2 motivation and multilingual identities. *The Modern Language Journal* 101 (3), 548–565. https://doi.org/10.1111/modl.12412.

Hiver, P. (2013) The interplay of possible language teacher selves in professional development choices. *Language Teaching Research* 17 (2), 210–227. https://doi.org/10.1177/1362168813475944.

Hiver, P. (2018) Teachstrong: The power of teacher resilience for second language practitioners. In S. Mercer and A. Kostoulas (eds) *Language Teacher Psychology* (pp. 231–246). Bristol: Multilingual Matters.

Hiver, P. and Dörnyei, Z. (2017) Language teacher immunity: A double-edged sword. *Applied Linguistics* 38 (3), 405–423. https://doi.org/10.1093/applin/amv034.

Hiver, P., Kim, T.-Y. and Kim, Y. (2018) Language teacher motivation. In S. Mercer and A. Kostoulas (eds) *Language Teacher Psychology* (pp. 18–33). Bristol: Multilingual Matters.

Hoang Van Van, Nguyen Thi Chi and Hoang Thi Xuan Hoa (2006) *Doi moi phuong phap day tieng Anh o trung hoc pho thong Viet Nam [Changing English Teaching Approaches in High Schools in Vietnam]*. Hanoi: Nha Xuat Ban Giao Duc.

Holliday, A. (1999) Small cultures. *Applied Linguistics* 20 (2), 237–264. https://doi.org/10.1093/applin/20.2.237.

Holliday, A. and Aboshiha, P. (2009) The denial of ideology in perceptions of nonnative speaker teachers. *TESOL Quarterly* 43 (4), 669–689. https://doi.org/10.1002/j.1545-7249.2009.tb00191.x.

Hornberger, N.H. (1994) Language policy and planning in South America. *Annual Review of Applied Linguistics* 14, 220–239. https://doi.org/10.1017/S0267190500002907.

Hornberger, N.H. (2006) Negotiating methodological rich points in applied linguistics research: An ethnographer's view. In M. Chalhoub-Deville, C. Chappelle and P.A. Duff (eds) *Inference and Generalizability in Applied Linguistics: Multiple Perspectives* (pp. 221–240). Amsterdam: John Benjamins.

Huensch, A. and Thompson, A.S. (2017) Contextualizing attitudes toward pronunciation: Foreign language learners in the United States. *Foreign Language Annals* 50 (2), 410–432. https://doi.org/10.1111/flan.12259.

Ibrahim, Z. and Al-Hoorie, A.H. (2019) Shared, sustained flow: Triggering motivation with collaborative projects. *ELT Journal* 73 (1), 51–60. https://doi.org/10.1093/elt/ccy025.

Ilieva, R. (2010) Non-native English-speaking teachers' negotiations of program discourses in their construction of professional identities within a TESOL program. *Canadian Modern Language Review* 66 (3), 343–369. https://doi.org/10.3138/cmlr.66.3.343.

Imhoof, M. (1977) The English language in Egypt. *English Around the World* 17, 1–3.

Inbar-Lourie, O. (2006) Mind the gap: Self and perceived native speaker identities of EFL teachers. In E. Llurda (ed.) *Non-Native Language Teachers: Perceptions, Challenges and Contributions to the Profession* (pp. 265–281). New York: Springer.

Islam, M., Lamb, M. and Chambers, G. (2013) The L2 motivational self system and national interest: A Pakistani perspective. *System* 41 (2), 231–244. https://doi.org/10.1016/j.system.2013.01.025.

Jeffreys, D. (ed.) (2016) *Views of Ancient Egypt since Napoleon Bonaparte: Imperialism, Colonialism and Modern Appropriations*. Abingdon: Routledge.

Jenkins, S. (2017) The elephant in the room: Discriminatory hiring practices in ELT. *ELT Journal* 71 (3), 373–376. https://doi.org/10.1093/elt/ccx025.

Kalaja, P. (2016) 'Dreaming is believing': The teaching of foreign languages as envisioned by student teachers. In P. Kalaja, A.M.F. Barcelos, M. Aro and M. Ruohotie-Lyhty (eds) *Beliefs, Agency and Identity in Foreign Language Learning and Teaching* (pp. 124–146). Basingstoke: Palgrave MacMillan.

Kamhi-Stein, L.D. (2016) The non-native English speaker teachers in TESOL movement. *ELT Journal* 70 (2), 180–189. https://doi.org/10.1093/elt/ccv076.

Kamhi-Stein, L.D., Maggioli, G.D. and de Oliveira, L.C. (eds) (2017) *English Language Teaching in South America: Policy, Preparation and Practices*. Bristol: Multilingual Matters.

Karahan, F. (2007) Language attitudes of Turkish students towards the English language and its use in the Turkish context. *Çankaya Universitesi Fen-Edebiyat Fakültesi, Journal of Arts and Sciences* 7, 73–87.

Karimi, M.N. and Norouzi, M. (2019) Developing and validating three measures of possible language teacher selves. *Studies in Educational Evaluation* 62, 49–60. https://doi.org/10.1016/j.stueduc.2019.04.006.

Karimi, M.N. and Zade, S.S.H. (2019) Teachers' use of motivational strategies: Effects of a motivation-oriented professional development course. *Innovation in Language Learning and Teaching* 13 (2), 194–204. https://doi.org/10.1080/17501229.2017.1422255.

Kieu Hang Kim Anh (2010) Use of Vietnamese in English language teaching in Vietnam: Attitudes of Vietnamese university teachers. *English Language Teaching* 3 (2), 119–128. https://doi.org/10.5539/elt.v3n2p119.

Kim, J.-I. (2017) Issues of motivation and identity positioning: Two teachers' motivational practices for engaging immigrant children in learning heritage languages. *International Journal of Bilingual Education and Bilingualism* 20 (6), 638–651. https://doi.org/10.1080/13670050.2015.1066754.

Kim, T.-Y., Kim, Y.-K. and Zhang, Q.-M. (2014) Differences in demotivation between Chinese and Korean English teachers: A mixed-methods study. *Asia-Pacific Education Researcher* 23 (2), 299–310. https://doi.org/10.1007/s40299-013-0105-x.

King, J. (ed.) (2016) *The Dynamic Interplay between Context and the Language Learner.* Basingstoke: Palgrave Macmillan.

Kormos, J. and Kiddle, T. (2013) The role of socio-economic factors in motivation to learn English as a foreign language: The case of Chile. *System* 41 (2), 399–412. https://doi.org/10.1016/j.system.2013.03.006.

Kormos, J., Kiddle, T. and Csizér, K. (2011) Systems of goals, attitudes, and self-related beliefs in second-language-learning motivation. *Applied Linguistics* 32 (5), 495–516. https://doi.org/10.1093/applin/amr019.

Kostoulas, A. and Mercer, S. (2016) Fifteen years of research on self & identity in *System*. *System* 60, 128–134. https://doi.org/10.1016/j.system.2016.04.002.

Kozlovets, M.A. (2008) Global'na migratsiya i polityka identychnosti ta gromadianstva [Global migration and the politics of identity and citizenship]. *Ukryins'ka Polonistyka* 5, 3–22.

Kramsch, C. (2013) Afterword. In B. Norton *Identity and Language Learning: Extending the Conversation* (2nd edn, pp. 192–201). Bristol: Multilingual Matters.

Kramsch, C. (2014) Teaching foreign languages in an era of globalization: Introduction. *The Modern Language Journal* 98 (1), 296–311. https://doi.org/10.1111/j.1540-4781.2014.12057.x.

Kubanyiova, M. (2015) The role of teachers' future self guides in creating L2 development opportunities in teacher-led classroom discourse: Reclaiming the relevance of language teacher cognition. *The Modern Language Journal* 99 (3), 565–584. https://doi.org/10.1111/modl.12244.

Kubanyiova, M. (2019) Language teacher motivation research: Its ends, means and future commitments. In M. Lamb, K. Csizér, A. Henry and S. Ryan (eds) *The Palgrave Handbook of Motivation for Language Learning* (pp. 389–407). Cham: Palgrave MacMillan.

Kubanyiova, M. and Feryok, A. (2015) Language teacher cognition in applied linguistics research: Revisiting the territory, redrawing the boundaries, reclaiming the relevance. *The Modern Language Journal* 99 (3), 435–449. https://doi.org/10.1111/modl.12239.

Kulyk, V. (2016) National identity in Ukraine: Impact of Euromaidan and the war. *Europe–Asia Studies* 68 (4), 588–608. https://doi.org/10.1080/09668136.2016.1174980.

Kumaravadivelu, B. (2016) The decolonial option in English teaching: Can the subaltern act? *TESOL Quarterly* 50 (1), 66–85. https://doi.org/10.1002/tesq.202.

Kuteeva, M. (2014) The parallel language use of Swedish and English: The question of 'nativeness' in university policies and practices. *Journal of Multilingual and Multicultural Development* 35 (4), 332–344. https://doi.org/10.1080/01434632.2013.874432.

Kuzio, T. (2005) From Kuchma to Yushchenko: Ukraine's 2004 presidential elections and the Orange Revolution. *Problems of Post-Communism* 52 (2), 29–44. https://doi.org/10.1080/10758216.2005.11052197.

Lamb, M. (2012) A self system perspective on young adolescents' motivation to learn English in urban and rural settings. *Language Learning* 62 (4), 997–1023. https://doi.org/10.1111/j.1467-9922.2012.00719.x.

Lamb, M. (2013) 'Your mum and dad can't teach you!': Constraints on agency among rural learners of English in the developing world. *Journal of Multilingual and Multicultural Development* 34 (1), 14–29. https://doi.org/10.1080/01434632.2012.697467.

Lamb, M. (2018) When motivation research motivates: Issues in long-term empirical investigations. *Innovation in Language Learning and Teaching* 12 (4), 357–370. https://doi.org/10.1080/17501229.2016.1251438.

Larsen-Freeman, D. and Cameron, L. (2008) Research methodology on language development from a complex systems perspective. *Modern Language Journal* 92 (2), 200–213.

Latif, M.M.M.A. (2018) English language teaching research in Egypt: Trends and challenges. *Journal of Multilingual and Multicultural Development* 39 (9), 818–829. https://doi.org/10.1080/01434632.2018.1445259.

Lauristin, M. and Vihalemm, P. (1997) Recent historical developments in Estonia: Three stages of transition (1987–1997). In M. Luaristin and P. Vihalemm (eds) *Return to the Western World: Cultural and Political Perspectives on the Estonian Post-communist Transition* (pp. 73–126). Tartu: Tartu University Press.

Levis, J.M., Sonsaat, S., Link, S. and Barriuso, T.A. (2016) Native and nonnative teachers of L2 pronunciation: Effects on learner performance. *TESOL Quarterly* 50 (4), 894–931. https://doi.org/10.1002/tesq.272.

Lewis, G. (1974) *Modern Turkey*. London: Ernest Benn.

Li, Q. (2014) Differences in the motivation of Chinese learners of English in a foreign and second language context. *System* 42, 451–461. https://doi.org/10.1016/j.system.2014.01.011.

Linde, C. (1993) *Life Stories: The Creation of Coherence*. Oxford: Oxford University Press.

Ling, C.Y. and Braine, G. (2007) The attitudes of university students towards nonnative speakers English teachers in Hong Kong. *RELC* 38 (3), 257–277. https://doi.org/10.1177/0033688207085847.

Liu, Y. and Thompson, A.S. (2018) Language learning motivation in China: An exploration of the L2MSS and psychological reactance. *System* 72, 37–48. https://doi.org/10.1016/j.system.2017.09.025.

Luna, F. (1984) El auge de las colectividades [The climax of the collectives]. *Nuestro Tiempo* 8, 65–80.

Ma, L.P.F. (2012) Advantages and disadvantages of native- and nonnative-English-speaking teachers: Student perceptions in Hong Kong. *TESOL Quarterly* 46 (2), 280–305. https://doi.org/10.1002/tesq.21.

MacIntyre, P.D. and Legatto, J.J. (2011) A dynamic system approach to willingness to communicate: Developing an idiodynamic method to capture rapidly changing affect. *Applied Linguistics* 32 (2), 149–171. https://doi.org/10.1093/applin/amq037.

Mälksoo, L. (2003) *Illegal Annexation and State Continuity: The Case of the Incorporation of the Baltic States by the USSR*. Leiden: Martinus Nijhoff.

Mann, S.J. (2016) *The Research Interview*. Basingstoke: Palgrave Macmillan.

Mansfield, P. (2003) *A History of the Middle East* (2nd edn). London: Penguin.

Martínez Agudo, J. de D. (ed.) (2018) *Emotions in Second Language Teaching: Theory, Research and Teacher Education*. Cham: Springer.

Mbaya, M. (2001) The spread of the English language in the French-speaking countries of Africa: The case of Senegal. *Journal of Humanities* 15 (1), 61–66. http://doi.org/10.4314/jh.v15i1.6284.

Medgyes, P. (2017) *The Non-Native Teacher*. Callander: Swan Communication Limited.

Mendoza, A. and Phung, H. (2019) Motivation to learn languages other than English: A critical research synthesis. *Foreign Language Annals* 52 (1), 121–140. https://doi.org/10.1111/flan.12380.

Mercaich Sartore, E., Sollier, M. and Soto, M. (2012) Motivation and its influence on language level performance: A case study on year 1 students at an English teacher training. In L. Anglada and D. Banegas (eds) *Views on Motivation and Autonomy in ELT: Selected Papers from the XXXVII FAAPI Conference* (pp. 70–81). Bariloche: APIZALS.

Mercer, S. (2014a) Re-imagining the self as a network of relationships. In K. Csizér and M. Magid (eds) *The Impact of Self-Concept on Language Learning* (pp. 51–69). Bristol: Multilingual Matters.

Mercer, S. (2014b) The self from a complexity perspective. In S. Mercer and M. Williams (eds) *Multiple Perspectives on the Self in SLA* (pp. 160–176). Bristol: Multilingual Matters.

Mercer, S. (2015a) Social network analysis and complex dynamic systems. In Z. Dörnyei, P.D. MacIntyre and A. Henry (eds) *Motivational Dynamics in Language Learning* (pp. 73–82). Bristol: Multilingual Matters.

Mercer, S. (2015b) Dynamics of the self: A multilevel nested systems approach. In Z. Dörnyei, P.D. MacIntyre and A. Henry (eds) *Motivational Dynamics in Language Learning* (pp. 139–163). Bristol: Multilingual Matters.

Mercer, S. (2016) The contexts within me: L2 self as a complex dynamic system. In J. King (ed.) *The Dynamic Interplay between Context and the Language Learner* (pp. 11–28). London: Palgrave Macmillan.

Mercer, S. and Williams, M. (2014a) Concluding reflections. In S. Mercer and M. Williams (eds) *Multiple Perspectives on the Self in SLA* (pp. 177–185). Bristol: Multilingual Matters.

Mercer, S. and Williams, M. (eds) (2014b) *Multiple Perspectives on the Self in SLA*. Bristol: Multilingual Matters.

Mercer, S. and Kostoulas, A. (eds) (2018) *Language Teacher Psychology*. Bristol: Multilingual Matters.

Ministry of Culture and Education of the Estonian Republic (1995) *Statistika Vihik*, 5, *Foreign Language Learning*. Tallinn: Ministry of Culture and Education of the Estonian Republic.

Moodie, I. and Feryok, A. (2015) Beyond cognition to commitment: English language teaching in South Korean primary schools. *The Modern Language Journal* 99 (3), 450–469. https://doi.org/10.1111/modl.12238.

Moser, M. (2015) Language policy and the discourse on languages in Ukraine under President Viktor Yanukovych (25 February 2010–28 October 2012). *East/West: Journal of Ukrainian Studies* 2 (2), 169–172. https://doi.org/10.21226/T2MK5P.

Moussu, L. and Llurda, E. (2008) Non-native English-speaking English language teachers: History and research. *Language Teaching* 41 (3), 315–348. http://doi.org/10.1017/S0261444808005028.

Mozgalina, A. (2015) More or less choice? The influence of choice on task motivation and task engagement. *System* 49, 120–132. https://doi.org/10.1016/j.system.2015.01.004.

Murphy, J.M. (2014) Intelligible, comprehensible, non-native models in ESL/EFL pronunciation teaching. *System* 42, 258–269. https://doi.org/10.1016/j.system.2013.12.007.

Mydans, S. (1995) Vietnam speaks English with an eager accent. *New York Times*, 7 May. See http://www.nytimes.com/1995/05/07/weekinreview/the-world-vietnam-speaks-English-with-an-eager-accent.html (accessed 20 October 2020).

Nashef, H.A.M. (2013) اهلا, hello and bonjour: A postcolonial analysis of Arab media's use of code switching and mixing and its ramification on the identity of the self in the Arab world. *International Journal of Multilingualism* 10 (3), 313–330. https://doi.org/10.1080/14790718.2013.783582.

Ngan Le Hai Phan (2018) Implications of the changing status of English for instructional models of English: A study of Vietnamese ELT teachers' reflections. *TESOL Journal* 9 (2), 368–387. https://doi.org/10.1002/tesj.331.

Ngan Nguyen (2012) How English has displaced Russian and other foreign languages in Vietnam since 'Doi Moi'. *International Journal of Humanities and Social Science* 2 (23), 259–266.

Ngan Nguyen Long and Kemdall, H. (1981) *After Saigon Fell: Daily life under the Vietnamese Communists*. Berkeley, CA: Institute of East Asian Studies.

Nielsen, P.M. (2003) English in Argentina: A sociolinguistic profile. *World Englishes* 22 (2), 199–209. https://doi.org/10.1111/1467-971X.00288.

Norton, B. (2000) *Identity and Language Learning: Gender, Ethnicity and Educational Change*. London: Longman/Pearson Education.

Norton, B. (2013) *Identity and Language Learning: Extending the Conversation* (2nd edn). Bristol: Multilingual Matters.

Norton, B. (2020) Motivation, identity and investment: A journey with Robert Gardner. In A.H. Al-Hoorie and P.D. MacIntyre (eds) *Contemporary Language Motivation Theory: 60 Years since Gardner and Lambert (1959)* (pp. 153–168). Bristol: Multilingual Matters.

Nuske, K. (2018) 'I mean I'm kind of discriminating my own people': A Chinese TESOL graduate student's shifting perceptions of China English. *TESOL Quarterly* 52 (2), 360–390. https://doi.org/10.1002/tesq.404.

Oder, T. (2008) The professional foreign language teacher in Estonia: Students' and principals' perceptions. *Teacher Development* 12 (3), 237–246. https://doi.org/10.1080/13664530802259297.

Önalan, O. (2005) EFL teachers' perceptions of the place of culture in ELT: A survey study at four universities in Ankara/Turkey. *Journal of Language and Linguistic Studies* 1 (2), 215–235.

Ortega, L. (2012) Epistemological diversity and moral ends of research in instructed SLA. *Language Teaching Research* 16 (2), 206–226. https://doi.org/10.1177/0267658311431373.

Ortega, L. (2013) SLA for the 21st century: Disciplinary progress, transdisciplinary relevance, and the bi/multilingual turn. *Language Learning* 63 (s1), 1–24. https://doi.org/10.1111/j.1467-9922.2012.00735.x.

Ozolins, U. (2002, April 16) *Post-Imperialist Language Situations: The Baltic States*. Barcelona: World Congress on Language Policies. See https://www.linguapax.org/en/publications-2/conferences-and-symposiums/world-congress-on-language-policies-linguapax-ix-2002/ (accessed 20 October 2020).

Papi, M. (2010) The L2 motivational self system, L2 anxiety, and motivated behavior: A structural equation modeling approach. *System* 38 (3), 467–479. https://doi.org/10.1016/j.system.2010.06.011.

Papi, M. and Abdollahzadeh, E. (2012) Teacher motivational practice, student motivation, and possible L2 selves: An examination in the Iranian EFL context. *Language Learning* 62 (2), 571–594. https://doi.org/10.1111/j.1467-9922.2011.00632.x.

Papi, M. and Teimouri, Y. (2014) Language learner motivational types: A cluster analysis study. *Language Learning* 64 (3), 493–525. https://doi.org/10.1111/lang.12065.

Park, G. (2012) 'I am never afraid of being recognized as an NNES': One teacher's journey in claiming and embracing her nonnative-speaker identity. *TESOL Quarterly* 46 (1), 127–151. https://doi.org/10.1002/tesq.4.

Parks, E. (2011) Vietnam demands English language teaching 'miracle'. *The Guardian*, 8 November. See http://www.theguardian.com/education/2011/nov/08/vietnam-unrealistic-english-teaching-goals (accessed 20 November 2020).

Parmegiani, A. (2010) Reconceptualizing language ownership. A case study of language practices and attitudes among students at the University of KwaZulu-Natal. *The Language Learning Journal* 38 (3), 359–378. https://doi.org/10.1080/09571736.2010.511771.

Pavlenko, A. (2007) Autobiographic narratives as data in applied linguistics. *Applied Linguistics* 28 (2), 163–188. https://doi.org/10.1093/applin/amm008.

Pavlenko, A. (2008) Russian in post-Soviet countries. *Russian Linguistics* 32 (1), 59–80. https://www.jstor.org/stable/40297130.

Pavlenko, A. (2011) Language rights versus speakers' rights: On the applicability of Western language rights approaches in Eastern European contexts. *Language Policy* 10 (1), 37–58. https://doi.org/10.1007/s10993-011-9194-7.

Pavlenko, A. (2013) Multilingualism in post-Soviet successor states. *Language and Linguistics Compass* 7 (4), 262–271. https://doi.org/10.1111/lnc3.12024.

Pham Hoa Khiet (2007) Communicative language teaching: Unity within diversity. *ELT Journal* 61 (3), 193–201. https://doi.org/10.1093/elt/ccm026.

Pham Minh Hac (ed.) (1991) *Education in Vietnam 1945–1991*. Hanoi: Ministry of Education and Training and UNESCO.

Pham Minh Hac (ed.) (1994) *Education in Vietnam: Situations, Issues, Policies* (2nd edn). Hanoi: Ministry of Education and Training.

Phan Le Ha (2004) University classrooms in Vietnam: Contesting the stereotypes. *ELT Journal* 58 (1), 50–57. https://doi.org/10.1093/elt/58.1.50.

Phillipson, R. (1992) *Linguistic Imperialism*. Oxford: Oxford University Press.

Placci, G., Barbeito, M. and Valsecchi, M. (2012) EAP students' motivation to learn English: What do they believe in? In L. Anglada and D. Banegas (eds) *Views on Motivation and Autonomy in ELT: Selected Papers from the XXXVII FAAPI Conference* (pp. 131–136). Bariloche: APIZALS.

Polat, N. (2014) The interaction of the L2 motivational self system with socialisation and identification patterns and L2 accent attainment. In K. Csizér and M. Magid (eds) *The Impact of Self-Concept on Language Learning* (pp. 268–285). Bristol: Multilingual Matters.

Polat, N. and Schallert, D.L. (2013) Kurdish adolescents acquiring Turkish: Their self-determined motivation and identification with L1 and L2 communities as predictors of L2 accent attainment. *The Modern Language Journal* 97 (3), 745–763. https://doi.org/10.1111/j.1540-4781.2013.12033.x.

Porto, M., Montemayor-Borsinger, A. and López-Barrios, M. (2016) Research on English language teaching and learning in Argentina (2007–2013). *Language Teaching* 49 (3), 356–389. http://doi.org/10.1017/S0261444816000094.

Pozzi, R. (2017) Examining teacher perspectives on language policy in the city of Buenos Aires, Argentina. In L.D. Kamhi-Stein, G.D. Maggioli and L.C. de Oliveira (eds) *English Language Teaching in South America: Policy, Preparation and Practices* (pp. 141–157). Bristol: Multilingual Matters.

Prybytkova, I. (2009) Hronika migratsiynyh podiy v Ukrayini do i pislia rozpadu SRSR [The chronicle of migration in Ukraine before and after the USSR breakdown]. *Sotsiologiya: Teoriya, Metody, Marketing* 1, 41–77.

Ramezanzadeh, A. and Rezaei, S. (2019) Reconceptualising authenticity in TESOL: A new space for diversity and inclusion. *TESOL Quarterly* 53 (3), 794–815. https://doi.org/10.1002/tesq.512.

Rannut, M. (2004) Language policy in Estonia. *Noves SL: Revista de Sociolingüística* Spring–Summer, 1–17.

Rao, Z. (2010) Chinese students' perceptions of native English-speaking teachers in EFL teaching. *Journal of Multilingual and Multicultural Development* 31 (1), 55–68. https://doi.org/10.1080/01434630903301941.

Rasool, G. and Winke, P. (2019) Undergraduate students' motivation to learn and attitudes towards English in multilingual Pakistan: A look at shifts in English as a world language. *System* 82, 50–62. https://doi.org/10.1016/j.system.2019.02.015.

Reid, D.M. (1977) Educational and career choices of Egyptian students, 1882–1922. *International Journal of Middle East Studies* 8 (3), 349–378. https://doi.org/10.1017/S0020743800025861.

Reisman, W.M. (1983) The struggle for the Falklands. Faculty Scholarship Series. *Yale Law School Legal Scholarship Repository* 726, 286–317. See http://digitalcommons.law.yale.edu/fss_papers/726 (accessed 20 November 2020).

Reznik, V. (2018) Language policy in independent Ukraine: A battle for national and linguistic empowerment. In E. Andrews (ed.) *Language Planning in the Post-communist Era: The Struggles for Language Control in the New Order in Eastern Europe, Eurasia and China* (pp. 169–192). Cham: Palgrave Macmillan.

Richter, T. and Steiner, C. (2008) Politics, economics and tourism development in Egypt: Insights into the sectoral transformations of a neo-patrimonial rentier state. *Third World Quarterly* 29 (5), 939–959.

Rothman, J. and Treffers-Daller, J. (2014) A prolegomenon to the construct of the native speaker: Heritage speaker bilinguals are natives too! *Applied Linguistics* 35 (1), 93–98. https://doi.org/10.1093/applin/amt049.

Rubenfeld, S. and Clémant, R. (2020) Identity, adaptation and social harmony: A legacy. In A.H. Al-Hoorie and P.D. MacIntyre (eds) *Contemporary Language Motivation Theory: 60 Years since Gardner and Lambert (1959)* (pp. 109–129). Bristol: Multilingual Matters.

Ruecker, T. and Ives, L. (2015) White native English speakers needed: The rhetorical construction of privilege in online teacher recruitment spaces. *TESOL Quarterly* 49 (4), 733–756. https://doi.org/10.1002/tesq.195.

Salakhyan, E. (2015) The attitude of Slavic speakers toward English(es): Native and non-native English judged from Germany and Ukraine. *English Today* 31 (3), 34–39. http://doi.org/10.1017/S0266078415000231.

Saldaña, J. (2016) *The Coding Manual for Qualitative Researchers* (3rd edn). London: Sage.

Samari, G.D. and Métangmo-Tatou, L. (2017) Négociation et reconfiguration des identités en classe de Langues et Cultures Nationales au Cameroun. *The Canadian Modern Language Review* 73 (4), 570–595. http://doi.org/10.3138/cmlr.4036.

Sampasivam, S. and Clément, R. (2014) The dynamics of second language confidence: Contact and interaction. In S. Mercer and M. Williams (eds) *Multiple Perspectives on the Self in SLA* (pp. 23–40). Bristol: Multilingual Matters.

Sato, R. (2019) Fluctuations in an EFL teacher's willingness to communicate in an English-medium lesson: An observational case study in Japan. *Innovation in Language Learning and Teaching* 13 (2), 105–117. https://doi.org/10.1080/17501229.2017.1375506.

Savignon, S.J. (2001) Communicative language teaching for the twenty-first century. In M. Celce-Murcia (ed.) *Teaching English as a Second or Foreign Language* (3rd edn, pp. 13–28). Boston, MA: Heinle & Heinle.

Savin-Baden, M. and Howell-Major, C. (2013) *Qualitative Research: The Essential Guide to Theory and Practice*. Abingdon: Routledge.

Schaub, M. (2000) English in the Arab Republic of Egypt. *World Englishes* 19 (2), 225–238. https://doi.org/10.1111/1467-971X.00171.

Schneider, E.W. (2016) Grassroots Englishes in tourism interactions: How many speakers acquire 'grassroots English' in direct interactions, and what this may mean to them, and perhaps to linguists. *English Today* 32 (3), 2–10. http://doi.org/10.1017/S0266078416000183.

Schreiber, B.R. (2019) 'More like you': Disrupting native speakerism through a multimodal online intercultural exchange. *TESOL Quarterly* 53 (4), 1115–1138. https://doi.org/10.1002/tesq.534.

Seidlhofer, B. (1999) Double standards: Teacher education in the expanding circle. *World Englishes* 18 (2), 233–245. https://doi-org.www.libproxy.wvu.edu/10.1111/1467-971X.00136.

Selec, A.M. and Abramicheva, Y.N. (2012) Cross-cultural education expectations and co-teaching in Ukraine. *ТЕОРЕТИЧНІ ОСНОВИ СУЧАСНОЇ ПЕДАГОГІКИ І ОСВІТИ* [*Theoretical Basis of Modern Pedagogy and Education*] 127, 20–23.

Selvi, A.F. (2011) The non-native speaker teacher. *ELT Journal* 65 (2), 187–189. https://doi.org/10.1093/elt/ccq092.

Selvi, A.F. (2014) Myths and misconceptions about nonnative English speakers in the TESOL (NNEST) movement. *TESOL Journal* 5 (3), 573–611. https://doi.org/10.1002/tesj.158.

Serafini, E.J. (2020) Further exploring the dynamicity, situatedness, and emergence of the self: The key role of context. *Studies in Second Language Learning and Teaching* 10 (1), 133–157. https://doi.org/10.14746/ssllt.2020.10.1.7.

Sharifian, F. (2009) *English as an International Language*. Bristol: Multilingual Matters.

Silverstein, M. (1996) Monoglot 'standard' in America: Standardization and metaphors of linguistic hegemony. In D. Brenneis and R. Macaulay (eds) *The Matrix of Language: Contemporary Linguistic Anthropology* (pp. 284–306). Boulder, CO: Westview Press.

Siridetkoon, P. and Dewaele, J.-M. (2018) Ideal self and ought-to self of simultaneous learners of multiple foreign languages. *International Journal of Multilingualism* 15 (4), 313–328. https://doi.org/10.1080/14790718.2017.1293063.

Smagulova, J. (2008) Language policies of Kazakhization and their influence on language attitudes and use. *International Journal of Bilingual Education and Bilingualism* 11 (3–4), 440–475. https://doi.org/10.1080/13670050802148798.

Smotrova, T. (2009) Globalization and English language teaching in Ukraine. *TESOL Quarterly* 43 (4), 728–733. https://doi.org/10.1002/j.1545-7249.2009.tb00200.x.

Snow, A.M., Cortes, V. and Pron, A. (1998) EFL and educational reform: Content-based interaction in Argentina. *Forum* (36) (1), 10–13.

Solano-Campos, A. (2014) The making of an international educator: Transnationalism and nonnativeness in English teaching and learning. *TESOL Journal* 5 (3), 412–443. https://doi.org/10.1002/tesj.156.

Subtirelu, N.C. (2019) Introduction: TESOL professionals and the struggle against xenophobia and White nationalism. *TESOL Quarterly* 53 (3), 816–818. https://doi.org/10.1002/tesq.524.

Sundqvist, P. (2009) *Extramural English Matters: Out-of-School English and Its Impact on Swedish Ninth Graders' Oral Proficiency and Vocabulary*. Karlstad: Karlstad University Studies.

Sundqvist, P. and Sylvén, L.K. (2016) *Extramural English in Teaching and Learning: From Theory and Research to Practice*. London: Palgrave Macmillan.

Swearingen, A.J. (2019) Nonnative-English-speaking teacher candidates' language teacher identity development in graduate TESOL preparation programs: A review of the literature. *TESOL Journal* 10 (4), e494. https://doi.org/10.1002/tesj.494.

Sylvén, L.K. (2004) *Teaching in English or English Teaching?* Gothenburg: University of Gothenburg.

Sylvén, L.K. and Sundqvist, P. (2012) Gaming as extramural English L2 learning and L2 proficiency among young learners. *ReCALL* 24 (3), 302–321. https://doi.org/10.1017/S095834401200016X.

Talmy, S. (2010) Qualitative interviews in applied linguistics: From research instrument to social practice. *Annual Review of Applied Linguistics* 30, 128–148. https://doi.org/10.1017/S0267190510000085.

Tao, J., Zhao, K. and Chen, X. (2019) The motivation and professional self of teachers teaching languages other than English in a Chinese university. *Journal of Multilingual and Multicultural Development* 40 (7), 633–646. https://doi.org/10.1080/01434632.2019.1571075.

Taranenko, O. (2007) Ukrainian and Russian in contact: Attraction and estrangement. *International Journal of the Sociology of Language* 183, 119–140. https://doi.org/10.1515/IJSL.2007.007.

Tarnopolsky, O.B. (1996) EFL teaching in the Ukraine: State regulated or commercial? *TESOL Quarterly* 30 (3), 616–622. https://doi.org/10.2307/3587705.

Tarnopolsky, O. (2015) Communicative-analytic method in teaching English to adults at commercial English schools and centers in Ukraine. *International Letters of Social and Humanistic Sciences* 65, 16–26. https://doi.org/10.18052/www.scipress.com/ILSHS.65.16.

Taylor, S.G. (2002) Multilingual societies and planned linguistic change: New language-in-education programs in Estonia and South Africa. *Comparative Education Review* 46 (3), 313–338. https://doi.org/10.1086/341160.

Teimouri, Y. (2017) L2 selves, emotions, and motivated behaviors. *Studies in Second Language Acquisition* 39 (4), 681–709. https://doi.org/10.1017/S0272263116000243.

Tennant, A. and Negash, N. (2010) *Language Improvement for English Teachers*. Senegal: The British Council.

Thompson, A.S. (2016) How do multilinguals conceptualize interactions among languages studied? Operationalizing Perceived Positive Language Interaction (PPLI). In L. Ortega and A. Tyler (eds) *The Usage-Based Study of Language Learning and Multilingualism* (pp. 91–111). Washington, DC: Georgetown University Press.

Thompson, A.S. (2017a) Don't tell me what to do! The anti-ought-to self and language learning motivation. *System* 67, 38–49. https://doi.org/10.1016/j.system.2017.04.004.

Thompson, A.S. (2017b) Language learning motivation in the United States: An examination of language choice and multilingualism. *The Modern Language Journal* 101 (3), 483–500. https://doi.org/10.1111/modl.12409.

Thompson, A.S. (2017c) Who is qualified to teach English? *Blog Post on TEFL Equity Advocates.* See https://teflequityadvocates.com/2017/05/26/who-is-qualified-to-teach-english-by-amy-thompson/ (accessed 20 November 2020).

Thompson, A.S. (2020) My many selves are still me: Motivation and multilingualism. *Studies in Second Language Learning and Teaching (SSLLT)* 10 (1), 159–176. http://dx.doi.org/10.14746/ssllt.2020.10.1.8

Thompson, A.S. (in press) Language learning in rural America: Creating an ideal self with limited resources. In A.H. Al-Hoorie and F. Szabo (eds) *Language Motivation: Extending the Landscape.* London: Bloomsbury.

Thompson, A.S. and Fioramonte, A. (2012) Nonnative speaker teachers of Spanish: Insights from novice teachers. *Foreign Language Annals* 45 (4), 564–579. https://doi.org/10.1111/j.1944-9720.2013.01210.x.

Thompson, A.S. and Aslan, E. (2015) Multilingualism, perceived positive language interaction (PPLI), and learner beliefs: What do Turkish students believe? *International Journal of Multilingualism* 12 (3), 259–275. https://doi.org/10.1080/14790718.2014.973413.

Thompson, A.S. and Vásquez, C. (2015) Exploring motivational profiles through language learning narratives. *The Modern Language Journal* 99 (1), 158–174. https://doi.org/10.1111/modl.12187.

Thompson, A.S. and Erdil-Moody, Z. (2016) Operationalizing multilingualism: Language learning motivation in Turkey. *International Journal of Bilingual Education and Bilingualism* 19 (3), 314–331. https://doi.org/10.1080/13670050.2014.985631.

Tin Tan Dang (2010) Learner autonomy in EFL studies in Vietnam: A discussion from a sociocultural perspective. *English Language Teaching* 3 (2), 3–9. https://doi.org/10.5539/elt.v3n2p3.

Tocalli-Beller, A. (2007) ELT and bilingual education in Argentina. In J. Cummins and C. Davison (eds) *International Handbook of English Language Teaching* (pp. 107–121). New York, NY: Springer.

Todd, R.W. and Pojanapunya, P. (2009) Implicit attitudes towards native and non-native speaker teachers. *System* 37 (1), 23–33. https://doi.org/10.1016/j.system.2008.08.002.

Trang Thi Thuy Nguyen and Hamid, M.O. (2016) Language attitudes, identity and L1 maintenance: A qualitative study of Vietnamese ethnic minority students. *System* 61, 87–97. https://doi.org/10.1016/j.system.2016.08.003.

Trent, J. (2012) The discursive positioning of teachers: Native-speaking English teachers and educational discourse in Hong Kong. *TESOL Quarterly* 46 (1), 104–126. https://doi.org/10.1002/tesq.1.

Trentman, E. (2013) Arabic and English during study abroad in Cairo, Egypt: Issues of access and use. *The Modern Language Journal* 97 (2), 457–473. https://doi.org/10.1111/j.1540-4781.2013.12013.x.

Trudell, B. and Klaas, A.R. (2010) Distinction, integration and identity: Motivations for local language literacy in Senegalese communities. *International Journal of Educational Development* 30 (2), 121–129. https://doi.org/10.1016/j.ijedudev.2009.08.006.

Tsang, A. (2019) Reconceptualizing speaking, listening, and pronunciation: Glocalizing TESOL in the contexts of World Englishes and English as a lingua franca. *TESOL Quarterly* 53 (2), 580–588. https://doi.org/10.1002/tesq.504.

Tuero, S., Innocentini, V., Forte, A., Bruno, C. and Martínez, A. (2012) Variability in reading performance as related to students' attitudes and motivation after failing an ESP course. In L. Anglada and D. Banegas (eds) *Views on Motivation and Autonomy in ELT: Selected Papers from the XXXVII FAAPI Conference* (pp. 121–130). Bariloche: APIZALS.

Turner, J., Reynolds, K., Haslam, S. and Veenstra, K. (2006) Producing individuality by defining the personal self. In T. Postmes and J. Jetten (eds) *Individuality and the Group: Advances in Social Identity* (pp. 11–36). London: Sage.

Ueki, M. and Takeuchi, O. (2013) Forming a clearer image of the ideal L2 self: The L2 motivational self system and learner autonomy in a Japanese EFL context. *Innovation in Language Learning and Teaching* 7 (3), 238–252. https://doi.org/10.1080/1750122 9.2013.836205.

Ushioda, E. (2009) A person-in-context relational view of emergent motivation, self and identity. In Z. Dörnyei and E. Ushioda (eds) *Motivation, Language Identity and the L2 Self* (pp. 215–228). Bristol: Multilingual Matters.

Ushioda, E. (2011) Why autonomy? Insights from motivation theory and research. *Innovation in Language Learning and Teaching* 5 (2), 221–232. https://doi.org/10.1080/1750 1229.2011.577536.

Ushioda, E. (2014) Motivational perspectives on the self in SLA: A developmental view. In S. Mercer and M. Williams (eds) *Multiple Perspectives on the Self in SLA* (pp. 127–141). Bristol: Multilingual Matters.

Ushioda, E. (2015) Context and complex dynamic systems theory. In Z. Dörnyei, P.D. MacIntyre and A. Henry (eds) *Motivational Dynamics in Language Learning* (pp. 47–54). Bristol: Multilingual Matters.

Ushioda, E. (2020) Researching L2 motivation: Re-evaluating the role of qualitative inquiry, or the 'wine and conversation' approach. In A.H. Al-Hoorie and P.D. MacIntyre (eds) *Contemporary Language Motivation Theory: 60 Years since Gardner and Lambert (1959)* (pp. 194–211). Bristol: Multilingual Matters.

Valmori, L. and De Costa, P.I. (2016) How do foreign language teachers maintain their proficiency? A grounded theory investigation. *System* 57, 98–108. https://doi.org/10.1016/j.system.2016.02.003.

Valsecchi, I., Barbeito, C. and Olivero, M. (2017) Students' beliefs about learning English as a foreign language at secondary school in Argentina. In L.D. Kamhi-Stein, G.D. Maggióli and L.C. de Oliveira (eds) *English Language Teaching in South America: Policy, Preparation and Practices* (pp. 183–205). Bristol: Multilingual Matters.

van Dijk, T.A. (2009) *Society and Discourse: How Social Contexts Influence Text and Talk*. Cambridge: Cambridge University Press.

Vasavakul, T. (2003) Language policy and ethnic relations in Vietnam. In M.E. Brown and Š. Ganguly (eds) *Fighting Words: Language Policy and Ethnic Relations in Asia* (pp. 211–238). Cambridge, MA: MIT Press.

Veciño, P. (2017) Integrating technology in Argentine classrooms: The case of a Buenos Aires teacher education school. In L.D. Kamhi-Stein, G.D. Maggioli and L.C. de Oliveira (eds) *English Language Teaching in South America: Policy, Preparation and Practices* (pp. 123–137). Bristol: Multilingual Matters.

Verschik, A. (2005) The language situation in Estonia. *The Journal of Baltic Studies* 36 (3), 283–316. https://doi.org/10.1080/01629770500000111.

Victor, D. (2016) Why 'all lives matter' is such a perilous phrase. *New York Times*, 15 July. See https://www.nytimes.com/2016/07/16/us/all-lives-matter-black-lives-matter.html (accessed 20 October).

Waddington, J. (2018) Teacher understanding and implementation of motivational strategies in ELT. *ELT Journal* 72 (2), 162–174. https://doi.org/10.1093/elt/ccx044.

Wardhaugh, R. (1987) *Languages in Competition: Dominance, Diversity and Decline.* Oxford: Oxford University Press.

White, C. and Cuong Pham (2017) Time in the experience of agency and emotion in English language learning in rural Vietnam. *Innovation in Language Learning and Teaching* 11 (3), 207–218. https://doi.org/10.1080/17501229.2017.1317256.

Wolff, D. and de Costa, P.I. (2017) Expanding the language teacher identity landscape: An investigation of the emotions and strategies of a NNEST. *The Modern Language Journal* 101 (S1), 76–90. https://doi.org/10.1111/modl.12370.

Write, W. (1974) *British-Owned Railways in Argentina.* Buenos Aries: Emecé.

Yağmur, K. (2001) Turkish and other languages in Turkey. In G. Extra and D. Gorter (eds) *The Other Languages of Europe: Demographic, Sociolinguistic and Educational Perspectives* (pp. 407–427). Clevedon: Multilingual Matters.

Yoo, I.W. (2014) Nonnative teachers in the expanding circle and the ownership of English. *Applied Linguistics* 35 (1), 82–86. https://doi.org/10.1093/applin/amt043.

You, C.J., Dörnyei, Z. and Csizér, K. (2016) Motivation, vision, and gender: A survey of learners of English in China. *Language Learning* 66 (1), 94–123. https://doi.org/10.1111/lang.12140.

Yuan, R. (2019) A critical review on nonnative English teacher identity research: From 2008 to 2017. *Journal of Multilingual and Multicultural Development* 40 (6), 518–537. https://doi.org/10.1080/01434632.2018.1533018.

Zabrodskaja, A. (2015) 'What is my country to me?' Identity construction by Russian-speakers in the Baltic countries. *Sociolinguistic Studies* 9 (2–3), 217–242. https://doi.org/10.1558/sols.v9i2.26885.

Zappa-Hollman, S. (2007) EFL in Argentina's schools: Teachers' perspectives on policy changes and instruction. *TESOL Quarterly* 41 (3), 618–625. https://doi.org/10.1002/j.1545-7249.2007.tb00094.x.

Zentella, A.C. (1997) *Growing Up Bilingual.* Oxford: Wiley.

Zhai, X. (2019) Becoming a teacher in rural areas: How curriculum influences government-contracted pre-service physics teachers' motivation. *International Journal of Educational Research* 94, 77–89. https://doi.org/10.1016/j.ijer.2018.11.012.

Zheng, X. (2017) Translingual identity as pedagogy: International teaching assistants of English in college composition classrooms. *The Modern Language Journal* 101 (S1), 29–44. https://doi.org/10.1111/modl.12373.

Index